Al Lopez

Al Lopez

The Life of Baseball's El Señor

by
WES SINGLETARY

with a foreword by
JEROME HOLTZMAN

McFarland & Company, Inc., Publishers
Jefferson, North Carolina, and London

Frontispiece: Al Lopez in his days as manager of the Chicago White Sox, circa 1959. (Courtesy National Baseball Library, Cooperstown, New York.)

British Library Cataloguing-in-Publication data are available

Library of Congress Cataloguing-in-Publication Data

Singletary, Wes, 1960–
    Al Lopez : the life of baseball's El Señor / by Wes Singletary ; with a foreword by Jerome Holtzman.
        p.   cm.
    Includes bibliographical references and index.
    ISBN 0-7864-0656-9 (sewn softcover : 50# alkaline paper) ∞
    1. Lopez, Al, 1908–   . 2. Baseball managers — United
States — Biography.   3. Baseball players — United States — Biography.
I. Title.
GV865.L67S55   1999
796.357'092 — dc21
    [B]   98-49360
                                                                          CIP

Manufactured in the United States of America

McFarland & Company, Inc., Publishers
  Box 611, Jefferson, North Carolina 28640

For Toni, my darling wife,
Patricia Judith, our wonderful daughter, and
Bertha Ruth, our little girl in heaven

"Everybody was proud of him."
—*Marcelo Maseda*

Acknowledgments

Al Lopez, the benevolent subject of this book, went well beyond kindness in helping me during the last six years. On numerous occasions, El Señor wrenched himself away from his beloved golf game, extending his warmth, time, and memories to me. His ready and good-natured assistance reminds one of why he is so revered both within and outside baseball.

Others in Tampa who have been helpful in either scheduling interviews or sharing their knowledge and memorabilia collections with me are Tony Saladino, "Tampa's Number 1 Baseball Man" (so dubbed by Mr. Lopez himself); Bertha Saladino, Tony's hostess-extraordinaire wife; Ted Webb, the "native" voice of Tampa Bay sports; Kyle Van Landingham, editor of the Tampa Historical Society's *Sunland Tribune*; Leland Hawes of the *Tampa Tribune*; and Al Lopez, Jr.

My deepest thanks go to Jim Jones, Distinguished Teaching Professor of History at THE Florida State University, for providing invaluable counsel and friendship to me during my rather lengthy tenure as his student. His approbation, reassurance, knowledge, and support of this project from the first were much needed, often sought, and vastly appreciated. Dr. Jones will remain to me an example of what a university professor *should* be about; personable, hands-on instruction supported by research gathered over a career, committed to providing the student all one has to offer. He is quite simply beyond the man.

I need also to thank the venerable Jerome Holtzman, longtime Chicago baseball writer and Hall-of-Famer, for preparing the foreword to this book. Given Mr. Holtzman's fifty-year association with the subject, few are as familiar with the material, and no one could have proven more appropriate or kinder than he.

Maxine Jones, Jeff Pasley, Nathan Stoltzfus, and Chuck Connerly, all of Florida State, conveyed valuable support as members of my doctoral committee. Joseph Moore, author of *Pride against Prejudice: The Biography of Larry Doby*, was helpful both in reviewing portions of the manuscript and in providing additional research. Paul Leslie of Nichols State University and Larry Gerlach of the University of Utah read early versions of the manuscript and were very encouraging. Charles Robertson, Will Benedicks, Monte Finklestein, Mary Louise Ellis, and Mark Goldman, all of Tallahassee Community College, also provided a great deal of support. Thanks to each of them.

The staffs of the National Baseball Library and Archives in Cooperstown, the Florida State Archives, the Inter-library loan department in Strozier Library at Florida State, the Tampa/Hillsborough County Public Library, the *Tampa Tribune*, the Oral History Project at the University of Florida, Corbis-Bettman Archives, the Cleveland Public Library, and *Tampa Bay History* were all more than helpful in obtaining photographs or research materials that I could not have done without.

I wish to thank the following former professional baseball players for allowing me the thrill of interviewing them and for corresponding with me on the subject: Bob Shaw, Frank "Red" Barrett, Earl Battey, Fred Hatfield, Al Smith, Walt Dropo, Charlie Cuellar, Marcelo Maseda, "Bitsy" Mott, Jimmy Bloodworth, Ted Beard, Ray Berres, Jack Cassini, "Nanny" Fernández, Don Gutteridge, Tom Saffell, and Manuel Onis.

Thanks also to the following family members and friends across the miles: Charles Singletary, Sr., Judy and Ray Fojaco, Joe Singletary, Lee, Tiffany and Taylor Singletary, Lorraine, Frank, Frankie and Devin Fernandez, Manuel and Patricia Zarate, Arnold and Bonnie Zarate, Paul and Mary Bvichman, Danny and Marilyn Zarate, Debra and John Merritt, Rose Carter, Marjorie Teel, Lauren Teel Handler, Paul Singletary, John Singletary, Cynthia and Cliff May, Ray Herrero, Danny Herrero, Louis Herrero, Michelle Highnote, Sam McIntosh, Steve McIntosh, Stan McIntosh, Gloria McIntosh, Raymond and Hazel Singletary, Billy Singletary, "Bubba" Singletary, Sherri Jurrell, Mike Salario, Candy Crawford, Vasili Efimov, Thierry Kobes, Joel Overton, A. J. Smith, Karen Miller, Tyler Turkle, Joe Martelli, Natalie Arias, Parker and Kayleigh Shebs, Marianne Valenti, Ray Harrison, Dr. Bernard Sliger, Rich and Annette Williams,

John Calacino, Bob "Leech" Lotane, Scott Harward, Todd Thomas, George Drady, Joe Bulgarella, Orlando Evora, Art and Tammy Skafidas, James and Jodee McIver, David Berry, Hillary Hodges, Brian Lynch, Robin Barber, Mark Solomon, Paul "Edwin" Burk, J. W. Ennis, Mike Fuller, Lee Woodard, Jose Gonzalez, Emil Piazzon, Fred and Beth Tedio and the Uptown Cafe regulars, David Browning, Jerry and Traci Cash, Ed and Christine Jonas, Stuart and Alisa Goldberg, Rev. Michael Ellis, Rev. Comforted Keen, Rev. David Sulleau and my "family" at Church of the Holy Spirit. Also, the late Raymond Gonzalez, Alex Abaroa, Howard Singletary, Glen McIntosh, Cal Carter, and Bertha L. Single-tary, my dear grandmother.

Last, the love and respect that I have for Toni Zarate Singletary, my darlin' wife, and the patience she has shown me throughout our years together cannot be sufficiently addressed on these pages, nor will I try. But I would like to note her multiple contributions to this book and publicly thank her for all she has given me. Toni's strong faith and loving heart, especially during difficult times, helps make everything our family enjoys in life possible. Similarly, our daughter Patricia Judith, an absolute gift from God and as beautiful as her mother, brings to my life a joy that heretofore could not have been imagined. Her laugh, eyes, dimple … everything says, "Hey, Papa, you've got it good!" I sure do, and I love that kid. Finally, the pending arrival of our late infant daughter Bertha Ruth, our firstborn, and the love and sense of urgency she inspired within me for eight months, pushed me to complete this book. While the book may not be perfect, she was. I miss her every day. For these reasons I dedicate *Al Lopez: The Life of Baseball's El Señor* to the three of them.

Contents

Foreword

Bibliophile that I am, I probably have opened as many as a thousand baseball books, but never before have I encountered one like this. It is, in effect, a remarkably detailed play-by-play of the life and times of Al Lopez, who is among baseball's noblemen, perhaps the noblest of all.

It has been my privilege to have known Mr. Lopez for the last five decades, since he arrived in Chicago to manage the White Sox in 1957. The Sox won the pennant two years later, their first since the 1919 Black Sox Scandal.

In the forty years between, the New York Yankees had hoisted 24 pennants on their flagpole and probably would have won eleven in a row, from 1949 through 1960, if not for the relentless pursuit of Señor Lopez, who twice broke their streak: in 1954 with the Cleveland Indians, and again five years later with the White Sox.

Marshall Smith in *Life* magazine described Lopez as a determined pursuer of legendary opponents (casting Casey Stengel as a bold *pistolero*):

> With all his limitless resources and daring the Yanqui [Casey Stengel] should feel safe from pursuit. But he does not. Every time he looks over his shoulder he sees the same inescapable figure. He is always there, always following. This pursuer is not a glamorous hero but a doleful, threadbare man wearing a big sombrero…. Alfonso Ramon Lopez never gives up.

This dogged perseverance has been the centerpiece of Mr. Lopez's existence. Of Spanish descent, the seventh son of a seventh son, he had a thirty-nine-year major league career, nineteen as a player, nineteen more as a manager. He had a .261 lifetime batting average and never had a season with more than eight home runs; nor did he ever reach a season tally of 60 RBIs.

Yet from the beginning it was apparent he was a force, a commanding personality. He captained three big league clubs, the first such appointment coming at the age of twenty-five. He was a catcher, the most hazardous and physically demanding position, and was acknowledged as the best low-ball receiver of his time. When he retired he held the record (since broken) for the most games caught. During his sixteen full seasons as a manager, his teams only three times finished lower than second.

"The big thing about Mr. Lopez, he never gave up," recalled outfielder Jim Landis, who played for him in Chicago. "And as long as he didn't give up, we couldn't give up, either."

Author Wes Singletary's offering is of major significance not merely because of its detailed account of a great man's life, on and off the field, but because it is rich in baseball history. There are many previously unpublished nuggets, such as Mr. Lopez's view of Willie Mays's widely heralded catch in the 1954 World Series, and other "insider" footnotes not found in the general baseball histories.

An example: In 1930, when the ball was juiced, the combined batting average in the National League was .303. A total of 71 players who appeared in 10 or more games batted .300 or higher. The next year the ball was deadened and the hitting was back to normal. The league average plunged to .277; home runs dropped 45 percent. Señor Lopez explains why:

> It was John McGraw's idea. He is the one who complained about it. He couldn't play his kind of baseball with the lively ball. Everyone was swinging for the fences. McGraw favored inside baseball — hitting, bunting, running, squeeze plays, stuff like that. I think the real reason they did it was to cut down on salaries. I hit .309 in 1930 and dropped to .269 in 1931 and they cut my salary.

Also some choice anecdotes:

> One day Early Wynn had been having a bad day and I had gone out to talk to him. If you went out to talk to your pitcher a second time he had to come out of the game. Well, Early was

in trouble and arguing with the umpire and he sees me coming the second time and just lets the umpire have it. The umpire told him that if he kept it up he would be gone. Early said, "What do you think Lopez is coming out here for, to bring me a ham sandwich?"

And, of course, the well-known story, which bears repeating, is also included: how Lopez, when he was 17, caught the legendary Walter Johnson in an exhibition game in Tampa. Before the game, the "Big Train," who threw 100 miles an hour, told him not to call for too many curveballs.

"Mr. Johnson, you throw whatever you want to," Lopez replied. "I'll put down the sign and if you don't want it then shake it off."

Johnson then informed his young catcher he would "let it out" only against Jack Fournier, the National League home run champion. This settled, Lopez "caught Johnson good."

Like Mr. Lopez, this biography is not merely good but excellent. I enjoyed reading it and so will you.

Jerome Holtzman
Evanston, Illinois

Introduction

In the fall of 1925, a barnstorming squad of big-league baseball players, traveling through Florida on a postseason exhibition tour, were convinced by Tampa civic leaders to bring their show to that city. Headlining the tour was "Old Barney" himself, the great pitcher Walter Johnson, weary from a six-game World Series loss by his Washington Senators to the Pittsburgh Pirates. The Senators, and Johnson personally, had a large following in Tampa, for they trained there each spring. After the final game of the series, it was reported that "the biggest crowd that ever kept tab on a World Series in Tampa stood by the *Tribune's* scoreboard ... and lost its heart ... [yet] loves Senators despite final defeat." The mayor of Tampa went so far as to send a conciliatory telegram on behalf of the city to Clark Griffith, owner of the club, congratulating his team on their season and expressing the sentiment that all Tampa was looking forward to their arrival come Spring.[1]

The *Tampa Tribune* advertised that the exhibition game would be held at Plant Field on Friday, October 30, at 3 o'clock, preceded at 1:30 by a parade of players down Franklin Street. It was also announced that the city had decreed the event "Walter Johnson Day" in honor of its hero.[2] Charlie Allen, the manager of the local class D club, the Tampa Smokers, arranged to have the lineups of the two teams composed of the traveling players themselves, other big leaguers who wintered in and around Tampa, and some local minor leaguers. When asked how he planned to fill out the rosters on such short notice, Allen replied, "Big leaguers are like ducks in Florida. If you take the trouble to get out and hunt 'em, you can find all varieties."[3]

Those players gathered by Allen seem to have vindicated his confidence. Among the major-league participants announced were Johnson, Al Schacht and Joe Judge of Washington; Jacques Fournier, William Ehrhardt, Milton Stock, and Bernie Neis of the Brooklyn "Robins"; Chick Fewster from Cleveland; Dave Bancroft and George Harper of the Boston Braves; and Freddie Lindstrom of the New York Giants.

Among the minor leaguers participating were veterans Gene "Old Folks" Hudgings and Jimmy Snead of the Tampa Smokers and their young, seventeen-year-old catcher, Alfonso Ramón Lopez. Lopez had just finished his first season of professional baseball with Tampa and was presently playing winter ball for a local amateur team called the Cuban Stars.[4] Upon being asked to catch, Lopez, thrilled but oblivious to recent headlines, asked who would be pitching. "Walter Johnson," they said. "Do you think you can catch him?" Lopez replied modestly that he didn't know but that he would try.[5] Walter Johnson, considered by some to be the fastest if not the greatest pitcher ever to play the game, presented a challenge to the most veteran receiver, let alone a teenage catcher. Lopez, however, had gained some experience working with Johnson as a batting-practice catcher for the Senators the prior spring, and because of this thought he could handle the job.

Enjoying their last glimpse of professional baseball before the off season set in, 4,000 spectators turned out on game day to revel in the perceptible "Halloween atmosphere" hanging over Plant Field. The contest itself, much to the organizers' delight, went off beautifully. Before the game, Johnson, pitching for the hometeam "Big Train," took Lopez aside and instructed him not to call for too many curve balls. Lopez answered, "Mr. Johnson, you throw whatever you want to; I'll put down the sign and if you don't want it then shake it off." Johnson then informed Lopez that he would "let it all out" only against Jacques Fournier, the National League homerun champ. That settled, the game began, and Lopez, surprising few, "caught Johnson good."[6]

"Old Barney" began fast, striking out former big-league infielder Heinie Scheer on three pitches.[7] He continued in much the same fashion, striking out three more while allowing three hits in a 10–2 victory over Fournier's "All Stars." For his part, Lopez walloped a triple and recorded four putouts in a complete nine-inning performance.[8] After the game Walter Johnson was heard to say, "That boy did real well back there; handled himself fine."[9]

Al Lopez was just beginning to handle himself in a manner others perceived as fine. This Tampa native and son of Spanish immigrants would go on to enjoy a lengthy and distinguished major-league career as a player and manager and would be enshrined in baseball's Hall of Fame.

During his major-league playing career of eighteen years in the National League and one in the American, he was on a first-division club nine times, yet most of those teams finished no better than fourth. The 1944 Pittsburgh Pirates gave him his highest finish, placing a distant second that year. His teams usually struggled because they rarely had good pitching depth and could never seem to obtain any. Chances were, if a deal could be made to obtain a pitcher, Lopez would be the player traded. Durability and respect typified his playing days, as he established a record for most games caught in a career of 1,918, a mark that lasted for many years.[10]

As a manager, his teams finished first or second in eleven of his first sixteen seasons. Beloved and appreciated by both his players and his opponents, Lopez managed by the "golden rule" that if the players respected him he would respect them. His 1954 Cleveland Indians won the American League pennant with a record 111 victories. In 1959 Lopez led an unheralded and seemingly undertalented Chicago White Sox club to his second American League crown. These were the only two teams in sixteen years to overtake the New York Yankees for the American League championship. Despite all this, however, in his hometown of Tampa, Lopez is best known as the man who began it all: the city's first major-league baseball player.

Recent history shows that there are few greater proving grounds for baseball talent than the playing fields of Tampa. Among the players emerging from this former cigar town are big-league baseball performers Steve Garvey, Wade Boggs, Dwight "Doc" Gooden, Fred McGriff, Gary Sheffield, Derek Bell, Tino Martínez, Luis González, and the two opposing managers in the 1990 World Series, Tony LaRussa and Lou Piniella. This is by no means an exhaustive list of major leaguers from Tampa, but a select sample serving to illustrate the breadth of talent in this area. Al Lopez paved the way for these players and is still known as Tampa's "Mr. Baseball."[11]

Al Lopez is not just a local hero; he was a pioneer in opening up baseball to the citizens of Florida and to individuals of Spanish, Cuban, and Italian ancestry, during a period when social barriers were only beginning to come down. Lopez, through his career in baseball, came to symbolize for many Latins, especially in Florida, the path to success. This book examines his remarkable rise along that path, a rise that took him from player to manager to the Hall of Fame.

We Played
Baseball, Mostly

The majority of Tampa's Spaniards originally immigrated from the Northwestern Spanish provinces of Asturias and Galicia during the late nineteenth century. This was in part due to the oppressed social conditions of that nation's poor, as well as exhausted farmland, declining agricultural prices, and a spiraling birthrate. Residents of Asturias and Galicia, together referred to as the "Nursery of Spanish emigrants," led the flight with 820,000 Spaniards leaving for the Americas between 1880 and 1920, 130,000 coming to the United States.[1]

In Cudillero, Asturias, Modesto Lopez, a young tenant farmer who had also worked as a doorman at a Madrid hotel, similarly felt the conditions of the time. With his new wife, Faustina Vásquez, he joined the migration west in the mid-1890s, selecting Cuba as their destination. Modesto, like others going before him, may have also sought to avoid Spain's compulsory military draft.[2]

Upon reaching Cuba, Modesto set out to learn a trade in the island's thriving cigar industry. Through kinship ties he was able to procure a position as an apprentice in one of Havana's better factories. And while temporarily hiding the fact that he was married, Modesto lived briefly in the factory, exchanging janitorial services for room and board. It was in this factory that Modesto Lopez learned the trade of *tabaquero*, or selector. This was a skilled position usually reserved for Spaniards, with Creole peasants, or native Cubans, handling the more menial tasks of stripping

Ybor City cigar makers. (Courtesy Tampa/Hillsborough County Public Library.)

and rolling the tobacco. The *tabaquero* selected the tobacco leaves provided to the cigar makers. At a time when all the cigars were handmade, it was crucial that the expensive tobacco leaf was parceled out according to the size of the cigar. If one was making a smaller cigar, for instance, the selector would provide them with less leaf so as to avoid wasting costly tobacco. The better, larger cigars were made with a bigger leaf. The selector also chose leaf by color. In any event, a skilled *tabaquero* like Modesto might save his factory a considerable amount of money.[3]

Modesto and his growing family, seven children and counting, lived in Havana until 1906. By that time, however, the developing expatriate cigar-making center of Ybor City, Florida, near Tampa, had begun recruiting skilled workers from Cuba for its own factories. Modesto, looking once again to "take a chance" on a better future, left his family temporarily in Havana and proceeded to Ybor City.

Founded in 1886 by the "visionary" Don Vicente Martínez Ybor, and aided by the arrival of fellow cigar manufacturers from Cuba, Ybor City had quickly become the destination for thousands of Spaniards traveling "increasingly familiar pathways" out of Spain, Cuba, and Key West. By 1910 the U.S. Census estimated that there were 2,337 Spaniards in Tampa, all buoyed by the solace found within the community's resonant Latin culture. Ybor City eventually boasted 122 cigar factories employing 10,000 workers sitting three to a team, and hand-rolling more than 250 million coronas, royals, perfectos, and panatelas a year.[4]

Traveling aboard the Henry B. Plant line steamer *S.S. Olivette*, Modesto, then twenty-nine years old, left Havana on February 3, 1906, arriving at the busy port of Key West the same day and continuing to Tampa. At Key West, Modesto informed U.S. immigration officials that he was a selector by trade, had $33 with him, and was traveling to the home of a friend, M. Auido, at 1410 8th Avenue, Tampa, Florida. What he left unsaid was that the "home" was a boardinghouse. In 1900 about 33 percent of Tampa's Spaniards, mostly single men, lived in boardinghouses; the percentage was unchanged a decade later.[5]

With Modesto in Ybor City, Faustina Lopez, then thirty-one years old, remained behind in Cuba with the couple's seven children, ranging in age from two months to nine years. While the separation was no doubt difficult, time passed and within three months, on May 12, 1906, Faustina, with $80 in her pocket and seven kids in tow, followed her husband out of Havana harbor aboard the same *S.S. Olivette*. Her tickets for passage through Key West to Tampa had been paid for in advance by Modesto, who, one can assume, eagerly awaited their arrival.[6]

Faustina, perhaps because of having recently given birth to a son, Emilio, was sick during the entire trip, and so the task of caring for the younger children fell to Amelia, the Lopezes' oldest daughter. Amelia accomplished her task with few problems, and within a brief period, the ordeal of separation behind them, the travel-weary family was reunited in Ybor City. Two years later, on August 20, 1908, the Lopezes welcomed the birth of yet another son, Alfonso Ramón.[7]

By this time the Lopezes had rented a house of their own at 2212 14th Avenue in Ybor City. A short time later they moved to 1210 12th Avenue, a dwelling they initially rented and later purchased. Segments of the Lopez family continued to occupy this home until 1960.[8]

Most of the Lopezes' needs could be met within the distinct confines of Ybor City without ever having to cross over into "Anglo" or "Cracka" Tampa. With streets running north and south, and avenues east and west, Ybor City stretched from Nebraska Avenue east past 22d Street and south from 2d Avenue to 26th Avenue. The claim "We came to Ybor City not Tampa!" was a cry shouted by many immigrants to the area and tended to signify not just their collective attitude, but the conditions that they faced together.[9]

7th Avenue, Ybor City, Tampa, Fla.

7th Avenue in Ybor City, Tampa, Florida, 1908 — the year Al Lopez was born. (Courtesy Florida State Archives.)

Anthony Pizzo, longtime resident of Ybor City and a chronicler of Tampa's ethnic history, remembers the community as a place where

> you could hear the light hearted chatter of Spanish and Italian workers trudging toward long days in the cigar factories; the rumbling of wagons and the clump of horse hooves through the brick streets delivering milk and loaves of bread before sunrise.... The steam-whistles of the Tampa Box Factory and the Latin-American Laundry; the Regensberg Cigar Factory clock tower striking on the hour, and the bell of Our Lady of Mercy Catholic Church calling its parishioners to mass.[10]

Many were the exotic fragrances in Ybor City that tingled one's nostrils. Again Pizzo:

> The aroma of bread being baked by Spanish, Cuban and Italian housewives in their backyard ovens, permeated the neighborhoods. The roasting of coffee-beans in the coffee-mills creating an aromatic smoke perfume filtering through the streets. The pungent smell of Havana tobacco being blended. The processing of guava plants, brewing the tropical fruit into jelly, paste, and "cascos de guayaba" or guava shells.[11]

Pizzo also recalls that the lively music drifting from the halls of El Centro Español, L'Unione Italiana, or El Círculo Cubano "wafted on the heavy night air during festive occasions and would always set hundreds of feet to tapping." Pizzo:

> It used to be so crowded on Seventh Avenue in Ybor on weekend nights that you could barely move. Shops would stay open and did brisk business until eleven at night. Young Latin men and women "dressed to kill" would promenade along the sidewalks with hopes of catching an admiring eye. Old-timers would sit on benches or in coffee shops talking the politics of Spain in Spanish and watched with amusement as the youngsters strutted by. Street vendors would shout the quality of their wares to all those who would listen.[12]

Ybor City's lively atmosphere provided Al Lopez with a childhood rich in the ways of boys. It was a simple time that allowed for almost anything. "You could go not too far from where you were and build your own baseball diamond in any of a couple of fields or lots," Lopez recalled. Or, if one so chose, one could go out past Buffalo Avenue, "where there was nothing but oaks," and catch flying squirrels.[13] Lopez remembers that "In those days there was an abundance of flying squirrels and we used to catch them by hand; they bit pretty good sometimes." He and his friends might also venture down to the Hillsborough River with its thick cover of woods and spend the day swimming and fishing.[14]

Whenever these youngsters got hungry from playing they might pick a watermelon or some oranges from a local field. Lopez elaborates, "We would put the watermelons in the river to cool them off and they would taste delicious." The local growers, however, did not find this casual thievery to be entertaining. Lopez recalls one agitated grower who took measures to prevent the looting:

> Across the street from where I went to school, Ybor Grammar School, there used to be an orange field. We used to try and sneak in there once in a while and pick us a few oranges. The man who owned the field was kind of mean and he was getting tired of those kids taking his oranges. So, he finally got himself an air gun and would fill it with rock salt. He wouldn't shoot you in the face or nothing but he would shoot you in the back or on the butt and that would burn to beat the band. I remember a kid I saw one day running from the orange grove

> all the way home just screaming, he thought he had been shot
> with a bullet and they finally had to get all the salt out of his
> wound before he quit screaming.[15]

Regardless of the exceptional heterogeneity found within Ybor's neighborhoods, the children of the various ethnic groups (Spanish, Cuban, Italian, and others) got along surprisingly well. "Once in a while there would be a battle or throwing stones or rocks, one group against another, but nothing vicious," said Lopez.[16] This was not always true with the adults in the community. In the Sulphur Springs section of Tampa, for instance, there were signs that read "No Latins or dogs allowed to go swimming." While such outside forces in "Cracka" Tampa might have served to draw Ybor's working-class Latins together,[17] ethnic divisions were a significant fact of daily life — with "thrifty" Spaniards generally occupying the upper strata, "fun-loving" Cubans the lower, and "goal-oriented" Italians mixed in between.[18]

Marbles and tops were always popular games with which Lopez and the other Ybor City children passed their days. Basketball was also played a great deal at a lighted park on the corner of Twelfth Avenue and Twelfth Street. And boxing was a popular sport too. Lopez recalls, "They used to have shows at Benjamin field and at the Cuban Club [El Círculo Cubano]. The Cuban Club had a good arena. There were some real good fighters coming out of Tampa then. Chino Álvarez was a great fighter; also a guy named Tommy Gómez came later."[19]

But in spite of the many interests enjoyed by Ybor's youth, Lopez remembers playing baseball "mostly." There was a playground on Thirteenth Avenue and Twentieth Street, in the Spanish district, and baseball was played there each day until it got dark. While Lopez had previously dabbled with the game somewhat, it was his older brother Emilio who formally introduced him to it while following the 1920 World Series. "I started watching him play [after the series] and I sort of followed him, hoping that I could be as good or better than he was.... He kind of gave me something to shoot at."[20] While Emilio Lopez had some baseball talent, he was not serious enough about the game and just played it for fun. Al Lopez, on the other hand, took the game quite seriously, thriving on the competition. "I guess I was a better competitor. I liked to win!"[21]

While baseball had been popular only among Ybor City's Cubans in the late 1880s, by the 1920s it had achieved communitywide acceptance. This was due in part to the influence of the cigar factories, which sponsored company teams. "The flexible schedules of cigarworkers ... served to increase attendance at ball games and heighten interest."[22] And while the game was initially perceived as frivolous by the "thrifty" Spanish, and unworthy of their time, baseball soon became a "community focal point," with factory workers, club members, and the general citizenry all joining in.

The game first appeared in Ybor City in 1887, but the roots of this fascination with the North American sport lay in Cuba, where baseball was introduced in the 1860s. Cubans organized teams and leagues in the late nineteenth century, as "baseball fever swept the country." In 1878 Emilio Sabourín, the "A. G. Spalding of Cuban baseball," helped organize the "Liga de Béisbol Professional Cubana," the world's second professional baseball league.[23] By 1889 it was noted that *béisbol* threatened to replace cockfighting as the Cuban national sport.[24] Thus many Cuban immigrants were already fanatical baseball fans when they arrived in Ybor City and were eager to preach the diamond gospel to their new neighbors.

During this inaugural phase, there were no organized little leagues for boys. Instead, they formed their own baseball clubs, competing against each other. The lack of available money, however, led them to go without suitable equipment, risking injury in the process. Lopez remembers:

> I got my nose busted a couple of times getting hit by foul balls because we didn't have any masks. I'd just go back there and catch. Sometimes everybody would pitch in a nickel or dime to buy a ball and then the ball would have to last. Even after hours of use the game played on as the kids wrapped black tape around the ball to make it last just a little while longer.[25]

As Lopez's developing skills matured, he began to play for a team that was organized by a local barber seeking to establish a rivalry with the team of a barber across town in West Tampa. The barber's wife made uniforms for the players, and games were scheduled whenever convenient. Making matters interesting was the fact that the West Tampa barber was married to the sister of the barber supporting Lopez's squad. The familial competition resulted in some good, aggressive baseball.[26]

Other local businesses and clubs, particularly cigar factories, sensing the publicity afforded by a good team, began putting together squads to play on the weekends in a municipal league that attracted many grown men onto its rosters. These games were played with a great deal of pride, often drawing a good crowd. Alex Scaglione, a Sicilian-born cigar worker,

Top: Newsboys at *La Traducción*, the Ybor City Spanish-language newspaper. A *La Traducción* sportswriter named Montoto encouraged sixteen-year old Al Lopez to try out for the Tampa Smokers. (Courtesy Florida State Archives.) *Bottom:* The 1924 Tampa Smokers. Caesar Álvarez is third from left in front row. (Courtesy Tampa/Hillsborough County Public Library.)

recalled that "the Italian Club, the Cuban Club, el Centro Asturiano, el Centro Español, ... all used to have baseball clubs. You should have seen the crowds on Sundays. Oh Lord, have mercy. It was good I tell you, we enjoyed it."[27] The lively competition found in these games also provided a great deal of experience to young players such as Lopez.

When the games were finished, Lopez spent many of his evenings attending dances or other social functions at one of Ybor's four popular "mutual aid society" clubhouses. Lopez:

> We had a fine life in Ybor back then. At that time we had four social clubs where everybody knew everybody and they had dances and shows. El Centro Español, el Centro Asturiano, el Círculo Cubano and L'Unione Italiana. They would have a dance every Saturday night and a matinee on Sunday. We would get a bunch of us together and go someplace to chip in and buy a bottle of whiskey for all of us to share. We didn't have to take a date or nothing like that. You would go there, and the girls would come with either a chaperon or their own group, sisters or what, and we would pick out a girl to dance with. The girls had this little booklet and you would write down your name in it stating what dance you preferred; the foxtrot, a waltz or whatever. It was all very simple.... If you wanted to take a girl out you would dance with her and ask her after the dance to go to a movie matinee. You would end up at the Tampa Theater watching a movie, with a date. I thought it worked out real good![28]

The 1924 Sacred Heart High School baseball team. Lopez is third from right in back row. (Courtesy Al Lopez.)

Lopez began his professional baseball career with the Tampa Smokers, the local minor-league team. While still a teenager, Lopez through his play around town had attracted the attention of a sportswriter named Montoto. Montoto worked for *La Traducción*, an Ybor City Spanish language newspaper, and encouraged the sixteen-year-old catcher to try out with the Smokers. Lopez at the time was working as a delivery boy for an Italian bakery owned by Angelo Ferlita and was eager for the chance.[29] The Smokers were just beginning to organize their Class D Florida State League team for the 1925 season and were in the market for promising young talent. The 1924 season had ended with the financially strapped Florida State League disbanding and people in the community hoped to reform the franchise and the league. Their games were to be played on Plant Field near the University of Tampa.[30]

An independent, partially subsidized minor-league club, the Smokers had recently been taken over by Dr. H. E. Opre, who operated a downtown real-estate investment firm at 307 Twiggs Street.[31] Opre took control of the Smokers from an ownership group known as the Tampa Athletic Association, which had initially organized the team for 1925. When told by these investors that the Smokers would certainly go under without financial support, Opre's civic pride was aroused and he decided to step in, seeing the team through the season, and if possible, to bring a pennant to Tampa.[32]

Initially, Opre had to discharge a large number of financial obligations before the club could be placed in good standing, and this he did from his own pocket. Even though Opre anticipated heavy operating expenses for the season, he hoped that the Tampa fans would turn out in larger numbers than ever before, thereby easing his costs.[33]

If the financial backbone of the Smokers was Dr. Opre, then its driving force was "Doc" Nance, who "was the guy that formed the team and ran the whole club," according to Lopez.[34] Ably assisted by Charlie Allen, Ray Parmely, Montoto, and other local newspapermen, Nance got busy and eventually rounded up more than seventy-five men to try out for the available roster positions. Of those first players selected, only Nance and Charlie Allen remained at the end of the season.[35]

Montoto gave Lopez a note of recommendation and told him to go see Doc Nance. Nance frequented the "Horseshoe," a downtown pool hall then owned by a merchant named H. E. Wellacott, which served as a center for bookmaking on horse races and ballgames. Officially labeled the "Horseshoe Cigar Stand and Billiard Parlor," it stood at 503 Franklin

Baseball in West Tampa, early 1920s. (Courtesy Florida State Archives.)

Street, close to the corner of Twiggs. Upon arriving, Lopez, a minor, was made to wait outside. Nance, who was in the back and expecting him, came out to meet the young prospect, and Lopez handed over the note from Montoto. After reading it, Nance asked, "How much money do you want to play?" Lopez replied, "I don't know anything about money or contracts or anything like this." Nance responded, "How does a hundred fifty dollars a month sound to you?" Astounded, the young catcher quickly accepted. Lopez then quit both Sacred Heart College [now Jesuit High School], where he had batted .323 that season, and his job at Ferlita's bakery to sign a minor-league baseball contract.[36]

Lopez's parents, Modesto and Faustina, did not object to his playing baseball for a living, since they were only moderately well off and had little hope of his attending college or even progressing further in high school. However, they did tell him that if he did not make it in baseball, he would have to get a job. With the threat of a cigar factory career looming on his horizon, Al Lopez set out to perform the only job that he ever wanted: to be a professional baseball player.[37]

It has been argued that baseball was more successful in helping to socialize and integrate Americans during the 1920s than ever before. While today Latins are pervasive on teams throughout the United States, it was not always so. Who, then, were these first Latin ballplayers? Upon the

Walter Johnson (left) and Bucky Harris of the Washington Senators, spring training in Tampa, mid–1920s. (Courtesy Tampa/Hillsborough County Public
Library.)

establishment of the first professional baseball league in 1871, the National Association of Professional Baseball Players, Cuban-born Esteban Bellan was rostered as a player for the Troy [New York] Haymakers. Bellan proved to be well ahead of his times.[38]

The first "big" Latin baseball star was the pitcher Adolfo "Dolf" Luque. Known alternately as the "Pride of Havana," or the "Havana Perfecto," Luque, a smart and crafty hurler, joined the Boston Braves in 1914 and began to earn a respectable 193–179 record over a twenty-year career in the majors that saw him pitch for several teams. Between Luque and the 1947 arrival of Jackie Robinson, another forty or so Latins played in the major leagues. There were also many Latin ballplayers struggling in the minors that might have played in the majors if there had not been the racial or ethnic quotas then in place. Even the Latins who made the big leagues were often ridiculed deliberately after arriving. Demeaning remarks, often involving their stereotypical eating habits and appearance, represented yet another manifestation of the game's historic discriminatory practices. As others have made clear, Latins were treated in much the same fashion as other "hyphenated" Americans — badly.[39]

In 1925 sixteen-year-old Al Lopez of the Tampa Smokers, "one of the youngest receivers in professional baseball,"[40] became part of the early entry of Latin ballplayers into the organized game. As noted earlier, although his parents were Spanish, Lopez grew up in a community that had a passion for baseball. Because of this, Latins turned out in large numbers to watch the Tampa Smokers play. The cigarmakers of Ybor City, arguably Tampa's strongest baseball fans, were paid piece rates. That is, they were paid for the number of cigars they had produced. The Smokers' games usually started at 3:15 p.m., so having made sure that their wages for the day were earned by 2:30, cigarmakers could leave their factories and journey over to nearby Plant Field for the contest.[41]

Tampa's Latins were also prone to wager on the ballgames, although the Smokers were hardly the only bet in town. Lopez remembers Tampa as "wide open" with regard to gambling. "Oh yeah, they bet like hell!" he says. "They loved to bet. At that time gambling in Tampa was wide open. There were gambling houses with roulette wheels, dice, any kind of gambling you could ask for."[42]

Along with Tampa, the Florida State League consisted of the St. Petersburg Saints, the Bradenton Growers, the Lakeland Highlanders, the Sarasota Gulls, the Fort Myers Palms, the Orlando Colts, and the Sanford Celeryfeds. Travel to and from the towns for the games was difficult because the roads were poor and the teams used private cars. The road to St. Petersburg was the easiest route; its recently constructed Gandy Bridge spanned Tampa Bay for the first time. As Lopez recalls:

> Before the bridge was built, we used to take Memorial Highway and go up around Clearwater, Largo, in there, just to get to St. Pete. It was about sixty miles and a terrible drive. Memorial Highway was just one-lane pavement. If another car was coming from the other direction, you would have to slow down and give him half of the road. When we went to Sanford it was another terrible trip. Tampa to Lakeland was a tough drive in those days. You had to pass through Mango, Seffner, Kissimmee, and then into Orlando, the other side of Lakeland, just to get there.[43]

Once the exhausting travel was behind them, the teams usually played in front of surprisingly large crowds. "We'd have 1,000 to 1,500 people at the games, but the prices were cheap," Lopez later emphasized. "The teams "were collecting $1,000 a game, probably a little more than that. By the end of the year a team might get lucky and break even. If they broke even during the season then they would profit if they sold one player."[44]

Lopez was almost sold before he ever played an inning for the Smokers. During spring training for the start of the 1925 season and shortly before reporting to the Smokers, Lopez was asked by the Washington Senators if he wanted a job as their batting-practice catcher for that spring. Lopez explained:

> In those days they [major league teams] didn't bring ten or eleven catchers to Spring Training like they do now. They would only bring two or three. But, because they took hours of batting practice and also had a number of pitchers to warm up, they would need some help. The manager that year was Bucky Harris and they offered me expenses plus $45 a week if I would just catch batting practice. I thought that was great because I would have done it for nothing. Just to put the Washington uniform on was a great experience. The Senators would also carry me to the exhibition games with them so that I could catch [pre-game] batting practice for them. I got to see great players then, guys like Zach Wheat of Brooklyn. Wheat was a picture at the plate, hitting.[45]

During this time, the catching and all-round hustle of Lopez caught the eye of Mike Martin, Washington's highly regarded trainer. He suggested to team owner Clark Griffith that it might be a good idea to purchase the contract of the young catcher, because "he loves to play ball and has good potential." However, when Martin asked the Smokers about buying the rights to Lopez, he was shocked to hear the asking price of $10,000. Martin responded that Lopez was an unproven kid and offered to pay $1,000 for him. Unproven or not, the Smokers refused and Lopez remained the property of the Tampa club.[46]

During that 1925 season with the Smokers, Lopez kept company with two other Spanish-speaking players on the team. Lopez:

> One Cuban boy, Oscar Estrada, they brought him from Cuba, played the outfield, pitched and played first-base. Good player. He was sold to the Boston Braves after the season. The other fellow I luckily roomed with, named Cesare Álvarez. He was an old man, about thirty-two. He had been pitching quite a while. He spoke English, but, you know, English like I did I guess [broken]. Cesare had married a Spanish girl from Tampa and she had her family here. While on the road, we would go out at night to eat or to a movie, because we played all day games. Get up in the morning, have breakfast, then go over to the ballpark and play your game.[47]

The Smokers played most of their away games in "Cracka" towns where fans would use colorful expletives to bait and with luck rile the opposing players, but it seems not to have bothered Lopez. He plainly suggests that whether the abuse was from the fans or the rival players, it was all part of the game. "They do that all over in baseball. They want to get under your skin. People would call me a 'Cuban Nigger' or something like that, and I'm not even Cuban." In retrospect, on the topic of racial or ethnic prejudice in baseball, Lopez thinks that maybe he was just too young to have been concerned when it was directed at him. "I treated everybody like I wanted to be treated. If a guy treated me badly then I just didn't bother with him. I never had this minority thing handicap me in any way. I'm Spanish and proud of it."[48]

During his first year of professional baseball, Lopez did not see much playing time. Because the Smokers were in a "good Class D" league, the sixteen-year-old found veteran minor-league catcher Gene "Old Folks" Hudgins playing in front of him. "Whenever 'Old Folks' was behind the plate," chimed the *Tampa Tribune*, "the pitcher in the box felt his confidence grow as he knew that he had a backstop with years of experience behind him and who knew the finer points of the game and just how to work a pitcher."[49] Lopez recalls sitting the bench until the "latter part of the season" because of the presence of the veteran Hudgins. "We played in the playoffs with St. Petersburg, and I had a good series that year," Lopez said.[50]

The Smokers, like many minor-league organizations, found their ballplayers when and wherever they could, being neither limited to the Tampa area nor confined by league rules. Says Lopez:

> They brought them from all over. In fact, my first year with the Smokers the team was supposed to have two rookies that had never played pro ball, and they were allowed to have two "classmen" — ballplayers who had played higher classification than "D" ball. So what happened was that we came up with some ballplayers who had played within the junior leagues which was class "B," and they changed some of their names to get them on our roster. One guy, Jimmy Snead, changed his name from Schneider to Snead, and things like that, because they wanted to get away with playing. They wanted to have a good team, which we did. We finally ended up with a good team but the league found out that we had too many classmen. We had four on our roster instead of the [maximum] two. Two of the four were pitchers and so was the manager [Jimmy Snead had taken over the managerial duties from Charlie Allen] and the catcher, Gene Hudgins. We finally ended up keeping the two pitchers. The manager then changed his name to maintain eligibility and the catcher was let go as a classman and that is when I got my break to start catching.[51]

Hudgins, with the approval of the St. Petersburg club, was brought back at the end of the season for the playoffs. By that time, however, Lopez was firmly entrenched as the team's starting backstop. "Young Alfonso Lopez" was described in the *Tampa Tribune* as having ably filled the place of catcher when Hudgins was released.[52] "He came through not only in the regular season but performed brilliantly in the series." In fifty-one regular season appearances, Lopez went to the plate 134 times, batting .224 with six doubles. But over the final two weeks of the season and league playoffs, Lopez performed like an experienced veteran and not the seventeen-year-old he had recently become. He tore up the opposition, batting .388 in the stretch (.294 in the league championship series).

During this two-week period the Smokers were locked in a pitched battle with the Lakeland Highlanders over first place for the second half of the season and the right to face the St. Petersburg Saints, the first-half champions, in the league playoffs. Amid the heat of a stretch run, the Smokers, with the inexperienced Lopez behind the "dish," began a nine-game home and home series with St. Petersburg, followed by a six-game home and home series against Lakeland.

In St. Petersburg, the Smokers took the first two games and advanced their league lead to two and a half games over Lakeland. They then extended the lead to three and a half by taming the Saints 10–2 in their final game of the regular season across the bay. Cesare Álvarez allowed just six hits while going the distance for Tampa.[53]

When the two teams returned to Plant Field, the Smokers opened it up by edging St. Petersburg 1–0 on the four-hit pitching of the Cuban, Oscar Estrada. Estrada, who during the season played as much in the outfield as on the mound, continued to show the form that made him a 1925 signee of the Boston Braves.[54] The following day, Tampa and St. Petersburg split their final doubleheader, thereby giving Tampa a narrow percentage point lead over second-place Lakeland, heading into their final regular season match-up.[55]

The next week in Lakeland, the Highlanders got six-hit pitching from their ace, Watt Luther, coming away with an unnerving 3–0 shutout over Tampa. Twice the Smokers filled the bases only to have their bats knotted by Luther's "viciously breaking" curveball. But Tampa battled back the following day as Lopez went three for three, leading a thirteen-hit attack to win, 6–4, and clinch the second-half league pennant. This gave the Smokers the right to play arch-nemesis St. Petersburg in the postseason.[56]

The next day, after the Smokers won a coin toss, it was announced that the playoffs would commence in Tampa the following week. But because El Centro Asturiano had already reserved Plant Field to stage a bull fight, the championship opener shifted to St. Petersburg.[57]

The playoffs began with Tampa edging the Saints 7–6 in a contest marked by "terrific slugging." The two teams combined for twenty-three hits, eleven of which were for extra bases. In game two, St. Petersburg, aided by two costly errors, tied the series at one each. The Saints ace, Hewitt, was masterful in allowing just four hits over nine innings. Game three was much the same, with St. Petersburg moving ahead for a two-game-to-one series advantage.[58]

Game four saw the Smokers' bats rekindle for thirteen hits, and Tampa won the contest 9–6, tying the series at two even. Pitching marked the following day's game as Álvarez strode to the mound for Tampa opposed by St. Petersburg's ace, Hewitt. The stingy Álvarez proved the better, allowing only three "widely scattered" base hits during the nine innings, and Tampa came away a 5–1 winner. During the match, the normally amicable Lopez and the veteran Charlie Allen were thrown out of the game for arguing balls and strikes with the umpire. After being called out on strikes to end an inning, Lopez, who was plainly disgusted, confronted the umpire upon returning to take his place behind the plate. The entire Tampa team soon crowded around the umpire shouting in defense of Lopez, with Charlie Allen, the former manager, being the most vocal of the group. After a few minutes the umpire called for a policeman, and three answered his call, escorting the ejected Lopez and Allen from the field. In game six, Oscar Estrada had one bad inning, but it was enough to give St. Petersburg the 4–1 win, knotting the series once again.[59]

Locked at three games apiece, the two best teams in the Florida State League squared off in the final and most exciting game of the season. The encounter moved along briskly until the seventh inning, when, with the score tied at one run, Hewitt of St. Petersburg hung a fat one to Horace Hicks, who ripped it down the first-base line for a triple. Emerson Welk followed with a triple of his own to left field, driving in Hicks and picking up the RBI. Bob Lee next blooped a single, bringing Welk home. Those two runs proved the difference, as the Smokers secured a 3–1 victory, thereby clinching the 1925 Florida State League championship and presenting Tampa the trophy for the first time in five years.[60]

Lopez began to emerge as a folk hero for Tampa Latins. "Clearly," write Gary Mormino and George Pozzetta, "he fostered a sense of pride among Latins who vicariously shared his success."[61] Lopez himself did not notice any special attention at first. He recalls, "I was just one of the local guys and I lived in the area. I played around the clubs, played dominoes with them. I never figured I was a hero, but I guess that maybe I was." Tony Pizzo recalled how groups would greet Lopez at the end of each season and parade him down Seventh Avenue in Ybor City. "Al Lopez was a real hero to everyone from Ybor City. It didn't matter that you were Spanish, Italian or what, we all stuck together." When asked if the people of Ybor City looked to Lopez with any special pride, Marcelo Maseda, a former professional baseball player and "alcalde" or unofficial mayor of Ybor City, responded, "Oh yeah! Everybody was proud of him."[62]

The 1926 season began with obvious high hopes for the Smokers and saw Lopez work himself into the starting lineup once again. Through the first two months of the campaign, however, the Smokers played just over .500 baseball with a record of sixteen and fourteen, good enough for fourth place. Near the end of May the Smokers showed some life, downing St. Petersburg 4–3 behind Lopez's game-winning tenth-inning RBI double, to complete a sweep. The *Tampa Tribune* reported that "Alphonz" might have stretched his hit into a triple, had the extra base been necessary.[63]

In spite of Lopez's heroics, the team continued to struggle, and by June 6, following two one-sided losses to first-place Sanford, they had slipped below .500 for the first time all season. In the second game, the Smokers mounted a minor ninth-inning rally only to have it snuffed out when former University of Tennessee ace Ben Cantwell, the league's top pitcher, was called upon to close it out for the Celeryfeds. Two days later Lopez himself contributed to the slide when in the midst of a pitching duel, he badly overthrew third base attempting to pick off a runner and allowed the deciding Sarasota run to score.[64]

A bright spot for the Smokers during the season's early months was the success of rookie pitcher Justo Dominguez. The Cuban hurler proved nearly untouchable, posting seven straight wins before allowing five runs on nine hits and suffering his first loss, to the Orlando Colts. Showing nerve, if not resiliency, Dominguez went to the hill the following day at Orlando and was chased in the second inning after giving up "a deluge of hits and runs." Lopez went one for three at the plate that day, raising his team-leading average to .362. The following afternoon Orlando made it three straight from the Smokers when the Colt sluggers "tapped the port-side slants" of Tampa's starting pitcher Kurtz for a total of eight hits, blanking the "downstaters" three to nothing. Once again, Lopez worked diligently, racing into the stands on three separate occasions to take foul flies, and going two for four at the plate.[65]

With little going right for the Smokers, it was reported that local businessman Robert E. Ellis had landed a 110-pound tarpon at Fort Myers.[66] This catch provided the perfect backdrop for the coming series against the "big fish" of the Florida State League, Ben Cantwell and his first-place Sanford Celeryfeds. Lacking the bats of past Tampa clubs, however, the weak-hitting Smokers tanked the three-game set, losing to Cantwell, his eleventh win, 2–0, followed by a doubleheader loss, 1–0 and 2–1. As the curtain dropped, the Smokers found themselves buried in sixth place with a 21–26 record.[67]

After slumping into seventh place the next week, it came as little surprise when Charlie Allen, twice manager of the Smokers for half a season, resigned his post "for the good of the club, inasmuch as the boys can't seem to play winning ball under me." Dr. Opre "closely followed" the resignation by announcing that Tommy Leach, the former Pittsburgh Pirate third baseman, was considered "as good as signed" to take Allen's place. It would be Leach's second go-around with the Smokers; he had also managed the club in 1920–22 and won a pennant in 1920. For his part, Leach let it be known that he would indeed assume the reins upon returning from Haines City, where he was completing some personal business.[68]

With second baseman Phil Tanner managing during the interim, the Smokers responded in "faultless" fashion, besting Ben Cantwell and Sanford, 5–3. After a runner reached third base behind an error, sacrifice, and a single to start the seventh inning, Cantwell, the "$5,000 beauty," walked Lopez, "all but throwing it out of the park," to get to light-hitting Bob Lee. The right fielder quickly made him regret the call, lacing a single to right and driving in the game's winning run. Afterward, the press reported that with Cantwell pitching, "curbstone circles" (bookmakers) had been spotting the Smokers two runs on all action.[69]

Two days later it was formally announced that Tommy Leach would officially take over the helm of the Smokers, beginning with the next day's afternoon affair against Sarasota. "I will be in Tampa Monday to take charge of the team," Leach said.[70] "Doc" Opre, expressing the optimism of the Smokers' faithful, exclaimed, "In Tommy Leach, we have an excellent pilot.... He showed that when he won a pennant for us in 1920, molding a championship team from absolute rookie material." Opre continued the endorsement by adding that if "Tommy wants more ballplayers ... [w]e will do our best to get them." Leach's initial worry was debuting without his hustling young catcher. With Sarasota coming to town to open a three game set, it was revealed that Lopez would miss at least one start and possibly more while recovering from minor surgery for an ear infection acquired while swimming the previous weekend. The concern proved legitimate because the Smokers, "minus a catcher," were "helpless" against the "hot mound work" of the Sarasota ace, Lanning. Lopez did not return to the Tampa lineup until a week later in a doubleheader with St. Petersburg that began the second half of the season. In the first game, Lopez went 0–4 in a 10–3 loss. After sitting out the second game, he recovered the next day, going 2–4 with a double to help his teammates get the 5–2 victory and an early 2–1 second-half league lead.[71]

The Florida State League's opening stanza had drawn to a close shrouded in a controversy involving Sanford, the eventual first-half champs. Pursuant to league rules, no club was allowed more than two "classmen" on its roster, or as Lopez mentioned in the quote above, ballplayers who had played higher than Class D baseball. Sanford, it was found, had played a majority of its games with its roster over the limit. League charges were brought against the Celeryfeds by St. Petersburg, Bradenton, Lakeland, and Fort Myers. This might have been expected, given the fact that St. Petersburg was penalized for the same thing earlier in the season and knocked from first place because of it. While some predicted that the "loop would be rocked to its foundations by 'sweeping investigations and penalties,'"[72] it did not occur. At a league meeting of club owners in Tampa, it was decided that given Sanford prexy J. B. Asher's claim that the offense was unintentional, only three St. Petersburg and Fort Myers losses would be tossed out, representing a total of six Sanford victories. Fort Myers, which had been on the verge of falling out of the league, "greatly appreciated" the concessions, for it moved them from third to second place in the league standings.[73] Dr. Opre, discussing the minor penalties doled out despite what some expected, reasoned that "The dove of peace still rules."[74] Apparently, the club owners viewed cooperation and goodwill as more immediate concerns to the league than ongoing rules violations. Remember, the league itself had collapsed during the 1924 run and all efforts were being made to ensure that it did not happen again.

In Tampa the league heads also took the opportunity to boost the salary limit for each club. It had been adhering to a $2,250-a-month payroll, but it now decided to raise the limit to $2,500. The latter figure was the regulation Class D league salary cap. While the $250 increase may have sounded like not much, it was argued by the owners that if divided equally among six regular players, it would mean an additional $25 a month in their [players'] pockets.

Following the Smokers' success against St. Petersburg over the July 4 weekend, they immediately fell back into their losing ways. Lakeland traveled to Tampa and quickly took advantage of Smokers pitching, scoring twelve runs on thirteen hits in a 12–8 win, and followed it up the next day with a 5–4 victory over veteran Smokers pitcher Cesare Álvarez. It was Álvarez's third defeat in five days as he struggled to correct Tampa's pitching woes. It got little better for the Smokers during the remainder of the month, and by July 22, after Álvarez lost again, this time to Rube

Brower and Sarasota, they found themselves in the second-half cellar with a 5–11 record.[75]

By mid-August, however, with the "dog days" upon them, Tampa's "Leachmen" began to recover, playing consistent .500 baseball for the first time all season and moving into fourth place at 18–16. Of note in this turn-around was the improved effort of Cesare Álvarez, who, as he had the prior season, saved his best for last in hurling a number of late-season quality games. With the sports pages trumpeting Jack Dempsey's return to the gym for his upcoming first bout with Gene Tunney, the Smokers got phys-ical against Sarasota, scoring six runs in six frames to defeat the Gulls 6–1. A week later Lopez, refusing the neutral corner, singled twice as Tampa topped St. Petersburg 6–3 and moved to within two games of first-place Orlando.[76]

The second-half surge gave "Doc" Opre reason to be optimistic about the fortunes of his club. Having recently lost an estimated $10,000 in the promotion of an exhibition football venture sold by Red Grange and his manager C. C. Pyle, Opre informed the *Tampa Tribune* that "I'm going to stick with baseball and make it a good thing."[77] He continued adding that because the Smokers were having a good year and attendance had been fair, the team had just about supported itself. These circumstances led him to hopefully confess that if the Smokers were to come through with a second-half pennant and play the Celeryfeds in a championship series, "he'll make a small piece of change."

The next day Opre's contenders began a series at Lakeland with a 4–2 win over the Highlanders. The light-hitting affair was marred somewhat in the sixth inning when Lakeland's player-manager Ellam, believing that Cesare Álvarez had thrown a couple of pitches too close to him, tossed his bat at the pitcher, resulting in Ellam's ejection. Lopez led all batters with three hits, including a double in the seventh that "started the works" for Tampa's game-winning rally. However, it was defensive efforts that paid the heaviest dividends. "Blackie" Blackstock, in left field, made "a beau-tiful one-hand catch of a hard hit ball" in the first inning, and Tanner at shortstop ran into center field and caught one over his shoulder to retire the side with two men on, silencing another Lakeland opportunity. It was also noted that Tampa's spectators outnumbered the home fans by "a large majority" and "cheered Tommy [Leach] and his charges continually." But the following week's efforts dealt a near "fatal blow" to Tampa's momen-tum when the Smokers dropped a crucial late-season doubleheader to Lakeland. On the mound for the Highlanders in the second game was

"Little" Walter Johnson, who proved "heroic," one-hitting the Smokers and holding Lopez and Tampa's two other top batters hitless, striking each out once.[78]

Notwithstanding the important loss, Tampa continued to scratch going into the final stretch and by Labor Day, following a two-game sweep of St. Petersburg, had moved back into contention, a game and a half behind the first-place Fort Myers Palms. Two days later, as the nation's moviegoers mourned the death of Rudolf Valentino, the Smokers closed to within half a game of first, beating Bradenton 5–0, while Fort Myers lost. The standings now showed Sanford in first with a 29–20 record, closely shadowed by Fort Myers at 32–23, Orlando at 30–22, and Tampa and Lakeland, both with identical 32–24 numbers. With the Smokers preparing to open their next-to-last home series of the season, against Sarasota, it was apparent that all contests were urgent. The Smoker–Gull series was originally scheduled for Sarasota, but both clubs agreed to switch it to Plant Field, thereby giving the "Leachmen" home-field advantage for the remainder of the year. It was also announced by Opre that inasmuch as the Sarasota series had been scheduled to be played on the road, season tickets and passes would not be honored, because all receipts were to go to the Gulls. In spite of the obvious importance of the present series, the *Tampa Tribune* noted that, barring a Smoker loss, the "crucial series" would come the following week against Fort Myers.[79]

Tommy Leach once again called upon Cesare Álvarez, his venerable workhorse, to take the hill in the opener against Sarasota's "Lefty" Owens. It was Owens who stole the early spotlight, starting like "a house afire" and holding the Smokers scoreless for the first five innings. An error by Denicke, the Tampa shortstop, staked Owens to a one-run lead in the first and it began to look as though the slim lead might hold up. In the sixth inning, however, the Smokers, led by Lopez, "solved [Owens's] delivery" and rushed four runs across the plate, giving Álvarez all the support he needed. With the bases full, Lopez, "the big cracker in the fireworks," belted a long, low drive to left field, the ball finding a resting place in the "bullrushes" near the foul line, scoring Tanner, Stanton, and Lee, with Lopez resting at third. Salvatz followed with a sacrifice fly to right that scored Lopez for the fourth run of the inning. In the eighth inning, Lopez's infield "tap" forced Stanton across with the Smokers' fifth and final run of the game, a 5–1 win. The *Tampa Tribune* reported the contest as a "case of the old reliable battery coming through." Álvarez, for his part, held the Gulls to one unearned run, "turning them back in clock-like fashion."[80]

The next day, on "an afternoon of golden moments," the Smokers kept it going, picking up a "twin win" over the Gulls, 5–4 and 5–2. Game one, which was filled with dramatics, brought the 1,500-paid-attendance crowd to their feet on multiple occasions. With two men on base and his team down by a digit, 4–3, in the bottom of the eighth, Manager Leach "placed himself into the fray," pinch-hitting for pitcher Lefty Kurtz. The count reached three and two on Leach, with the old Pirate fouling back three, before he found the pitch he wanted. Connecting, he sent a streaking drive to center that "seemed labelled for at least two bases." The two runners crossed the plate and Leach drew up at second as the "bespectacled" Gulls player-manager Harry Manush made a desperate dive toward the descending ball. Manush caught it just off the ground with his glove hand outstretched, "way to the left." By some "freak of acrobatics or juggling," he held the ball, stumbling at least ten feet in the process. Leach's blow had fallen short, leaving the Smokers still a run behind.

In the ninth inning, after Smokers relief pitcher Red Craig had retired the Gulls, Tampa came to the plate with one last chance. Denicke led off with a walk, followed by Tanner, who was hit by a pitched ball, also taking his base. This brought young George Stanton, the center fielder, to bat. Stanton, who initially squared to bunt, missed the first two pitches. But with two strikes and bunting no longer an option, he took a ball before "smashing" a drive between left and center fields, scoring Denicke standing, and Tanner sliding in for the winning run. In the bleachers the hat was immediately passed by the jubilant crowd and liberally filled. After the game at an impromptu ceremony, Tommy Leach called Stanton to home plate and presented him with his reward. As the "great little Smoker manager" turned the fans' contribution over to his player, it became difficult to determine who the fans were applauding the most. The *Tampa Tribune* referred to the "golden" moment as one of those in baseball that "only seldom are allowed the fans, and which seldom are forgotten."[81]

Compared to the first game, the second was relatively easy for the Smokers. Red Craig, the winner of game one, made it two in a row, being hit often, but managing to hold the score down in a 5–2 decision. Four Sarasota base hits gave the Gulls two runs in the first. But Tampa got three runs in the bottom half of the inning and "the game might as well have ended there." The Smokers collected two more runs in the third against Rube Brower, who like Craig, was pitching his second consecutive game. With two down in the inning, Lopez singled and advanced to score on Salvatz's base hit. Lopez had initially stopped at third. However, upon realizing that the plate was left uncovered, he raced home and scored, beating the Gulls catcher, Armstrong, on the play. Salvatz then stole third, rubbing salt in Armstrong's already wounded psyche, and scored on Blackstock's single to center. Armstrong, the dazed Sarasota receiver, then ended the inning by throwing out Blackstock on an attempted steal. With the game in hand, umpire Bradley called it at the end of Sarasota's fifth inning because of darkness. With their victories, the Smokers passed Fort Myers (who had lost to St. Petersburg) in the standings and "were crowding the edges of first place," eleven points behind Sanford. They had also earned the next day off and looked ahead to their season-ending showdown against the Palms.[82]

With the Smokers idle, Sanford took advantage of the opportunity to stretch their lead by easily defeating Bradenton, 4–1. Having been virtually tied with Tampa the day before, the "Feds" extended their lead to a half game with the key win. With only percentage points favoring Sanford, the Smokers needed to make up a full game on the Celeryfeds to "nose out a victory." Tampa could win the pennant only by taking two of the three games from Fort Myers while Sanford dropped all three to St. Petersburg at Sanford; or, if Sanford won one, Tampa must take three. By sweeping the series, the best percentage Tampa would obtain was .613. If Sanford won two, the Celeryfeds would take the pennant with a percentage of .618. The league championship would then go uncontested to Sanford, who were also the first-victors.[83]

Recognizing the stakes, manager Leach called on the "right-hand chunking" of Cesare Álvarez to face Fort Myers before 1,500 fans in the first game of the season-ending set. Álvarez was opposed by Joe Domingo, the former Tampa Hillsborough High School baseball and football star, who had been a Smoker jinx all season. Seeming "fully cognizant ... of the shortness of the time in which to win" the pennant for the second half of the season, the Smokers jumped on Domingo in the first inning. "Skinny" Denicke led off with a walk, Tanner popped out, and Stanton singled through second. Lee then walked, filling the bases, and Lopez sacrificed Denicke home for the first run of the contest. In the third, Denicke walked again and promptly stole second. He scored on successive sacrifice flies by Tanner and Stanton. In the fourth, Lopez, Salvatz, and Blackstock rapped out consecutive singles. Barnes's sacrifice fly to center scored Lopez, and Salvatz followed Lopez home when Overstreet, the Palms' catcher, let the throw from center field get through him. Álvarez was then hit on the wrist and took his base. Denicke followed with a single

to right, sending Blackstock home and Domingo to the showers. It was
Tampa's fifth and final run. Meanwhile, Álvarez was dealing the Palms
misery in "concentrated doses." For six innings he sent his foes down in
order, finally allowing a dink bunt single in the seventh, when Lopez, who
surely could have handled the play, chose to let it roll foul; and it didn't.
Three scratch hits and one clean one off Álvarez represented the sum total
of Fort Myers' offense.[84]

As Tampa was winning, Sanford was being held to a draw, affording
the Smokers a few more points in their last-minute bid for the second half
pennant. With the tie, Sanford remained fifteen percentage points ahead
of Tampa. A victory the following day coupled with a Sanford loss would
give the Smokers a narrow lead, with one day remaining.[85]

The upshot was that the Smokers and Palms returned to the diamond
once again recognizing that Tampa's pennant hopes hinged on a win and
a Sanford loss. Showing a "grimness" inspired by knowledge that a single
defeat meant elimination, the Smokers met the challenge, earning a "hard-
won" victory on "Blackie" Blackstock's tie-breaking RBI double in the
ninth. With the score knotted at one all, Tampa's Lee got things going
with his third hit of the game, a clean drive to right. Lopez followed and
attempted a sacrifice bunt, but the Palms catcher overthrew first, putting
Lopez on and moving Lee to second. Overstreet, the Palms' catcher, "paid
his debt" by gunning down Lee at third on Salvatz's bunt, with Lopez taking second. Blackstock then came "to the rescue" by slashing a "wicked
drive" to center that soared several feet above the outfielder's head and
pushed Lopez across with the winning tally. At Sanford, however, the Celeryfeds won the first game 9–1 and were well on their way to another when
the game was stopped in the seventh inning on account of darkness with
the score tied, 1–1. A doubleheader between Sanford and St. Petersburg
was arranged for the next day to finish out the regular season, while Tampa
and Fort Myers played their last game, at Plant Field. If the Saints and
Celeryfeds played both scheduled games, Tampa could win the pennant
if they defeated the Palms while Sanford lost two. A win for Tampa and
one loss for the Celeryfeds would also catch the Smokers up in the game
column, but Sanford must lose a game to settle matters in Tampa's favor
due to Sanford's favorable winning percentage.[86]

The final day of the 1926 Florida State League season dawned in
Tampa with high hopes. The Smokers began it by blanking Fort Myers,
5–0. All eyes then shifted to Sanford, where one loss by the Celeryfeds
was necessary to send the Smokers into the postseason. Anxious for the

results, some of Tampa's players, including Lopez, ventured into the press box to call the *Tribune* office. But what they learned left them soured. Sanford had clinched the second-half pennant, playing a one-to-one tie with St. Petersburg in another rain shortened encounter. The second game scheduled between the Celeryfeds and Saints was also canceled, possibly sparing the "Feds" the all-important loss. While the hard-charging Smokers now seemingly held a half-game lead over the Celeryfeds in the win column, Sanford's winning percentage remained higher, giving them the advantage. Even the nature of the draw was cheap, coming as it did on an error in the seventh by "Luckey," the Saint's ill-named catcher.[87]

One of the greatest uphill battles in the history of the Florida State League was thus lost just when it seemed that victory was within the grasp of the climber. Dr. Opre, when questioned regarding Sanford's failure to make up rainouts and other postponements that "marred" their record, graciously conceded that "Sanford has won the pennant as far as I am concerned. Of course, we have the more admirable record. We have played all our games — hard ones and easy ones — and we have half a game lead over the Celeryfeds." A postseason series between the two clubs was briefly considered but never came about because Sanford decided instead to play against an all-star team led by former Chicago Cubs shortstop Joe Tinker.[88]

In only his second season of professional baseball, Al Lopez had performed well, batting .315 over 116 games. During the early part of the season when the club was struggling, he remained a rock, providing veteran leadership beyond his years. After the arrival of Tommy Leach, Lopez, returning from surgery, showed his value behind the plate and was a factor in the team's improved pitching the second half of the season. His rooming and working with Cesare Álvarez for two seasons and the maturity gained from the experience had also benefited the club. These factors led the sportswriters covering the Florida State League to select Lopez as the league's "best catcher."[89]

After the 1926 season in Tampa, Lopez, in a move reflecting his emerging status in professional circles, was drafted by the Jacksonville Tars organization in the higher-classification B league. He explains, "If you're not sold you can only play two years in one league, then you are subject to the draft. So the Jacksonville team which had just started the year before drafted me to come up to Jacksonville."[90] With two championship-caliber seasons behind him, Al Lopez found himself leaving home for the first time, traveling up Highway 301 to become a member of the Southeastern League's Jacksonville Tars for the 1927 season.

Up Through
the South

At Jacksonville the durability that Al Lopez would demonstrate throughout his career began to surface. He caught 128 of the 154 games in 1927 for the team — an outstanding number for a minor-league catcher. While his batting average dipped to .276 from the .315 he hit at Tampa in 1926, he continued to collect extra-base hits: ten doubles and ten triples for the season. For this, Lopez was chosen his league's outstanding catcher for the second consecutive year.[1]

The 1927 season began on an up note for Jacksonville when it was announced at a preseason meeting of club owners that the Tars would be one of four Southeastern league clubs to open its schedule at home, playing a four-game set with the Albany Nuts at Durkee Field. League president Cliff Green made it clear that he expected an "exceptionally good season" and that "everything was in readiness for the opening on April 11."[2] The first mention of Lopez in the Jacksonville press came in early April when the *Florida Times-Union* reported that he would be on the "receiving end" of Ben Cantwell's opening-day deliveries.[3]

The Tars themselves got a taste of Lopez's ability on April 9 when they took on the Macon Peaches of the South Atlantic League in an exhibition contest between Lopez's present and future teams.[4] Ben Cantwell and Johnny Bates held Macon in check while Lopez, Pat Collins, "Teen" Gallegos, and Bill Narlesky provided the offense in a 9–6 victory. Lopez collected two hits in the affair and was described afterward by Frank Wright of the *Florida Times-Union* as being "pep personified" and a "sparkplug on the field." Regarding Lopez's receiving skills, Wright noted that he "looked real good behind the bat."[5] As the "Sally" League was a higher classification than the Southeastern, the win, exhibition or not, was a confidence booster for the Tars heading into the season.

Lopez began the year platooning behind the plate with veteran catcher Arnold Townsend. However, in an early-season move described by team president Charles R. Griner as "necessary to bring about a winning club," Townsend was released on May 2, thereby giving Lopez the job outright.[6] Lopez responded the same day by belting a "gorgeous" three-run homer that beat the Savannah Indians, 7–5. With such timely hitting, Lopez, referred to as the "young Cuban catcher," was said to be "showing splendidly," and winning the "plaudits" of the Jacksonville fans, much as he had in Tampa.[7]

During the campaign's first month, the Tars' playing improved. They hovered around second or third place, getting the important victories when necessary. An example of this came on the final day of April, when "Bear-Cat Ben" Cantwell shut out second-place Savannah, 1–0. Described as the "prettiest baseball played in Jacksonville this year," Cantwell allowed the Indians three hits, two of which came after the "elongated right-hander" had retired two batters in the inning. Three days later "one good Indian," Tars hurler "Chief" McBee, held "nine other Indians," Savannah, to four hits in a 7–0 victory that clinched the confidence-inspiring series for Jacksonville. The win also moved them into second place as they traveled north the following day to begin a series at Savannah. The Tars hot streak continued with consecutive victories at Savannah, 7–6 and 14–3, that kept Jacksonville in the hunt for first place. Cantwell once again exhibited his dominance in game two, registering his seventh victory of the year and further assisting the cause with a home run. By the end of the series, Jacksonville was firmly in second place, a half game behind Albany.[8]

Jacksonville next traveled from Savannah to Selma, Alabama, to take on the Cloverleafs. Once again the often-used Ben Cantwell went to the mound to start the series, holding Selma to one run on six hits and winning 5–1. In garnering his eighth triumph of the year, Cantwell allowed only two men to advance as far as second after the second inning. A base on balls, an infield out, and a single past third in the second inning prevented Cantwell's notching another shutout. The "hard swinging bat" of Lopez registered a triple and a single, the triple coming to open the seventh. This victory proved crucial; it gave Jacksonville sole possession of first place. Two days later the Tars strengthened their grip on first with a

3–2 victory over Selma. During this stretch, the remarkable battery of Cantwell and Lopez continued to impress, Cantwell getting his ninth win on May 13 and Lopez belting his eighth triple the next day. Cantwell's latest victory, coupled with his 1926 season-ending nine-game winning streak with Sanford, gave him eighteen consecutive wins.[9] While the streak came to an end on May 26 with a 7–3 loss to Pensacola,[10] Cantwell rebounded nicely, closing out the month with a doubleheader victory over Selma for his tenth and eleventh wins. In those two contests, Bear-Cat Ben allowed just seven hits in sixteen innings and led his teammates in batting for the day, going three for six. Lopez, catching both ends of the hot doubleheader, could not match Cantwell's performance, allowing a run in the first game on a passed ball and being called out during the second after missing first base on a double to left field.[11]

Lopez began June slugging, homering on consecutive days at Golden Park against Columbus during 3–1 and 19–8 Tars wins. His second homer came as a pinch hitter in the top of the ninth inning, adding pain to the Foxes' misery. By this point in the season, Lopez was third on the club in batting with a .370 average. His at-bats, however, were considerably more than the two hitters in front of him; Lopez with 135 to that point, Cantwell and Bourg with 53 and 77 respectively. The closest Tar hitter to him with comparable at-bats was shortstop Bill Narlesky, usually hitting third in the lineup, batting .339 in 194 attempts.[12]

On June 3 Cantwell won his fourteenth game of the year but looked weary in the process, allowing eighteen hits against Columbus. In the loss, the Foxes touched Cantwell for four doubles and a homer. The following day the rigors and overuse of the season caught up with Cantwell, as he lost (15–13) for just the second time, in a relief appearance at Montgomery. After some deserved rest over the next month, partially because of a leg injury caused by a line drive, Cantwell rebounded, winning nine of his next ten outings. In the process, Jacksonville continued to extend their league lead, with a 63–30 record by mid-July. During this stretch Lopez aptly displayed the defensive skills he was becoming noted for. Two examples came early in a mid-June pitching duel between Cantwell and "Lefty" Rube Benton of the Albany Nuts. In the second inning, with no outs and two runners on base, Lopez's "great throw to Narlesky," the shortstop, trapped the runner off second. Later the same inning, as Chaplin (the batter) struck out, Lopez whipped the ball to second baseman McMillan to catch a runner at the "midway station." Both plays proved pivotal in preserving Cantwell's 1–0 shutout victory. The following day, in a 9–3 loss,

Lopez again showed his fielding brilliance with a "wonderful foul catch" against the grandstand. By mid-June, Lopez, also continuing to impress at the plate, was batting sixth in the league with a .363 average.[13]

The pacesetting Tars stumbled somewhat to close out July, losing eight games against just one win during the final two weeks of the month. However, Cantwell's twenty-fourth victory on August 1 provided some needed momentum, and the club began to nose up, winning four of their next six. Cantwell's 24–5 record at August 1 was striking. An examination reveals that he spread his talents and victories evenly among league opponents. He beat Albany, Selma, and Savannah each on four occasions; Columbus and Montgomery on three each; and Pensacola on two. Montgomery was the only club to touch Cantwell for more than one loss, winning twice. During the twenty-nine games in which Cantwell received credit, he allowed only 66 runs or an average of 2.28 per contest. This figure includes both earned and unearned runs. These limited tallies came off a total of 202 hits and 66 bases on balls. Cantwell also struck out 113 men, for an average of 3.9 per game. All the while, Cantwell's teammates supported him with error-free ball a mere six times. When taken with his stellar numbers at Sanford the year before, it was becoming obvious to most that Ben Cantwell would soon be applying his talents in the major leagues. Even the Associated Press took note, sending out a news story and picture of Cantwell through its feature wire service to members.[14]

Cantwell's performance was not the only indicator that a move out of the minors would be coming soon. According to league rules, if Cantwell was still with Jacksonville on September 15, any Class A ballclub would have the right to draft him at the "draft price" of $1,800. Recognizing this, and looking to avoid what could be a considerable loss of profit, Jacksonville club president Charles Griner traveled to New York and conferred with several major-league magnates regarding the possibility of selling Cantwell's contract. While there, Griner contacted John McGraw and the New York Giants, who were looking to shore up their major-league roster for the coming pennant stretch. McGraw was more than aware of Cantwell, his club having been stymied in five innings of shutout ball by the Jacksonville ace the previous spring. After New York scout Dick Kinsella traveled to Montgomery on July 29 to watch Cantwell perform (ironically, a 3–1 loss), the Giants had seen enough, paying Griner $25,000 for Cantwell's contract. The sale was typical of the period in being conditional and enabling McGraw to look Cantwell over for thirty days, after which time the total sum of the purchase must have been paid or the player would be returned. The $25,000 paid for Cantwell was believed to have been the largest ever paid for a Class B player.[15]

The profit earned from Cantwell's sale proved timely for Griner, since he was interested in purchasing another baseball club. The August 2 *Florida Times-Union* reported that Griner, after several invitations from Florida State League president J. B. Asher, would travel to Tampa to discuss purchasing the Smokers, which had recently been given up by Dr. Opre because of a perceived "lack of interest manifested in Tampa baseball." It was widely understood that the city of Tampa would offer Plant field free of rent to any responsible person willing to assume control of the orphaned team. While Griner remarked that he had no formulated plan regarding the Smokers, nor would he until he had seen the "lay of the land" in that city, he believed that the Tampa franchise could be made into a paying proposition. For reasons left unrevealed, Griner never took over the Smokers.

The biggest question confronting the Tars organization after the sale of Cantwell was how they would perform without him. Initially, Griner thought that Rube Marquard, the erstwhile New York Giant hurler, might be lured onto the Jacksonville roster. In spite of his age, it was presumed that Marquard could still be a winner in the Southeastern league. Marquard, however, never signed with Jacksonville, and so the club was forced to the trading table in an attempt to lesson the blow of losing their top pitcher. On August 6, Jack Wilson, the Tars third baseman, was sent to the Waycross Railroaders for pitcher Dave McKinney, who, in spite of his 11–11 record, was considered one of the league's better hurlers. To replace Wilson, the Tars called upon nineteen-year-old prospect Leo Bader, who himself was sold for $5,000 to Brooklyn later in the season.[16] In other moves designed to prepare the Tars for the final dash of the season, Jacksonville acquired pitcher "Lefty" Miller and veteran second baseman Joe Brennan. Brennan had been the manager at Savannah.[17]

For their part, the Tars players showed little sign of requiring a shakeup, going nine and six during the next three weeks and extending their lead over second-place Montgomery to nine games. On August 10 Lopez played the outfield and went one for four in a 7–3 loss to Waycross. The reason for the position shift was more than likely to grant the catcher a well-deserved rest. It was fitting that Lopez was awarded a break on that day in that it was also the day that 15,000 Ybor City cigarmakers chose to strike in protest against the death sentences imposed upon Nicola Sacco and Bartolomeo Vanzetti.[18] An estimated 5,000 cigarmakers, including several hundred women and children, jammed the Ybor City Labor Temple to hear speakers in Italian, Spanish, and English praise the condemned men. Few of the Sacco-Vanzetti sympathizers appeared on the streets in the early part of the day, and it was only at three o'clock, the hour set for the mass meeting, that crowds began to gather.[19]

With strikes of another kind all about him, typically coming in groups of three, Lopez endured a minor slump in early August and found himself getting a spot of bench time because of it. In the midst of the slump and facing Apalachicola native Ned Porter, a wild-throwing New York Giants prospect, Lopez went zero for four, striking out twice in a 6–5 loss. Lopez fared little better a week later, going one for four against Porter, who, although two years removed from the University of Florida campus where he captained the baseball squad, still lacked good control. With their catcher struggling — Lopez's average slid to .314 by late August — the Tars were forced to stiffen, winning six of seven.[20]

With all the attention afforded Cantwell by major-league scouts, it is not surprising that other Tars players gained big-league notice as well, particularly Lopez. Every time Cantwell pitched, there to receive him was the hustling young backstop that Washington had already tried unsuccessfully to obtain. Lopez, who in spite of his recent slump was having a very good year, remembers:

> Cantwell was having a great year. A record of 25–5 or close to it by the early part of August. He would have won 40 games had he pitched all year. All the big league scouts at that time would come out to see him. In those days each team had only a few scouts and they would send those scouts into wherever a ballplayer was hot. Every time we played we must have had 6–8 scouts in the stands watching. Especially when Cantwell was pitching. For some reason or another, the Brooklyn scout, fellow by the name of Nap Rucker, took a liking to me. He notified the front office about me and said that he liked the catcher better than the pitcher. They told him if he liked the catcher to go ahead and buy him. So they made a deal for me for $10,000 and I was sold to the Brooklyn Dodgers.[21]

Lopez also recalls the deal as one of his first exposures to the realities of baseball high finance. "At the time they only gave the Jacksonville guy [Griner] $1,000 down and the rest would follow if they kept me. The Jacksonville guy told me that he would let me have a tenth of it if I made good. I said that's fine. I never did get anything."[22]

The Brooklyn Dodgers in spring training ca. 1927, Clearwater, Florida. At the time they were often called the Brooklyn "Robins," a name that acknowledged the strong influence of their manager, Wilbert Robinson (here shown front and center). (Courtesy Florida State Archives.)

The *Florida Times-Union* announced the sale with a headline declaring "Brooklyn Robins Purchase Al Lopez from Tars for $10,000." Described as the "battery mate par excellence of Ben Cantwell," the newspaper revealed that Lopez would finish the season with Jacksonville and report to the Robins at the start of 1928 spring training. From then until May 15 he would have the opportunity of "displaying his wares" to Wilbert Robinson, the well-known Brooklyn manager. As was the case with Cantwell, the contract was conditional and if Lopez were to not stick with the Brooklyn organization, he would then be returned to Jacksonville. Nap Rucker, the veteran scout who signed Lopez, was very enthusiastic about the catcher's chances. The seasoned bird dog announced that as the present crop of Brooklyn receivers "were on the downgrade," Lopez, only nineteen, "looks like a sure bet for the Robins."[23]

The Tars swept into September with a Labor Day doubleheader win over Pensacola, thereby preserving a nine-game lead over Montgomery that "practically clinches matters." With losses the next week to Selma and Montgomery, however, the Tars' lead shortened by a game and "the pennant was put on hold." That week it was announced the "Teen" Gallegos, "the fleet footed Jacksonville outfielder," had been awarded the Kunsberg trophy, as the most valuable player for the Tars during the 1927 season. The fans voted for Gallegos 285 times, outdistancing Bill Narlesky, who had 279 votes, and Lopez with 234.[24]

With the pennant still "on hold," Jacksonville continued its stall, hitting safely only three times at second-place Montgomery, losing 3–1, and "leaving flag race up in the air." Ironically, on the same day, former ace Ben Cantwell bested the St. Louis Cardinals 9–3 in his first New York Giants start. The race, however, came to an end the following day when Jacksonville clinched the pennant with an 11–7 victory over Columbus. The deciding day's contest was marked by offense — particularly from the losing Foxes, who bettered the Tars with fifteen hits. The Tars, lacking a stopper like Cantwell to turn to, were forced to use three pitchers during the slugfest. The championship won, Jacksonville resumed its late-season swoon, losing the next three before Babe Phelps, a recently signed pitcher, hurled a shutout against Pensacola on the next-to-last day of the season. The Tars, before one of the largest crowds of the year and with Lopez at first base, then closed out the season, losing 6–1 to Pensacola.[25]

The season, only the second in the Southeastern League's history, was viewed by league president Cliff Green as being quite novel and an enormous success. "The Southeastern League," according to Green, "has accomplished its aim to furnish high class and clean amusement ... and in the span of two years has taken a prominent place in organized baseball."[26] Among the league's innovations was the initiation of a movement to hold a national "flood sufferers day" in minor leagues throughout the United States to aid victims in a series of Mississippi floods. Also, it featured a kids' section in each league ballpark to which "boys" were admitted without charge.

To further support Green's argument that the Southeastern League was among baseball's best, on the field as well as off, a postseason series was arranged between Jacksonville and the Greenville Spinners to decide a champion of the South. The Spinners, champions of the South Atlantic or "Sally" League, were fresh from a postseason series victory over Portsmouth, champions of the Virginia League. For weather and time considerations (diminishing daylight hours), it was agreed that all games would be played at Durkee Field in Jacksonville and being at 3:30 p.m.[27]

The series began quietly with Greenville winning game one 1–0. The shutout featured a pitching duel between Al Yeargin, the "lanky Spinner righthander," and Johnny Bates. These two hurlers held the respective clubs to a total of six hits, Bates allowing four and Yeargin two. Greenville's lone run came in the fourth inning when Spinners right fielder Daniels doubled to right center and was then driven in by fellow outfielder Fitzberger, who punched a single to left. The next day Babe Phelps, Jacksonville's "gigantic moundsman," tossed five-hit baseball to earn the victory, evening the series at one game apiece. Phelps, who entered the contest after a line drive glanced off starter Dave McKinney's pitching hand, had the fans "hanging on his name," and the Spinners puzzled into the ninth. Lopez provided most of the Tars offense with two clutch-run scoring singles.

Two days later Greenville again took the edge in the series, winning 10–4. Coming off a weekend's rest, Johnny Leggett, the Spinner catcher, led all batsmen, going three for four, including a bases-clearing triple in the first inning "that carried the fleet Gallegos into the Chesterfield sign" in deep left field. Then in the fifth Leggett knocked two men in with "one of the longest hits ever seen here," the ball caroming off the left-field fence. The *Florida Times-Union* declared that all "four balls hit by Leggett would have been home runs in almost any other park in the league." Lopez once again led Jacksonville batters, collecting three singles in four at-bats.

The Tars fought back the next day, winning 6–3 to even the series at two games all. Johnny Bates, pitching on three days' rest, took the measure of the Spinners in a contest marred by a heated dispute between umpire Ted Clark and Greenville manager Frank Walker. During the seventh inning, Rodríguez, Greenville's second baseman, took exception to umpire Clark's positioning himself in the middle of the diamond and requested that Clark move. His reasoning was that with two outs and a man on third, Clark was obstructing his view of the runner. Clark, however, saw it differently and stayed put. Upon this refusal, Walker, playing center field, "opened up" on the umpire and was ejected before reaching second base. The infuriated Walker, fuming over the umpire's refusal to move and the subsequent ejection, refused to leave the playing field until police were called in to escort him away and restore order.

With no travel days to contend with, the two clubs went at it again the following day, Jacksonville winning 3–2. Babe Phelps, a newcomer and the Tars' "prized dark steed," went to the mound that day reviving memories of Ben Cantwell with his ability to continuously pitch his way out of trouble. Phelps twice retired the Spinners with the bases full before finally allowing Greenville a run in the eighth. Both teams left eleven runners on the sacks in the low-scoring affair. With a series lead of three games to two, one more win would secure the championship of the South for Jacksonville. However, Greenville, pounding out fourteen hits against three Jacksonville pitchers, forced a seventh game, "swamping the Tars 9–2" in game six.

After a day off, the indefatigable Phelps again took the mound at Durkee Field, looking to claim a Jacksonville championship with his "easy going style." While an argument might have been made over how much ease Phelps had displayed while disposing of the Spinners in his prior outings, his teammates knew better. The hurler's arm had been severely taxed in the earlier games and just how long he could last was the question being asked. When the game began, however, all queries were satisfied: "If Phelps tossed with a sore arm, what a pitcher he must be when his flipper is in the glow."[28] Only six hits were registered by Greenville batters on this day, the same day on which another Babe added his sixtieth home run of the season for the New York Yankees. Two doubles were among the Greenville hits, and these were the only runners to advance as far as second base in the 3–0 Tars victory.

Along the way, Jacksonville provided errorless support, something no other Tars hurler enjoyed during the series. Against three Greenville pitchers, Jacksonville collected seven hits, three by Leo Bader. The scoring took place in the first, third, and sixth innings.

In the first, Art Bourg led off with a hit through the middle, followed by Leonard's single to center field. Bill Narlesky then reached first on an error after laying down a bunt toward third to advance the runners. With the bases full and no outs, Mike Burke hit into a double play that scored Bourg from third.

In the third inning, Jacksonville pushed across run number two without a base hit. Leonard walked to start off the inning and was followed by Narlesky. The hit-and-run was on, and Narlesky advanced Leonard to second and wound up safe at first on an error. Burke then bunted toward third, again advancing the runners while being thrown out at first. Gallegos was then intentionally walked to set up the double play, but the strategy backfired when Bader "bombed a long fly" to center field, scoring Leonard easily and moving Narlesky to third. The inning ended with Gallegos being thrown out at second on a double-steal attempt.

In the sixth, Bader beat out a hit to start the inning and Seehorn followed with a single to center that moved Bader to third. With Lopez at the plate, the double steal was put into effect; Seehorn made his move, and when the Greenville catcher tossed to second, Bader "lit out" for home. The shortstop, who had cut off the catcher's throw, returned the ball to the plate in ample time for the putout. For a moment it looked as though Bader was out. But Bader's deft slide knocked the ball out of the catcher's hand and Jacksonville had its last run of the 1927 season and the championship of the South.[29]

For their efforts, each player on the winning Tars roster received only a $40 share of the proceeds. This figure was denounced by the *Florida Times-Union* as a "black eye," especially in light of the support granted the club by local fans in this series "so full of good baseball." Contributing mightily to the effort was Lopez, who led the team in hitting with a .368 average, while refusing to allow a stolen base.[30]

For many devotees of minor-league baseball, the end of a season marks a melancholy passage, because so much in it is transient and fleeting. There are no permanent assignments in the "bush," nor often the kind of personal affinity between fan and player that lingers for several seasons. What exists is a continuous procession of hope, moving along a path to somewhere else. What happens when the current cortege passes on? Will the sorrow or elation of the bygone summer return next spring? What emotions might the new sequence convey? For its enthusiasts, the allure of the minor-league game is the perpetual renewal encapsuled in these questions. The *Florida Times-Union* expressed this sentiment after the 1927 campaign when it lamented that "Today the Tars will start disbanding. Already some of them are on the road to their homes; some of them will not return. The final game of the year has been played and the curtain drawn on professional baseball *until next season*" (emphasis added).[31] In that brief, somber farewell, the bases were cleared at Durkee Field, the standings evened, and the innings erased. The regeneration of the game had begun.

Lopez reported to spring training the following season determined to reward Nap Rucker's faith in him and to possibly earn a position with Brooklyn's AA Southern League affiliate, the Atlanta Crackers. Atlanta, however, was still a year away for the nineteen year old. Though Lopez drilled with the club throughout the spring, it was decided that in spite of his flashy defensive skills, his bat could use another year of seasoning. The verdict came after an early April exhibition rout of the Crackers by the parent Brooklyn "Robins," so nicknamed for their manager "Uncle" Wilbert Robinson. Atlanta's team president, Colonel Rell J. Spiller, met with Robinson after the game to discuss the makeup of the Crackers' roster and in doing so opted to send Lopez to Macon in the Sally League.

However, a proviso was attached stipulating that Atlanta could exchange a reserve catcher named Angley for Lopez at any time, if Angley failed to hit at the level expected. Lopez then traveled to Macon and, with Colonel Spiller in attendance, caught in the opening-day 9–1 victory against Columbia.[32]

At Macon and only two years away from home, Lopez proved that he was in professional baseball to stay with an outstanding season including a .326 batting average over 114 games caught. His most impressive statistic, however, was his sudden power display of fourteen home runs. While some of these were of the in-the-park variety, never again in his minor- or major-league career would Lopez hit that many homers in a single season.[33] Whether it was the improvement in round-trip production or simply his continued excellence behind the plate, Lopez was called up to the major leagues by Brooklyn for the last two and a half weeks of the 1928 season.

Having been raised in Tampa and having played only in the small southern towns of Tampa, Jacksonville, and Macon, Lopez was amazed when he arrived in Brooklyn:

> I got off at the station and luckily I ran into two guys that belonged to Brooklyn and had just been called up from Atlanta at the same time as I was (from Macon). It was lucky for me because I was only nineteen years old and we took the subway, one of them (player) had been there before, we took the subway and rode underneath the river, and up at the Brooklyn side of the island we got off. It was the first station we came to and by God there was a hotel right on top of the station, quite an experience. I thought that was amazing.[34]

Less than amazing was his bat production at Brooklyn in the closing weeks of the 1928 season. Lopez played in three games and came to the plate twelve times, but his hot Georgia bat seems to have stayed in the South. He "wore the collar" or went hitless in all twelve plate appearances. Lopez remembers that he didn't play much initially:

> I sat around on the bench the final few weeks, not doing anything until the last weekend of the season. We were playing the Pirates and all of a sudden Wilbert Robinson put me in to catch. I found out later that the reason I caught was because Burleigh Grimes, the last of the great spitball pitchers, was facing us that day and none of the other catchers liked to hit

against him; Burleigh was kind of mean. I caught that day and went 0 for 4. The next day we had a double-header and "Robbie" [Wilbert Robinson] let me catch both ends. This is when the Pirates had Pie Traynor and Glenn Wright on the left side of their infield. Well, I was strictly a pull hitter and I hit some good hard shots to the left side. I'd take off for first figuring I had myself a hit, but each time, to my astonishment, I saw that peg zinging into the first baseman's glove. I knew, I just knew, that at Macon those would have been hits. It was practically impossible to hit a ball past Traynor and Wright. I was 0 for 8 in that double-header and went home that Fall wondering what a fellow had to do to get a base hit in the big leagues.[35]

Considering his age and relative inexperience, Lopez had accomplished something simply being at the plate in a big-league uniform. To that point in major-league history, only twelve men from Florida could make the same claim.[36]

Based upon his improvement shown during the 1928 season, Lopez was promoted to the Atlanta Crackers for the 1929 year. If the Brooklyn organization had any doubt that Lopez was a top prospect, it was dispelled at Atlanta. He ripped Southern League pitching, hitting .327 over 490 at-bats. He also banged ten home runs, nine triples, and twenty-one doubles while knocking in 85 runs.[37] For this powerful minor league season, Lopez was paid the hefty sum of $575 a month.[38]

The question of whether Lopez would play for Atlanta or Brooklyn in 1929 had lingered through much of spring training. The reason was that in spite of his having been promised to Atlanta for the coming campaign, Wilbert Robinson kept him with the major-league club until right before the regular season commenced. On March 18 the *Atlanta Constitution* reported that Lopez and shortstop Leo Bader, Lopez's teammate at Jacksonville in 1927, would report to training in Macon on that date and would be in Atlanta by the first of April. The newspaper continued to report Lopez's imminent arrival for the next week. However, a week later, Lopez was still in Brooklyn's lineup when the Dodgers played host to the Columbus, Ohio, club of the American Association. The following day it was reported in Atlanta that Lopez was set to arrive "within the next few days," regardless of his continued work with Brooklyn. Yet two days later, with the *Tampa Tribune* proclaiming "Tampa Boy 'Comes Home' Today," in response to Lopez's scheduled start against the Washington Senators in Tampa, Lopez was still not a Cracker. Speculation about when and if Lopez would arrive in Atlanta continued through the remainder of the month.[39]

With the immediate future of his roster in air, Colonel Spiller traveled to Florida on an "ivory hunt," in search of Wilbert Robinson. Spiller planned to ask just what were the chances, if any of obtaining Brooklyn prospects Nick Cullop, a hard-hitting outfielder, and Lopez. Atlanta manager Wilbur Good was especially interested in Lopez because of the promise, not two weeks old, of having his services. The *Atlanta Constitution*, however, reported that "Uncle Robbie" was "becoming weary of telling correspondents that he doesn't know the whereabouts of Lopez or when he will report." In Florida, Spiller heard from Robinson, but it was not the answer he had wished to hear. With the catching situation in Brooklyn questionable because of the sore arms of Butch Henline and Hank DeBerry, Robinson was strongly considering keeping Lopez when the club broke camp and returned north. Robinson then added that if Atlanta did not get Lopez, they would receive veteran National League receiver Johnny Gooch.[40]

While Johnny Gooch would have made a splendid backstop for the double-A squad, the Crackers preferred Lopez because of his "youth and hustling." The Southern League, as did the Florida State League and others, also had a "class rule" that stipulated a roster player limit of eighteen, with five of the men being Class B players, or players ascending to the double-A level from Class B. It was hinted in the press that Atlanta had violated this rule the prior summer and did not wish to do so again. Furthermore, with four Class B pitchers already on the roster to go with Lopez, the Crackers would have met their roster quota and could then concentrate on filling the other positions with veteran Class A ballplayers.[41]

All this guesswork, of course, did not sit very well with the Atlanta press or fans. The *Constitution* reported on March 30 that the "concrete facts of the Crackers' condition are clouded over by speculation." "Wilbert Robinson," it judged, "has the annoying habit of promising you something and then forgetting about it. He announced in the papers that Lopez had been sent to Atlanta and Lopez is still catching exhibition games for Brooklyn." Colonel Spiller, however, returned to Atlanta on the last day of March "with a coat of tan, empty gas tank and promises from Wilbert Robinson ... to the effect that he would leave an outfielder and catcher [there] when his team comes through town April 6." It was again widely assumed that the catcher would be "Alfonso Lopez, youthful wizard of the mask." On March 30 Lopez was in the Robins' lineup against the St. Louis

Browns at West Palm Beach.[42] A few days later, it was reported that Brooklyn had been delayed on the way to an exhibition game in Florida by a freight wreck. "Uncle Robbie" and his players ultimately reached the game site "by way of a team of horses and several bicycles." Commenting on Brooklyn's effort, Ed Danforth of the *Atlanta Constitution* quipped that he hoped "Robbie does not send the Crackers help by the same method."[43]

As Spiller and his manager faced opening day with something less than equanimity, the conjecture over the long-promised reinforcements increased. Robinson confirmed "over long distance telephone" to Ralph McGill of the *Atlanta Constitution* that he would be leaving Lopez, outfielder Jim Rosenfield, and Jim Richardson, "a tall, ungainly right-hander from the Eastern League," in Atlanta. The news could not have come sooner for manager Wilbur Good, who discerned the problems his club faced behind the plate and acknowledged that its fortunes hinged on the acquisition of Lopez and some outfield help. "If I get Lopez," Good remarked, "I'll be alright ... Lopez has a lot of pepper."[44]

Robinson's "long distance" promise was realized the second week in April when Uncle Robbie turned these Atlanta "orphans of the storm" into his "fair-haired boys." The gist of the agreement reached between Brooklyn and Atlanta found Lopez and Rosenfield reporting to the Crackers, with Spiller refusing the pitcher Richardson. Commenting on the assignments, Robinson, "getting his throat all parched from eating parched peanuts," announced that Lopez was as good a catcher as he had on his squad. "All he needs," said Robinson, "is one more year of seasoning. He is a great prospect. He will hit for you too." Admitting that there were no outstanding clubs projected in the Southern League, the *Atlanta Constitution* predicted that the "new" Crackers would be a good hustling ball club with a chance to win.[45]

The Crackers got their first look at their new catcher during an April 10 exhibition game. Lopez hit the ball "sharply and well" all day but collected just one hit. As usual, it was his defensive work and his handling of the pitching that elicited the most praise from the fans who had gathered. While the performance didn't set any seasonal standards, it was apparently enough to convince Spiller and Good that Lopez was indeed the catcher they had pined for. The following day the club announced that Cliff Knox, a reserve catcher competing for a roster position, was being farmed out to Spartanburg of the Sally League.[46]

In Atlanta, Lopez found an old friend and mentor in Cracker assistant coach Tommy Leach. Leach, the veteran Pittsburgh third baseman, had coached Lopez during the latter part of the 1926 season in Tampa and thought very highly of him. During his career, beginning at Louisville in 1898 and finishing with Pittsburgh in 1918, Leach had the opportunity to play with and view some of the game's greatest players. Yet in 1929 Leach, speaking "unhesitatingly," told Ralph McGill of the *Atlanta Constitution*, that Honus P. Wagner was the greatest ball player that baseball ever knew. This might not seem surprising given the fact that Leach played alongside Wagner from 1898 until 1912, fourteen years. However, having played against or seen the likes of Walter Johnson, Cy Young, Ty Cobb, Napoleon Lajoie, Christy Mathewson, Tris Speaker, and Babe Ruth, Leach was in a unique position to judge.

> Hans could do everything.... He was the greatest. The others can do one or two things, but Hans could do everything and do it well. He was a great first baseman, he played there for a while and there was none better. He was a marvelous outfielder. He was the greatest shortstop, probably greatest infielder that baseball has ever seen. He could pitch or catch and do either well. He could steal bases as well as Cobb. He could hit as well as any man the game has had. He led the league eight years and hit better than .300 for 17 consecutive years. Yes, Wagner was the greatest.[47]

On the day Babe Ruth married Claire Hodgson, a former resident of Athens, Georgia, the Crackers opened their season on the road at Chattanooga. In front of 8,000 fans, including former New York Highlanders manager Norman Elberfield, known in baseball as the "Tabasco Kid," Joe Kiefer, Atlanta's starting pitcher, chilled the Lookouts 6–2 "as cold wave sweeps the park."[48] Lopez gathered a hit and an RBI for the Crackers in the "stunning victory." The next day, with Dick Bonelly pitching, Atlanta won 10–0. It was the second defeat of Chattanooga in as many days and was more convincing than the first. Only thirty-four Lookouts went to the plate against Bonelly, five coming away with "well-scattered" hits and one for extra bases. Lopez, "the fine young Cuban arm," spent the afternoon "knocking down Lookout hopes." He threw two men out as they wandered too far off base, both in critical moments. He caught the only runner who attempted to steal second base and he made a catch of a difficult pop fly. Lopez also homered with two men on base, leaving the natives talking "nothing but Al Lopez when the game was done."[49]

Atlanta planned a raucous gala for the home opener, all devised to improve its chances of winning the league "attendance cup," awarded each year to the Southern League city that turned out the largest opening-day crowd. Especially important was beating Birmingham. The slogan "Beat Birmingham" was heard so much that one might have thought the Crackers were playing the Barons rather than the Lookouts. The year before, Atlanta's inaugural gate had totaled 14,138, placing it second to Birmingham, who found, after several days of counting, that 14,174 tickets had been sold — just more than Atlanta. To Atlanta the loss was a sour one, smacking of "queer dealing." It was speculated that Barons officials had awaited Atlanta's attendance report before selling themselves enough tickets to win. In any event, Atlanta's civic pride was quickened and it grew determined to claim the trophy in 1929.

I. N. Ragsdale, the mayor of Atlanta, proclaimed a half-day holiday to allow city employees to attend the contest. At Ragsdale's urging, county employees were also given the half-day off. The mayor also suggested that as many businesses as possible grant permission for their employees to go to the game, or if it was not possible to close for the afternoon, businesses should at least allow a number of employees to attend. Downtown merchants following suit were Florsheim's shoe store, Emerson shoe store, Moss Insurance Agency, Muench jewelers, Briarcliff florist, J. B. Withers Cigar Co., and the Ku Klux factory and office.

On the morning of the game, the *Atlanta Constitution* portrayed the town as "Baseball-Mad" and "popping overnight with old-fashioned baseball spirit" after the two wins at Chattanooga. The Junior Chamber of Commerce estimated that 20,000 would attend the opener, up 5,000 from the previous year. The "ballyhoo" was set to begin at eleven o'clock with Lopez attempting to catch baseballs dropped from the top of the Flatiron building. Further merriment included the appearance of Marion Grant, "the accomplished and beautiful actress of the Fulenweider Players," to throw out the first ball of the year. "Miss Grant," it was noted, "has been pitching and hopes to throw a real strike."[50]

Wilbur Good chose "Climax" Blethen as his starting pitcher, with Lopez behind the plate. Blethen allowed three runs on two walks, an error, a sacrifice, and a single, all in the second inning. After the rough start, however, he settled down, shutting out Chattanooga the rest of the way in the 4–3 victory. It was the third straight win over the Lookouts. It was won by a surging rally in the ninth inning that left the smaller-than-expected crowd of 15,000 "wrung dry of emotion." The crowd was large enough to win the president's trophy; it rained in Birmingham, limiting attendance there to 9,000. Behind 3–2 in the ninth, Atlanta's Johnny Jones beat out a hopper to shortstop, followed by Lopez's sacrifice bunt and pinch hitter Frank Haley's double to deep right, scoring Jones with the tying run. With the crowd singing "When Johnny Came Marching Home," Jack Sheehan drove Haley in with the winning run. Ralph McGill wrote that had it not been for the "cat-like" Lopez with his great confidence and throwing arm, the story might have been different. Lopez "shot down" Chattanooga players in the game "as a skilled sharpshooter shoots down marks set up for him." He caught one man off base and he caught three attempting to steal — two of them in the ninth inning with the Lookouts attempting to pad their lead.[51]

Two days later the Crackers, having lost the day before, made it four out of five with a come-from-behind 15–12 victory over Chattanooga. In "one of the most remarkable games ever played on Spiller field," the Crackers, down seven runs (12–5) with two outs in the seventh inning, "leaped onto the Lookouts and let fly." Atlanta's rally began when Sheehan walked to start the inning. Max Rosenfield and Poole went down in order, but not before Poole moved Jack Sheehan to third base on a botched double-play grounder. Dick Wade then reached first on an error, scoring Sheehan from third. Had Chattanooga's Wally Dashiell made the play on Wade's grounder, the inning would have ended before it began — but that did not happen. Bill Marriott next came through with a single, giving the crowd something to yell about, and the rally caught fire. Johnny Jones came to bat and drove Wade in. Lopez, a single and triple already to his credit, then doubled, scoring Marriott and Jones. Frank Haley, pinch-hitting again, scored Lopez. Maurice Archdeacon doubled next to score Haley, Sheehan drove in Archdeacon, and Rosenfield brought Sheehan home with what ultimately proved enough to win, the thirteenth run.[52]

In the contest Lopez was a "hitting fiend," batting for the cycle with a single, a double, a triple, and a home run. Having already contributed to the game-winning rally in the seventh, Lopez added the homer in the eighth with a "hard smash to center field." Cy Bell, staff writer for the *Atlanta Constitution*, noted that the crowd, "already hysterical, began to gibber and make squeaking noises. They were all out of volume." Bell continued by remarking that Lopez's popularity was well deserved, for he "must be the best catcher in the league." Lopez truly was off to a terrific start for the Crackers. He caught each of the first five games, collecting seven hits in sixteen at-bats for a .438 average, including nine RBIs and two homers. However, it was his "great throwing arm" and his "cat-like" style behind the plate that had Atlanta's followers stamping him for the majors. In the five games, Lopez caught six men stealing, picked two off base with quick throws, and handled two bunted balls flawlessly. It was beginning to look as though Wilbert Robinson was not kidding when he said "I am leaving my best catcher."[53]

The Crackers, it seems, could have used a few more of Robbie's best, because after the great start, they settled into unexpectedly mediocre play, leveling off at .500 by midsummer. It was Bobby Jones and his winning of a third U.S. Open golf championship, in record fashion, that had Atlanta talking, not the sagging Crackers. In fact, a citywide celebration was scheduled to honor the achievements of "Mistah Jones, Sah!"[54] The entire Cracker team had been suffering through a batting slump that buried them in fifth place, nine games behind pace-setting Birmingham. Colonel Spiller, inspired by the challenge of his club's .500 average, became determined to pursue a hard-hitting outfielder who might help the club. Lopez, for his part, had been cooling at the plate, his average falling to .325 with seven home runs after 76 games.[55]

Spiller was also upset over the collapse of a proposed sale of his club to Clark Griffith, owner of the Washington Senators. Griffith, the "Old Fox," had previously agreed, having left a $5,000 binder, to purchase the Atlanta franchise and all its associated amusement facilities and properties from Spiller for a reported $650,000, but then he reneged on the agreement, citing Southern League opposition to the sale. When Spiller took the matter before baseball commissioner Judge Kenesaw Mountain Landis, the former federal jurist announced a hands-off policy.

The club thought to have "frightened" Griffith into not buying the Crackers was Birmingham. The Barons had profited handsomely from a close working relationship with Washington and obviously did not wish to see it end. Ed Danforth wrote in the *Atlanta Constitution* that "Birmingham never had a ball club until the Senators began sending them players." With a Washington-Atlanta entente no longer a threat, the Barons could resume acquiring players from the "Nats," now at the expense of the Crackers. A case in point occurred when Washington released Stuffy Stewart, a thirty-two-year-old journeyman, to the Barons. This release, occurring shortly after Griffith had backed off the purchase, was solid proof that Griffith had "washed his hands" of any intentions toward Atlanta and had resumed cordial relations with Birmingham. Had the purchase of the Crackers been realized, Stewart, no doubt, would have been sent to Atlanta and provided the needed outfield punch that Spiller had been looking for.

As it was, the first-place Barons were strengthened by his arrival and the Crackers seemingly hurt. (Atlanta eventually received Nick Cullop from Brooklyn to strengthen its outfield.)[56]

Within three weeks all seemed to have been forgotten as the "Crax," reviving their early-season form, bested Birmingham three straight at Spiller field. These wins gave Atlanta four out of six over the Barons for the week. The final contest was a hard-fought game and for a time it looked as though Crackers hurler Climax Blethen would be unable to "stem the tide of Baron hits," but he did. From the fourth inning on Blethen "mowed the Barons down as if he had been shooting at them with an old-fashioned scatter-bore gun." Only sixteen men faced him in the final five frames. A single by Yam Yaryan, the veteran Barons catcher, was the only hit allowed in that time. Only two of the outs left the infield. The 10–4 Atlanta win was the fifteenth victory for Blethen, "the lean little right-hander," and it firmly placed the Crackers back in the pennant hunt.[57]

Three days later "Atlantans saw their first game of night baseball ... at Spiller field when Grinell, a local amateur nine, defeated the American Athletics, 12–5, before 1,500 fans." On the same day, the Crackers won their fifth straight, a 4–3 decision at the Memphis Chicks. Lopez led the offense, going two for four with an RBI, which gave him five hits in two games. The next day President Herbert Hoover proclaimed effective the Kellogg-Briand Pact, a treaty renouncing war, or the threat thereof, as a manner of international conduct. The Crackers, strictly adhering to the intent of the policy, renounced its own offense in a 6–1 loss, concluding their five-game winning streak. This loss returned the Crackers to their tepid routine, and by the beginning of September they were six games behind, still clutching fifth place.[58]

With stock markets staging "an impressive advance," the Crackers split a Labor Day twin bill at Mobile, winning the first 5–1 and losing the second 4–3. In spite of a 7–2 "trouncing" of Birmingham a week later, a victory in which the team showed "a dash and determination that was unusual," the Crackers found themselves buried eleven games back in the standings and with little hope of catching up. Lopez, however, showing the consistency at the plate that "Uncle Robbie" was looking for, went two for three in the contest. The *Atlanta Constitution* remarked that the "ability of Lopez ... to hit in the pinches ... was the feature of the Crackers offense."[59]

In their final home games of the season, the "Crax" lost game one of a doubleheader with Nashville, 8–6. The second game was called on account of darkness with the score tied at three all. They then traveled to Chattanooga to finish the year where they began it, against the Lookouts. As they had in April, the Crackers proved the better team, beating the Lookouts 7–6. With both clubs out of the running, the usual "diamond burlesque" that marked the final game of the season was absent. Instead both teams settled down to see how quickly they could get through it and in this aspect they succeeded "right well." Despite a total of twenty-five hits, the game finished in one hour and twenty-five minutes. A three-run spurt in the fourth inning followed by a similar burst in the seventh put Chattanooga out front, 6–5. The Crackers, however, "put on an uprising in the ninth to rush two men across and win." Playing second base for the first time all season, Lopez collected two hits in the finale, one triple to right field. With the Atlanta press and southern attention now turning to college football (particularly Georgia Tech football) the Crackers ended the 1929 season in fifth place, fifteen games back. The optimism of spring had been spent like shells in a dove hunt, and in the end there was little left but the casing. With his cartridges shot, but looking ahead nonetheless, Colonel Spiller remarked that it would be terrible for his club if Lopez were to be recalled by Wilbert Robinson at Brooklyn, but he expected it.[60]

Lopez fondly remembers his years in the minor leagues. While there are many horror stories in baseball folklore about beating the bush and life on the bus, Lopez frankly believes that players during his period had it easier:

> When you're young and all, you think that it's fun but actually you look back and [maybe it wasn't]. The minor leagues, after I left them, got pretty tough traveling because they travel in buses. I was very fortunate because in Tampa we traveled by private car but when I went to Jacksonville we traveled by train most of the time. It was great, then I went to the South-Atlantic League with Macon and that was train. Atlanta traveled by train also. That was great compared to like they do now. They go now and play night games all the time. We used to play all day games because there was no lights. Played all day games at three o'clock. Now they play a night game, they're on the bus and down the road again. Or maybe a double-header finishing with a nightcap and then jump and maybe go 400 miles on a bus. Oh yeah, I was very lucky.[61]

In addition to luck, Lopez possessed the necessary skills and maturity to advance into the majors. After catching roughly 500 games in the minor leagues and just four years removed from his debut with the Smokers, Al Lopez looked forward in 1930 to joining Wilbert Robinson and his "Daffiness Boys" in Brooklyn as a full-time member of the big leagues.

3

The Fella Which
Caught As Good
As Any of Them

In 1930 the Brooklyn Dodgers were led by the rotund, avuncular Wilbert Robinson. Robinson, christened "Uncle Wilbert" by sportswriter Damon Runyon, yet dubbed "Uncle Robbie" by the Brooklyn faithful, took over the Dodgers in 1914 as a fifty-year-old castoff of John McGraw and the New York Giants.[1] Lopez remembers Robinson as being almost paternal in his treatment of younger players. "He was a nice man; like a father to me. He treated me real nice and he wanted me to sit next to him my first year when I started catching in 1930. Just sit there and we'd talk things over. He'd watch the ballgame and I'd sit next to him"—learning.[2]

It is not rare in baseball when a manager, seeking to point out the game's nuances to a protégé, will have the player sit next to him on the bench during games. This is especially true of young catchers who, as the manager's liaison with the field, must learn the skills and limitations of opposing hitters. The only way to learn such traits is through repeated observation. Tony LaRussa, another Ybor City native and major-league manager, explains that "every player has a past that reveals his skills, limitations and tendencies…. You can look it up, especially if you have been disciplined about writing it down."[3] Once these traits are recorded, the player can be confronted in a fashion designed to minimize his strengths

59

or highlight his weaknesses. Through Robinson's mentoring, Lopez began to develop a "book" on hitters around the league, growing more in tune with his manager.

From his pine observation perch, Lopez also witnessed, and still recalls, many of the comical traits for which "Uncle Robbie" was famous:

> In those days he used to bring in tin packs of 'Lucky Strike' tobacco, they used to give it to him, and he would sit it next to him. He would wear pin stripe pants and a silk shirt with a tie to manage in. Two tone shoes. He'd hang his coat up in the dugout. He used to wear expensive clothes. He was a big guy with a scar on his face. False teeth upper and lowers. He used to come in there [the dugout] and before the game he would open up and start chewing tobacco. As the inning progressed he put more tobacco in his mouth. If it was a long inning, you can imagine, he'd have a mouth full of tobacco. So he would spit it all out and go to the fountain, we used to have a little fountain with a spigot for water, he'd go over there and take both of his plates out and wash them off there all over the fountain and we wouldn't drink water for the rest of the day.[4]

Robinson already had behind him a substantial career as a player and coach upon coming to Brooklyn. He had broken in as a catcher with the Philadelphia Athletics of the American Association in 1886 and gone on to play for seventeen seasons, most of them with the Baltimore Orioles. In his distinguished career, Robinson caught more than 1,300 games and batted a respectable .273. His greatest day as a player came in 1892 when he went seven for seven and drove in eleven runs during a nine-inning game. But it was his natural feel for the game's subtleties and his easy disposition that lent him his particular value and endeared him to John McGraw, a teammate on Ned Hanlon's notorious Baltimore Orioles.[5]

The Orioles of the 1890s were a raffish group, and none more so than the combative John McGraw. Stanley Cohen describes them as playing "with a jagged intensity, a reckless disregard for their own bodily welfare, and an utter disdain for their opponents." To this assembly of rogues and derelicts came the "affable serenity" of Robinson. "He leavened the mood of the team, eased the tension, and on more than one occasion stilled the passions of a beleaguered umpire."[6]

Robinson's friendly disposition enticed McGraw to summon him from retirement in 1911. Robinson had been working in his family's meat market in Baltimore for several years when the call came. The Giants were in the midst of a pennant race with the Cubs and seemed to be buckling under the impact of McGraw's hard-driving manner. Sensing this, McGraw asked Robinson to join the club informally, in the hope that his good-natured humor might leaven the mood in the Giants clubhouse. Robinson was a hit with the players from the outset, becoming more popular as the season progressed. The Giants eventually won the pennant by seven and a half games and the players expressed their appreciation to Robinson by voting him a substantial share of their World Series money. The following season, he signed on as a coach, serving as McGraw's "alter ego" until 1913.[7]

After the final game of the 1913 World Series, one in which the Philadelphia Athletics beat the Giants four games to one, Robinson joined McGraw and other members of the old Baltimore Orioles in a reunion of sorts held at a local New York saloon. That evening, McGraw, having had too much to drink, advised Robinson that he had looked bad several times on the coaching lines that afternoon. McGraw, Robinson countered, had made more mistakes during the series than everybody else on the team put together. McGraw, or "Little Napoleon" as he was accurately dubbed, fired Robinson on the spot, ordering him to "get the hell out." Robinson obliged him, but only after dousing him with a beer on the way to the door. The two erstwhile friends did not speak to each other again for seventeen years.[8]

Charles Ebbets of the Brooklyn Dodgers was convinced that McGraw had made a mistake and immediately signed Robinson to manage the Brooklyn club beginning with the 1914 season. For the next eighteen years, Robinson would attempt to model teams on his ideal of good pitching and strong up-the-middle defense. "Uncle Robbie's" 1916 "Robins," featuring the splendid Hall of Fame hitter Zach Wheat, ex-Giant pitcher Rube Marquard, and the all-around hustle of Casey Stengel, won the National League pennant with a 94–60 record. The "Robins" were, however, subdued in the World Series four games to one by the defending champion Boston Red Sox. Robinson led Brooklyn to another National League crown in 1920 but once again met defeat, this time to Tris Speaker, Stan Coveleski, and the Cleveland Indians, five games to two.

The latter series was the apex of Robinson's success and popularity. Only twice in the next ten years did a Dodger team finish with a record above .500. Many of these squads became known more for their on-the-field antics than for their play. "Outfielders mystified by the course of fly balls, batters unable to decipher a coach's signs, runners losing direction on the base paths," became commonplace and expected at Ebbets Field.[9]

These were Brooklyn's "Daffiness Boys," a name pinned on them by sportswriter Westbrook Pegler, and if anyone epitomized this label it was the hurler Charles Arthur "Dazzy" Vance. Vance, who is remembered by Lopez as one of the best pitchers he ever saw, came to Brooklyn in 1922 as a hard-throwing thirty-one-year-old rookie. Although Vance earned a reputation for his wildness both on and off the mound, his fastball and curve were as good as anyone's. Between 1922 and 1930, Vance, on an aging Brooklyn club, posted 157 victories while leading the club in earned run average three times.

Another of these "Daffy" Dodgers was Babe Herman, an outfielder who ironically had what many considered the purest swing in baseball. While it was said that he treated a glove "like a foreign object," he had few weaknesses at the plate. From 1928 to 1930 Herman posted batting averages of .340, .381, and .393, respectively, with a total of 68 home runs and 334 runs batted in. Yet, when the name Babe Herman is mentioned, "the mind first conjures images of a befuddled outfielder getting clocked on the head by fly balls and a base runner so oblivious to circumstance as to run a three-base hit into a triple play."[10]

These were the Brooklyn Dodgers to whom Al Lopez had first reported at the end of the 1928 season and then joined to stay in 1930. After finishing in sixth place for five consecutive seasons, 1930 evolved into a "modest revival" for the Dodgers. Lopez recalls, "We had a bunch of guys that were great players. [Del] Bissonette hit I think .330, Glen Wright [the former Pittsburgh Pirate and the best shortstop Lopez ever saw] hit .321. Wright was a fourth place hitter, shortstop you know. Babe Herman hit .390 or something like that [.393] and didn't even win the batting title, we had a good hitting ballclub."[11]

In fact the Dodgers were an above-average-hitting ballclub that year. Babe Herman hit .393, first baseman Del Bissonette .330, Glen Wright .321, Lopez himself hit .309, second-baseman Jake Flowers .320, the great outfielder Rube Bressler .299, centerfielder Johnny Frederick .334, and third-baseman Wally Gilbert a respectable .294. Improbable as it may seem, Babe Herman's .393 average only netted him a second-place finish behind Bill Terry of the New York Giants for the league batting crown. ("Memphis Bill," the big Giant first baseman, batted .401 that season. No other batter reached the .400 plateau again until Ted Williams of the Boston Red Sox did it with a .406 average in 1941 and no one has done it since.) Despite their hitting, however, Dodger pitching was only modestly capable, even though its staff featured five pitchers who won in double figures. Vance was 17–15 with a league-leading 2.61 ERA, followed by Dolf Luque at 14–8, Watty Clark 13–13, Jumbo Elliott 10–7 and Ray Phelps 14–7.

Coming out of spring training that season, it was noted in the press that "Alfonso Lopez, 28-year-old Spaniard" would be behind the bat in the coming season for Brooklyn. The stated age was off by seven years; Lopez was twenty-one. The mistake is understandable given Lopez's five years of professional baseball to that point. The same article commented that Lopez had come very close the previous year to being retained by Brooklyn. It also remarked that Lopez was handling pitchers with "big league skill" and was showing the best throwing arm in camp, his throws to second arriving as "strikes." The defensive abilities Lopez demonstrated in the minors were what was most expected of him even though his bat was thought to be ready for the challenge as well. As to how many games Lopez might catch, the speculation fell toward the high side. His stamina was unquestioned, having caught 143 games the previous summer in the Southern League, where "it gets hot."[12]

The 1930 season began slowly for Brooklyn. The Dodgers lost their first three games and failed to post a win until April 21. The victory came on the "coldest day of the early season," as the Dodgers gave "6,000 shivering fans" a 15–8 victory over the Boston Braves. Del Bissonette homered and tripled, driving in seven runs to pace Brooklyn. Pitching for the Dodgers was Dolf Luque, who held the Braves to five hits over the first seven innings before being knocked from the mound by a George Sisler line drive. Three days later, the cold weather that had been affecting play all over in the early part of the season resulted in the cancellation of Brooklyn's game with the Philadelphia Phillies.[13]

Lopez, who had not seen much action in the early going, caught his first game on April 27, a 7–0 loss to the New York Giants. The *New York Times* reported that he "turned in an excellent performance, throwing out the 'speedy' Ed Marshall on an attempted steal." How speedy Marshall was may be a point of contention, as he failed to steal any bases at all in 1930 and stole only four in his brief career.[14]

Firmly in the cellar at two and seven, the Dodgers finally shook off the chill the following day, besting the Giants 6–4. Lopez belted a game-tying triple in the sixth and Harvey Hendricks drove home the winning run in the ninth inning. Lopez continued hot the next day, going four for five in a twenty-two-hit Brooklyn onslaught, resulting in a 19–15 win over New York. The latter high-scoring game with the Giants was a microcosm

Publicity photo of Al Lopez (left) and Dolfe Luque in uniform for Brooklyn. (Courtesy Tampa/Hillsborough County Public Library.)

of Brooklyn's season. In spite of the offense provided, no lead was safe, because the pitching generally refused to hold it. Dazzy Vance was the only Dodger starter to average less than four earned runs a game over the course of the entire season.[15]

With the emphasis on offense, the Dodgers surged ahead and by mid-season held a two-game lead over the Chicago Cubs, with the Giants in third place followed closely by St. Louis in fourth. When asked whether the Dodgers were on their way to a championship, the confident Robinson retorted, "No, I'm not predicting any pennants for Brooklyn ... but, I'm not forecasting any pennants for any other club in the National League either; don't forget that!" The following Saturday, Gallant Fox won the Arlington Classic for three-year-old thoroughbreds, Bobby Jones captured his fourth U.S. Open golf championship, and the "Robins" preserved their thin two game lead with a 10–4 victory over the Giants played before 50,000 fans at New York's Polo Grounds. Lopez was hitting a crisp .337 on this date and drawing rave reviews in the process.[16]

Near this point in the season, Ralph McGill, the *Atlanta Constitution* reporter who had covered Lopez the previous year (and who later became one of the South's most respected journalists), wrote that the "Ybor City

Kid" was already showing himself to be a great catcher. Commenting on a perceived dearth of quality catchers in the majors, McGill guessed that Lopez would soon be ranked alongside Mickey Cochrane as one of the game's best receivers. McGill noted that Robinson himself, while respectful of Lopez's talents, had not planned on using him as a regular. But Lopez, McGill acknowledged, had other ideas, and upon getting an opportunity made the most of it, outhitting his competitors and proving to be the "honey of the lot."[17]

The Dodgers held onto first place until late August, when their lack of pitching caught up with them, allowing the Giants, Cubs, and Cardinals back into the race. Moving into September, Brooklyn split a twin bill with the Braves, falling from third to fourth place behind Chicago, New York, and the surging St. Louis Cardinals. As the nation watched two French flyers, Diendonne Coste and Maurice Bellonte, complete the first Paris-to-New-York transatlantic flight, the Dodgers settled into fourth. Although Lopez continued to hit well, batting .330 as late as September 21, the Dodgers, lacking the necessary pitching, failed to make a move on the leaders and were eliminated from the race by September 24.[18]

Brooklyn topped the Boston Braves 6–3 before 10,000 appreciative fans at Ebbets Field on the season's final day. The day also marked the return to the pitching mound of Babe Ruth. Ruth, baseball's immortal home-run champ, had not hurled a game in ten years. Proving more than up to the task, the "Bambino" allowed no earned runs in seven innings of work and the New York Yankees defeated the Boston Red Sox 9–3. Ruth, the *New York Times* reported, "dealt speed and curves that bewildered Boston and his superb fielding started two double plays."[19]

The final National League standings for Lopez's rookie season found St. Louis finishing on top with a 92–62 record, nosing out Chicago by two games and New York by five. Brooklyn, finishing in fourth place, was able to take some solace in the knowledge that the Dodger faithful spun the turnstiles for an Ebbets Field attendance record of 1.1 million fans.[20] Lopez himself had by the season's end secured the starting catching duties on a full-time basis. His .309 batting average became a career high for him, as did his 130 hits. In fact, Lopez so impressed the Dodger management and coaches with his "exceptional defensive skills" and all-around hustle that after the following season they traded twenty-two-year-old Ernie Lombardi, a promising catcher who went on to his own Hall of Fame career, to the Cincinnati Reds.[21]

When asked to describe the attributes that made Brooklyn commit to him early in that rookie season, Lopez explained that he was simply a young man who tried hard. He remembers:

> I was a young rookie coming up and I tried to catch the same way I always had, they must have signed me because they liked my style of play. I used to always back up first base on throws, show a lot of hustle. I was small, and once, when I ran to back up first base on a throw, one of the umpires said, "What are you doing running in back of first base like that, you're holding up the game; they don't overthrow like that." They overthrow alright. He wanted to keep the game going faster.[22]

The next season, 1931, was another "humdrum" year for the Robins. Although they once again finished in fourth place, they were never really in the race. Brooklyn ended the season trailing St. Louis by twenty-one games, convincing Dodger management that after eighteen years of "Uncle Robbie," it was time for a change. Robinson's firing brought to a close one of the more colorful eras in Brooklyn baseball history. Max Carey, a former base-stealing wizard with the Pirates and a player whom Robinson had acquired at the end of the 1926 season, was chosen to succeed him.

Throughout 1931, the Dodgers, unaware that it might be the final season of Robinson's tenure, continued to perform in a "daffy" fashion. Lopez told author Donald Honig of such an incident:

> One day I had an argument with umpire Bill Klem over a close play at home. We had a pretty good go at it, and that was that. The next day there was a picture in the paper of that play and it showed Klem was wrong. One of the guys, I think it was Mungo [rookie pitcher Van Lingle Mungo], cut the picture out, taped it over home plate and covered it with dirt. I didn't know anything about it. Just before the first pitch was thrown, Klem went around to clean off the plate. I was crouched there watching him. He bent down and started whisking his little brush back and forth. He uncovered a corner of the picture, turned his head and gave me a dirty look. Then he went on brushing, his hand moving slower and slower, his face getting redder and redder. Little by little he cleared off the whole picture. I tried not to laugh because I could see how mad he was. He thought I had done it and boy, was he burned up. "You dumb busher," he said. "I didn't do it, Bill," I said. But I don't think he even heard me because he just kept chewing me out.[23]

Lopez in uniform for Brooklyn, ca. 1931. (Courtesy National Baseball Library, Cooperstown, New York.)

The umpire in question, Bill Klem, was known to have a short fuse regarding any form of harassment. Chief Myers, a former New York Giants catcher, once recalled that:

> If Klem was umpiring behind the plate, all you had to do was
> call him "Catfish" and out of the game you would go. That's

all. Just that one word and you were out. I'm not quite sure
why. Maybe it was because he had rather prominent lips, and
when he'd call a ball or strike he'd let fly a rather fine spray from
his mouth. Sort of gave the general impression of a catfish, you
know. He was sensitive about it, to say the least![24]

If Mungo, as Lopez believes, actually put the picture of Klem on
home plate, it would not be surprising. Van Lingle Mungo, an outspoken, rebellious sort who possessed an overpowering fastball, is remembered by Lopez as having gotten into trouble a lot because of his excessive
drinking. Hailed as the next Dazzy Vance, Mungo was also the most
difficult pitcher to catch that Lopez ever worked with. Lopez:

> Because he was so fast and he, you'd give him a target high and
> well, he hit me on the instep one day and I had given him a
> target high and tight with two strikes on the batter and he hit
> me on the instep, with a man on third base! Luckily the ball
> hit me [or the runner may have scored]. He was laughing like
> hell because he hit me on the instep. He was outspoken, but a
> real nice guy.[25]

Lopez's offensive statistics declined slightly in 1931, but his reputation as a handler of pitchers grew. His .269 batting average was the result
of what Lopez believed to be a dead-ball conspiracy designed to get the
game back in the park. Lopez explains:

> They changed the ball! They wanted to deaden it. It was
> McGraw's idea. He is the one that complained about it. He
> couldn't play his kind of baseball with that lively ball, every-
> one was hitting homeruns and stuff like that. I think it hurt
> me especially because I weighed only 165 pounds. McGraw felt
> that you couldn't play inside baseball, hitting, bunting, run-
> ning, squeeze play, stuff like that. Everybody was swinging for
> the fence. You need virgin wool on that ball to make it go and
> they would use old wool. It hurt everybody, not just me. I
> think that the real reason they did it was to cut down on
> salaries. I hit .309 in 1930 and dropped to .269 in 1931 and
> they cut my salary.[26]

Among 1931's batting leaders, Bill Terry of the Giants, who had led
the league with a remarkable .401 average the previous season, fell to .349,

a fifty-two-point drop. Lopez's teammates, Babe Herman and Lefty O'Doul, went from .393 to .313 and .383 to .336. Chuck Klein of the Phillies dropped from .386 to .337. However, Chick Hafey of the Cardinals and the Cubs' Charlie Grimm, among others, improved their numbers going from .337 to .386 and .289 to .331 respectively. Some of the reductions noted above may have been caused by factors such as O'Doul's being traded to Brooklyn prior to the 1931 season or Terry's simply returning to his norm after having posted a career year. Lopez himself, in spite of dropping to .269 that season, bettered his career average by eight points. While McGraw and other National League luminaries might very well have sought to bring the game back inside with a dead ball, the above speculated reasons could have also played a role.

The drop in Lopez's batting average seems not to have affected his golf game. In Tampa, that off season, Lopez joined "golf's prestigious hole-in-one club," with a 230-yard stroke at the Airport Golf Course.[27] Golf had become a passion with Lopez (it would be a lifelong passion) and he sought every opportunity during the off season to pursue it. Manuel Onis, another native of Tampa who found his way into a Brooklyn Dodgers uniform, remembers that he and Lopez would play golf throughout the off season. "Al and I spent the winter playing golf at Macfarlane Park, in West Tampa. The city had a nine-hole golf course there. You only needed to use an iron, a putter, and a pitching wedge. That's all it took."[28]

As the Depression worsened in 1932, with Americans' personal incomes having declined more than $42 million from three years earlier and unemployment continuing to rise, the Brooklyn Dodgers placed third, lessening to an extent the misery of its borough faithful. Responding to the crisis, Max Carey, the Dodgers' rookie manager, provided work relief to a makeshift array of hopefuls who, on paper, inspired little optimism of autumnal glory. Yet this club, a paradigm of transient utility, managed to scratch out more wins than losses, finishing the campaign over .500 at 81–73. Newly acquired outfielder Lefty O'Doul, who had won a batting championship with the Phillies in 1929, won another in this, his second year in Brooklyn, hitting .368. Mungo and Vance both had solid if not spectacular seasons, combining for twenty-five wins, while a maturing left-hander named Watty Clark led the staff with twenty victories. Lopez, catching in 126 games, batted .275, up six points. He improved in virtually every offensive category, collecting eighteen doubles, six triples, and forty-three RBIs.

Recalling his early years played during the Depression, Lopez remembers good and hard times. Not necessarily his hard times, although the Depression did make it more difficult to negotiate a contract, but the difficulties suffered by his neighbors, particularly in Ybor City. Lopez:

> Well, it [the Depression] eventually hurt the player salaries because it was really rough during the Depression. Early in my career at Brooklyn, I was making about $10,000, which was good money. I was fortunate. I personally didn't feel the Depression at all. But when I would come home and see all of these families that were friends of ours in Ybor City, some going to bed at night without food, that was a serious bad thing.[29]

Mormino and Pozzetta note that the Great Depression struck the Ybor City cigar industry with "particular force," because much of the market for "high-priced, quality cigars" dried up. As the Depression worsened, cigarettes, being less expensive to make and subsequently cheaper to purchase, captured more of the tobacco market. In response, Ybor City's cigarmaker work force diminished across ethnic lines. The result was a deepening of hardship, discontent, and labor strife among Ybor City's largely immigrant populace.[30]

If the Dodgers' 1932 third-place finish kindled any hopes for the near future in Brooklyn, they proved to be short lived. Max Carey's club plunged to sixth place in 1933, remaining in the second division for the next six seasons. At the plate, Lopez once again showed improvement and enjoyed one of his finest years with a robust (for Lopez) .301 batting average. This was the second and last year in which Lopez would hit .300 or better over an entire season.

After failing to win a pennant in either of his two years at the helm, Max Carey was dismissed the following spring and replaced by his assistant, Charles Dillon "Casey" Stengel. Stengel, who broke in with Brooklyn as a player in 1912, was thrown out during his rookie season trying to steal second off catcher Jimmy Archer of the Chicago Cubs. Upon coming into second, Stengel threw a particularly hard slide into the veteran Cubs second baseman Johnny Evers. The shrill Evers, appalled at Stengel's brashness, told the rookie that the next time he came in like that, he would shove the ball down his throat. Stengel responded that he had done it that way in the minors and was not about to change now. He also told Evers to look for him, because he would be around for a long time. Stengel proved to be around longer than either of them imagined he would be. Recognized throughout his career for a sometimes unorthodox style, Stengel now hoped to instill some life into the listless Dodgers.[31]

As the Dodgers' skipper, Stengel was provoked by the club's poor work ethic. "Some of these fellows," said Stengel, "think that one workout a day is enough. Well, it's not, not in my book." Stengel subsequently made his "book" required reading on the part of his players. Roscoe McGowen noted that in one such "workout" Stengel had virtually the entire team ranged along the shortstop side of second base, taking turns practicing their lead. It was, believed Stengel, training for both the base runners, the infielders who had to cover the bag, his catcher, and the pitchers. All were "crisply" instructed by Stengel on their responsibilities. "Make your throw good," shouted Stengel to his pitchers. "This is a protection play and what protection is there in a ball going into center field?" It was obvious from the start that Stengel expected his men to be physically and mentally fit to perform and would be "annoyed" with anything less.[32]

Stengel and Lopez became fast and lasting friends at Brooklyn. In fact, a few seasons after Stengel's arrival, the two became business partners in an oil well in Texas. The story is told by Lopez to Maury Allen in Allen's entertaining biography of Stengel. Lopez:

> Stengel and I went to dinner one evening at Joe's, a restaurant under the Brooklyn Bridge, famous for the best home-fried potatoes in Brooklyn. A journeyman Dodgers outfielder named Randy Moore was with us. Stengel asked Moore what he would be doing after his baseball career ended. "Well, my father-in-law has some oil wells back home in Naples, Texas. I might get involved in that." Casey said he might be interested investing a few bucks into some oil wells, too, if there was room. "Let's put the Mexican [Lopez] in it too," said Stengel. Casey was fired by the Dodgers the next year and was out of baseball. Moore had broken his leg and quit. He went into the oil business and one day he called Casey. He asked if Casey was serious about investing. Casey said he was, got Edna [Stengel's wife] to approve a ten-thousand-dollar investment and went in with Moore. I went in for a thousand bucks.[33]

Lopez found the gregarious, sometimes giddy nature of Stengel to be both entertaining and refreshing. The usually fettered Lopez no doubt saw in Stengel traits that he himself could not possess, yet admired in others. The ability to speak on end about any subject; the relative ease in which

Spring training 1934: Lopez, holding out for a better Dodgers contract, works out with the Cincinnati Reds. (Courtesy National Baseball Library, Cooperstown, New York.)

Stengel dealt with the public and media; his innate sense of allowing intuition to quell intellect. And while Lopez did not understand everything Stengel did as a manager, he respected the latter's ability to instinctively apply reason, albeit his own, to a given scenario. For a percentage player like Lopez, this style often represented too many gambles, but it looked good on Stengel and Lopez respected that. Stengel on the other hand, lauded the diligence with which Lopez pursued his craft and relished the example of hard work set by his catcher. As in love, baseball sometimes makes for strange bedfellows, and Stengel and Lopez were certainly no exception.

Lopez began spring training in 1934 at his home in Tampa, where he was holding out for a better contract. His actions may have seemed particularly puzzling to his neighbors in Ybor City, many of whom, as Lopez acknowledged, were out of work and going to bed hungry. But Lopez, believing his salary demands to be just, was determined not to be taken advantage of by management despite the hard economic conditions. During the holdout, Stengel, who must have thought he had witnessed everything there was to see on a baseball diamond, was nonetheless surprised by what took place in an exhibition game with the Philadelphia Athletics. The starting pitcher for Connie Mack's club was none other than Mildred "Babe" Didrickson, the 1932 Olympic javelin and 100-meter hurdles champion. In one inning of action, Didrickson, who had been receiving pitching tips from veteran spitballer Burleigh Grimes, displayed a "graceful, easy delivery that would do credit to any hurler." After walking Danny Taylor and hitting Johnny Frederick, however, the defense was forced to her rescue, "astounding" the spectators with a 6-4-3 triple play. With runners on first and second, Joe Stripp lined a hard one to Dib Williams at shortstop, who relayed it to Williams at second and on to Warstler at first, catching both runners off base for the outs. Didrickson gladly gave way to Roy Mahaffey to start the second, and after the game she retreated to a local golf course, where she had promised to give a demonstration of her driving power.[34]

Brooklyn's business manager, Bob Quinn, arrived the following day bearing the news that Lopez and the club were still at odds over the catcher's contract. Lopez's last communication to Quinn, in reply to the business manager's request for him to come to Orlando and talk things over, had sounded uncompromising. "If you think a meeting with you," wired Lopez, "would help to bring an agreement on the salary I asked for, I would be more than glad to come to Orlando. Otherwise I prefer to stay here." Lopez's response, while not overly optimistic, was taken by Quinn with a grain of salt, as he knew that his club was visiting Tampa the next day anyway and felt that he would see Lopez then. With Lopez sitting in the stands, "still a determined holdout," the Dodgers, largely on a bad throw by Clyde Sukeforth, a backup catcher, lost 3–2. After the game Lopez, "nattily dressed and looking in the pink of condition," announced that he would travel to Orlando the next morning to talk things over with Quinn. While expressing reservations that a deal could be reached, Lopez agreed to meet with Quinn because Stengel had asked him to. "Casey asked me to go and talk things over with Quinn," said Lopez, "and I guess that's the best thing to do, so I'll run over in the morning." By lunchtime the following day, Lopez and Quinn had reached a compromise deal bringing the catcher a one-year contract for a figure close to $13,000. Lopez's original demand had been for $15,000 and Brooklyn had countered with $11,000. It was reported that Lopez would arrive in camp the next day and be ready to play as soon as Stengel needed him. This fact became "evident to anybody watching him" when after reporting, Lopez worked an hour and a half behind the plate in batting practice.[35]

With the season approaching, Stengel's top priority became finding enough pitchers to erect a solid staff around Mungo, his ace hurler. This was especially difficult, given the limited number of quality arms in camp. Under persistent questioning on his rotation, Stengel admitted that the Dodgers might have to begin the year with no more than eight pitchers rostered. "We can start with eight, can't we?" asked Stengel. "I figure you can't overwork a pitcher during the early part of the season when the weather is cold, so eight of 'em ought to stand the gaff." In the end, however, the limitation he faced regarding good pitching in camp mandated that he keep ten. Among those named by Stengel to join Mungo as starters were Ray Benge, Ownie Carroll, and a rookie, Emil "Dutch" Leonard. Aside from Mungo and Leonard, the staff was "inadequate" at best, collectively posting minimal career numbers. The bankrupt condition of this coterie so embodied Stengel's dilemma and the economic distress then gripping the nation that it may have been aptly referred to as a "Hoover" pitching staff.[36]

Another harbinger to Brooklyn's season occurred at the end of March when a cadre of Stengel's regulars were beaten by an assortment of reserves in an intrasquad game. Lopez managed the Yannigans, as the reserves were called, "instilling them with his fiery spirit." He also played right field and collected one of the two singles recorded off Ray Benge in contributing to the Yannigans' 1–0 victory. The game did prove useful to Stengel, how-ever, in that he was able to carry out his plan of making Len Koenecke the leadoff man and he was able to get a good look at recently signed Hack Wilson. Playing left field for Lopez's team in his initial appearance of the spring, Wilson, the former Chicago Cubs strongman, went back against the left field fence to rob Tony Cuccinello of a double.[37]

In spite of Stengel's maneuvers, Brooklyn was given little chance by anyone of finishing near the top of league standings. Most expected the Dodgers' hated rival, the New York Giants, winners of the previous year's pennant, of repeating with little challenge. They were led by "Memphis Bill" Terry, the player-manager first baseman, who had taken over the club in 1932 upon John McGraw's retirement. Before spring training began, Roscoe McGowan, who regularly covered the Dodgers for the *New York Times*, asked Terry his opinion of Brooklyn. Terry, after noting that he had not "heard a peep out of there," asked McGowan "Is Brooklyn still in the league?" The comment, considered by Terry to be no more than a "mild joke," was not viewed the same way in Brooklyn. Later in the spring, while previewing the coming season with John Kieran of the *New York Times*, Terry had the opportunity to recant some of what he had earlier said. However, upon watching two of Stengel's "kaleidoscopic Dodgers" fight for possession of one base twice in the same afternoon, "Memphis Bill" could not help but laughingly remark, "How long have these fellows been down here? They're in midseason form already." The acerbic after-taste of Terry's comments stayed with Dodgers followers throughout the season.[38]

Brooklyn provided the Giants' skipper with little reason to believe his assessment might be wrong. The day Terry's comment was reported by John Kieran, Brooklyn blew a two-run lead in the eighth inning against Philadelphia and lost 4–2. The Athletics rally consisted of an error by Brooklyn shortstop Lonny Frey to start the inning, followed by Tony Cuc-cinello's fumble and subsequent wild throw on what should have been a routine out to retire the side scoreless. The next day, the twenty-one-year-old Frey suffered a concussion and was taken to the hospital after being hit in the head with a pitch during *batting practice*.[39]

The following day, "inspired" by Lopez's three hits and "spurred on by verbal evidence" that Stengel's patience was "practically exhausted," the Dodgers bested the Boston Red Sox 9–5. Brooklyn followed that perfor-mance with another victory over Boston, prompting Roscoe McGowen to write that "Stengel's earnest efforts toward making his players capable of out guessing their opponents [has] borne more fruit." The highlight of the contest was Brooklyn's flawless execution of two run-producing double steals. Both double steals, taken against Rick Ferrell, the all-star American League catcher and future Hall of Famer, "caught the Red Sox napping and astonished several hundred spectators." The two outings gave Stengel the encouragement he had been seeking as the club moved toward opening day. Stengel also made the "long expected appointment" of Lopez as captain of the Dodgers, providing the catcher with an additional $500 for the season as well as the honor due him.[40]

While many in the press and around the league were writing the Dodgers off as pennant contenders, Stengel would not concede anything. Much as "Uncle Robbie" had four years earlier, Stengel commented that he was not predicting a pennant for Brooklyn, but "that doesn't mean we are planting ourselves in the second division before the gong rings." Stengel:

> Everybody may have to wait until that 154th game is played before the race is decided, and the Dodgers will be in there making trouble. We'll have a better punch than before. Sam Leslie will be a better ballplayer and the same is true of Cuccinello and Stripp. With Jordan, that makes a pretty good infield. We've got the best catcher in the league in Al Lopez and one of the best pitchers in Mungo. Wilson and Frederick will give that new lively ball a few trips. Hack's a winning ballplayer — a fellow who still thinks he can do it. I like that kind. All my boys will give the best they've got.[41]

Stengel's remark that the season would go to the wire with Brooklyn in there "making trouble" proved more prophetic than the "Old Professor" could have known. However, most prognosticators believed the Dodgers would finish no better than the second division, in a "merry scramble" with Philadelphia and Cincinnati for the bottom three positions.[42]

The Dodgers opened the season convincingly, besting the Braves 8–7 before 28,000 Ebbets Field patrons. The opening-day ceremonies were accompanied by fireworks, "an enthusiastic gentleman in a field box back of first base setting off a string of firecrackers several feet long" just as the players lined up "to start the flagpole march." Adding further to the excitement, a large piece of bunting on the upper stands just behind the Brooklyn dugout caught fire and the blazing fragments fell into the seats below with the spectators scrambling for safety. After the two team captains, Lopez and Pinky Whitney, raised the flag as the national anthem was played, the game got underway, but not before umpire Ernest Quigley forgot to have the first ball thrown out by borough president Raymond V. Ingersoll. The contest itself kept those in attendance on the edges of their seats until the final out was called. In the final frame, Boston scored three runs, the tying run was on third, and the winning run was on first when Whitney lined directly into Joe Stripp's hands at third, ending the game. Danny Taylor and Hack Wilson homered for Brooklyn off Ed Brandt, driving in five of Brooklyn's eight runs, but both left the game late with leg injuries.[43]

Brooklyn lost 3–2 in the second game of the Boston series and played to a 1–1 draw in the finale. The tie came when Quigley, the umpire, called it in the eighth inning on account of fog. With a record of 1–1–1, the Dodgers next played host to Philadelphia, sweeping them in a three-game series. In the first contest, rookie hurler Dutch Leonard blanked the Phillies 5–0, behind Len Koenecke's two home runs. Mungo followed that by performing "astonishingly," allowing no walks or hit batsmen, in a 3–1 Dodgers victory. The next day, a four-run Brooklyn rally in the eighth inning secured another win for Stengel's team. Down by a run at 4–3, Sam Leslie started the rally, smashing a triple to center field. At that point, Phillies manager Jimmy Wilson removed his pitcher, bringing in Cy Moore, a former Dodger, in relief. Moore responded by walking Cuccinello and allowing a single to Lopez that scored Leslie for the tying run. Moore then fanned Munns, but Koenecke's hard drive to right field drove home the Dodgers fifth run. Moore next walked Jordan, and Frederick followed with a single over second, scoring Lopez and Jordan. The Dodgers, sporting a 4–1–1 record, then headed out of Brooklyn until May 17.[44]

Away from the familiarity of Ebbets Field, the Dodgers hit the skids, losing four of their next five in Boston and Philadelphia. At Boston the Braves swept Brooklyn 5–3, 9–4, and 2–0. Only in game three did the Dodgers mount any threat of winning. Dutch Leonard, having been bumped by Mungo in the previous day's rotation, got the start and allowed two runs out of the box in the first inning. After that, however, the rookie settled down, allowing only four scattered hits and no Boston runner past second over the next eight frames. The Dodgers threat came in the ninth inning, when with one out, Leslie walked, Cuccinello lined hard to center field the second out, Lopez doubled, and Glenn Chapman walked to load the bases. With the sacks full, however, Lonny Frey slashed into a force play, ending it. In Philadelphia, two days later, the Dodgers extended their losing streak, bowing to the Phillies 10–8. The losses knocked Brooklyn into fifth place, trailing league leaders Chicago and New York. In spite of a narrow win at Philadelphia the next day, it was looking as though Bill Terry knew what he was talking about.[45]

Brooklyn's poor play continued into the summer, and by July 1, heading into a two-game series with the Giants at the Polo Grounds, the Dodgers were slouched in sixth place, saddled with an eight-game losing streak. Commenting on Brooklyn's woeful record, however, John Drebinger of the *New York Times* wrote positively that "whatever the troubles and misfortunes of the Dodgers may have been, they still seem able at a moment's notice to step up and knock over the one pitcher in baseball that most teams are unable to beat at all." He was referring to New York's ace left-hander, Carl Hubbell, who was slated to start game one of the two-game set. Before the season opened, the Dodgers held an all-time advantage over Hubbell, winning twenty times against him and losing only nine. In fact, Bill Terry usually refrained from pitching Hubbell against "the Flatbush brigade" for that very reason. Yet in "a moment of overexuberance," Terry chose to start Hubbell and the Dodgers did not disappoint, routing "King Carl" 8–4. The victory was only the second scored by the Dodgers in nine games with the Giants so far that season.[46] The next day the Giants came back strong with homers by Travis Jackson and Lefty O'Doul, summarily relieving Brooklyn of the prior day's good feelings by winning this game 5–4.[47]

Lopez in 1934 displayed a defensive versatility that heretofore had been absent. Aside from catching more than 100 games, Lopez saw action at both second and third base. The increased activity showed; the number of games Lopez played in climbed to 140 for the season. Lopez's performance that year was good enough to earn him a spot in the All-Star game, his first, to be played at the Polo Grounds in New York City.

The rosters for the All-Star game were chosen by Bill Terry and Joe Cronin, the opposing managers, "in an effort to put the strongest possible teams together." Among the forty players chosen to participate in "baseball's spectacular mid-season show" were ten players from the Giants and Yankees alone. Because of this, it was said that the contest might offer a preview of the expected "subway series" to come. Terry and Cronin's selections varied little from a fan poll conducted by newspapers throughout the country. Terry differed only by starting the Giants' Mel Ott over Wally Berger of the Braves in the outfield, while Cronin went with Al

Simmons in the outfield rather than Earl Averill, the fans' selection. It was also argued that the National League enjoyed an edge, on the basis of pitching, but the American League sluggers might be able to offset it. Outside of the pitchers and catchers, American League batters averaged approximately .348 while the Nationals countered at .344. If Pittsburgh's Arky Vaughan was replaced at shortstop by Travis Jackson, as Terry threatened to do, then the National League average dipped to .334.[48]

This particular midsummer classic was only the second in baseball's history, the first coming the year before. The catchers represented what may have been the finest assemblage of backstop talent ever gathered on one diamond.[49] Terry chose as catchers Lopez and Gabby Hartnett, another Hall of Famer, who with Lopez shares National League records: most seasons with more than 100 games caught — twelve — and most consecutive years catching 100 or more games — eight. Terry opted for a pair of catchers rather than three in order to have an additional infielder. Cronin designated Mickey Cochrane, Bill Dickey, and Rick Ferrell as his receiving trio. At one time or another either Cochrane or Dickey has been considered

Left to right: Van Lingle Mungo, Babe Ruth, Al Lopez, early 1930s. (Courtesy National Baseball Library, Cooperstown, New York.)

among the greatest catchers of all time, and Ferrell, certainly no slouch, is in the Hall of Fame with them. "Black Mike" Cochrane, known as much for his tenacious leadership abilities as anything, played on five-pennant winning clubs in seven years. On two of those teams (Detroit in 1934–35) he was the player-manager. From 1925 until his career was ended by a Bump Hadley fastball (which almost killed him) in 1937, Cochrane averaged .320, the best mark for any catcher. Bill Dickey caught 100 games or more for thirteen consecutive years, surpassing Lopez and Hartnett in that regard. This clutch hitter had a career average of .313, with 202 home runs and 1,209 RBIs, on New York Yankees teams featuring Babe Ruth, Lou Gehrig, and Joe DiMaggio. Ferrell had been the all-star catcher the year before and caught all nine innings. He resembled Lopez in that durability was his game — he held the American League record at the time for most games caught with 1,805.

The matchup itself featured some of the brightest stars baseball has ever known. Babe Ruth, Lou Gehrig, Jimmie Foxx, Mel Ott, Charlie Gehringer, Dizzy Dean, Lefty Gomez, and other notables participated in this classic encounter. The game is remembered best, however, for the pitching of Carl Hubbell, the New York Giants left-hander deluxe. Over the first two innings, Hubbell struck out Babe Ruth, Lou Gehrig, Jimmie Foxx, Al Simmons, and Joe Cronin in order before allowing Bill Dickey to ground out. "King Carl" eventually gave up two hits in his three innings of work, but he allowed no runs as the National League took a 4–0 lead on homers by St. Louis Cardinals "Gas House Gang" teammates Frankie Frisch and Joe Medwick. Down four runs, the American League rallied against Lon Warneke and Van Lingle Mungo for four runs apiece in the fourth and fifth innings. While the Nationals were able to narrow the gap somewhat, sending three runs across in the fifth against the Yankees' Red Ruffing, Cleveland's Mel Harder came on for the Americans and closed the door. The American League scored a final run in the sixth off Dizzy Dean, but that was it as the American League won the contest 9–7.[50]

With Terry choosing Hartnett to start the game, Lopez witnessed Hubbell's brilliance from the bullpen. In spite of a badly swollen right thumb, he entered the game in the sixth inning to catch Dizzy Dean, but he failed to distinguish himself at bat, going zero for two with a strikeout.[51]

Despite earning his first All-Star game appearance, the season was another disappointment for Lopez, as the Dodgers finished a dismal sixth for the second consecutive year. Lopez batted .273 for the season with career highs in doubles, 23, and home runs, 7; He also drove in 54 runs. The problem confronting Brooklyn was not so much losing to the league's better clubs; that was expected. It was the losses to the lesser ones that hurt. Their record against fellow second-division rivals was terrible, especially given the necessity of winning those games. By midseason Brooklyn had lost a combined sixteen games to Boston, Philadelphia, and Cincinnati and things got little better. Although Boston rebounded from fifth to fourth place, the others finished the season in seventh and eighth place respectively. For Brooklyn to improve its chances of climbing out of the league's low-rent district, it would first have to win the games it was capable of. That done, they might then set their sights on the league leaders and hope for the upset. Whatever the plan, it was obvious to most that any attempt by Brooklyn to regroup its fortunes would have to wait another year; or would it?[52]

Bill Terry's New York Giants had begun the season fast and consistent, holding a six-game lead as late as Labor Day. However, with St. Louis turning on the gas late to catch them, New York's lead diminished. After two wins at Boston on September 21, the Cardinals stood three and a half games behind New York. Two days later the Giants were beaten by Boston and their lead shrank to two and a half, with six games remaining. On September 26 New York, needing to win its three remaining games to clinch, was shut out by Curt Davis of the Phillies 4–0. With St. Louis beating Pittsburgh, New York's lead was reduced to one. The next day the Cardinals and Giants both lost, preserving New York's slim lead. By the final weekend of the year, however, St. Louis had closed to a "flat-footed" tie with New York.[53]

The pennant came down to the season's final two days with St. Louis facing Cincinnati and the Dodgers visiting the Polo Grounds. The Cardinals began the faceoff with Paul Dean scoring his nineteenth victory of the season, besting the Reds 6–1. Brooklyn then topped New York 5–1 behind the fastball of Van Lingle Mungo. Before the game began, Stengel received a telegram with fifty signatures that read "You'll win the undying gratitude of Brooklyn fans if you knock Bill Terry and his Giants flat on their backs." Stengel was so moved by the message that he read it aloud to his team and then called a special closed meeting, asking all newspapermen to leave. It was presumed that Stengel then spoke with his players regarding the promised gratitude. When the Giants emerged from the clubhouse for their practice, they were greeted not by the warm cheers of a home crowd, but instead a "tremendous roar of derision." John Drebinger reported that in spite of poor weather limiting attendance to "less than a third of what it might have been," a "staunch flock of [Brooklyn] adherents" came to the Polo Grounds for no other purpose than to show Bill Terry that they were still very much in the league.

On the rain-drenched diamond, the defending world champion Giants never got on track, struggling "feebly, as if finally weighed down by the utter futility of it all." Mungo, proving masterful all afternoon, limited the Giants to one run, a seventh-inning George Watkins homer that in the end meant nothing. Meanwhile, the Dodgers seemed content to take them one at a time, at least until the ninth, when two runs came across. Mungo opened the Brooklyn scoring in the fifth, slashing a single to right field, moving to second on a passed ball, and racing home on a single to center by Lonny Frey. The next inning, Cuccinello started with a walk, moved to second on a sacrifice by Taylor, and came home on a single by Mungo. After posting another run in the seventh, Brooklyn tallied twice more in the ninth, scoring one off Al Smith, who Brooklyn fans shouted should be replaced by Herbert Hoover, and the other on a bases-loaded walk by Dolph Luque. Terry had turned to the veteran Cuban hurler, figuring that with his dark skin and smallish size, he would be difficult to see in the afternoon shadows. As the game ended, the only sound that could be heard was "the jeering wails of the gleeful Flatbushers." New York was now a complete game behind St. Louis and their only hope was to win the next day with the Cardinals losing, thus finishing in a tie and forcing the first playoff series in major-league history.[54]

On the final day of baseball's regular season, the Giants' dream of "continued world domination" crumbled simultaneously on two fronts. The Cardinals, with Dizzy Dean on the mound, "walloped" the Reds 9–0, while Brooklyn closed the door on the Giants, scoring three runs in the top of the tenth, winning 8–5. The end result was a pennant for Frankie Frisch and his Cardinals and a trip to the World Series, where they would face the Detroit Tigers. Betting odds went off at three to five, favoring the Cardinals' chances.

In the parallel St. Louis game, Dizzy Dean, the Gas House Gang's brash young ace, confronted a bases-loaded, no out situation in the ninth by striking out two and getting another to foul out. It was his thirtieth win and seventh shutout of the season. After the game, celebrating Cardinals shouted, "Brooklyn is in the league now ... and how!"[55]

The Dodgers–Giants game transpired before an almost-capacity Polo Grounds crowd of 45,000, many of whom came equipped with cow bells, horns, whistles, and rattles. The Giants took an early lead, posting four runs in the first inning. Giants hurler "Fat Freddie" Fitzsimmons later padded his own lead with a fourth-inning home run. But the Dodgers, as they had the day before, began pecking away, scoring one run in each of the second, fourth, and sixth innings. They followed that by pushing two across in the eighth to tie the game. The aroused fans of both clubs remained involved throughout; the left wing of the stands — the Brooklyn rooters — booed Terry furiously every time he came to bat, and the Giants faithful followed suit, booing Lopez. The climactic tenth inning began when Sam Leslie singled to left, replaced by pinch runner Johnny McCarthy, who moved to third on Cuccinello's double. With New York's Carl Hubbell on in relief, Johnny Babich struck out and then Joe Stripp was intentionally walked to load the bases. Lopez next drove a "hot smash" to Blondy Ryan at shortstop, who fumbled the play, scoring McCarthy and keeping the bases filled. Glenn Chapman then smacked a deep drive to George Watkins in center field, scoring Cuccinello and sending Stripp to third; Lopez was held at first. Buzz Boyle followed with a single to right, scoring Stripp and moving Lopez to third. Frey then struck out to end the inning, but not before three runs had scored, putting the game out of reach. The victory, ending as it did any hope of a pennant for the Giants, was one of Brooklyn's finest, and it certainly won the "undying gratitude" of the Dodgers fans. Meanwhile, the Giants "went out in darkness and defeat, and night fell over the abandoned Polo Grounds." With the season over, the only thing left for them to do was refund the price of the World Series tickets they had begun selling the week before.[56]

For his part, Bill Terry failed to offer any excuses for his club's late-season slide. "No, I can't explain how it happened," he said. "The slump just came on us and it was too late to do anything about it. But I'm not blaming anybody and have no alibis to offer. For the mistakes we made I'll take the full responsibility."[57]

Lopez characterized Terry's season-opening comment as one of those things that can come back to haunt a manager. "I think he was sorry later on that he ever said it," Lopez said. "Terry's remark never bothered us players, but it burned the fans up.... [I]t couldn't have been any wilder out there if we had won the pennant ourselves."[58]

The temporarily quelled Brooklyn faithful would have to wait some time before being swept up in emotion of that sort again. Performing miserably, Brooklyn crawled up a notch to fifth in 1935, slumbering through a 70–83 record. Mungo, continuing to assert himself in the rotation, posted a 16–10 record with four shutouts. He also finished third in the league in strikeouts with 143. Lopez had another solid season behind the plate, catching more than 100 games and continuing to earn the respect of those around him. His .251 batting average, however, was a personal low. These were the years when Lopez's leadership, hustle, and all-out effort led Stengel, his manager, to label him "the fella which caught as good as any of them."[59]

Under Stengel, Lopez got an advanced education in percentage baseball. He learned most of Stengel's tricks and developed one or two of his own. In Brooklyn (then later playing in Boston), Lopez and second baseman Tony Cuccinello worked one play that made them seem prescient even to their teammates. With a runner on first base, Cuccinello would watch the opposing first-base coach out of the corner of his eye. When he saw him wink, the standard steal sign in those days, "Cooch" would double his right fist along his right leg. Lopez, reading the sign, would promptly call for a pitchout, whip the ball to Cuccinello, and nail the runner halfway to second.[60]

Lopez became so adept at playing the position the way Stengel wanted that the manager soon had his catcher running the ball club from behind the plate, calling pitches, moving men, and keeping the team on its toes. With Lopez in there, "I could sit back and nap," said Stengel. One third baseman commented that Lopez moved him before every pitch for a full season. This shift was based on Lopez's belief that a batter who was ahead in the count would expect a fastball and swing early, thereby increasing the chances of the pitch being pulled down the line. Conversely, when a batter was behind in the count and anticipated a breaking pitch, he would swing late and hit the pitch toward the opposite side of the diamond. Lopez continued to employ this strategy throughout his career as a player and later as a manager.[61]

Lopez was also growing into a guru of sorts for young pitchers. It wasn't just his ability to catch the hard, low pitch, as Mungo could attest, but his innate intuitiveness about a pitcher's idiosyncrasies and about how a pitcher could best use his talents on a given day. Bill Posedel, winner of fifteen games in 1939 with Lopez catching, told a *Life* magazine reporter almost twenty years later that Lopez "nursed you, led you, worried for you, and won for you. Because he was the best low ball receiver in the business, pitchers could rear back and throw hard with men on base without fear that the pitch would go into the dirt and roll to the backstop."[62]

Aside from these skills, Lopez, like Stengel, was also developing an eye for young baseball talent. However, as with every scouting venture, those you think might make the grade do not always pan out. Manuel Onis remembers Lopez as bringing him to the attention of Stengel and the Brooklyn organization. Onis:

> 1931 is when Al Lopez recommended me to a friend of his that was manager in Johnstown, Pennsylvania, and he took me with him. [Johnstown] was a minor league team, but I have forgotten what level.... The following year I went into what they called the Florida-Georgia League. I was catching at the time, which was 1934, for Jacksonville. I got a call from Al Lopez and he says, "Can you come up here?" I said, "Sure." Man, I was excited. He said, "They want to look at you, because I recommended you." Casey Stengel was the manager at the time in Brooklyn. So I said, "Well Al, I don't have no fare. I got no money for the ticket." I didn't have it either so Al sent me a ticket. So I got on the train to New York and Al met me at the railroad station.... The next day he took me to the ballpark. I can still close my eyes and see Ebbets Field; I felt on top of the world.... I was there two months in 1934, no, a month in 1934 and they sent me to Allentown, Pennsylvania, to play. I played out the season there and then went to Brooklyn. Al had a little automobile and we used it to drive home.... [The next season] [W]e went to Orlando to train. I had a nice training session there. I hit .359 in sixteen ballgames and I caught most of them; I was ready.... Well anyway, the club liked me, so when camp ended they carried me right on up to Brooklyn with them. Once there, we were Lopez, Babe Phelps and myself at catcher.[63]

Onis stayed with Brooklyn only briefly, but in doing so he posted an unheard-of lifetime 1.000 batting average, going one for one at the plate. Again, Onis:

> [W]e were sitting on the bench during one game, in about the seventh or eighth inning, and Casey leaned over and he looked at me and says, "You wanna catch?" Of course, I told him that is what I am here for. He said, "Well go on in there." I went in and put my stuff on and man, I was shaking. I can't explain the feeling and you can't realize the feeling that I had at that time, when he told me to get in there.... So I went in there to catch ... and we went ahead and played the inning out and went

back to the dugout and my time came to bat. I went up there and I couldn't stand at the plate; I was so nervous. George Magerkurth was the umpire, stood about 6'2", a big, huge man. Lefty Brandt was pitching.... He threw me a pitch and it was a strike. So I stepped out of the batter's box, stooped over to get some sand in my hands and Magerkurth stepped by me and he said, "Get up there and hit, son." Then he walked off, didn't even look at me or nothing, but I heard him. So that kind of gave me a little strength, you know? I turned back on the plate and this guy Ed Brandt threw me a curveball and I hit it right over the third baseman. Jeez, I ran to first base and I got there and couldn't get off the base. I didn't want to get picked off; I didn't know what to do. I stayed right there at first base because nobody could move me over. Later, Al told me that when I got the hit, Casey had turned to him and said, "Where did you get this guy?" ... I stayed there [Brooklyn] until cutting. That is the only year that the major leagues cut the roster to twenty-four. It had always been twenty-five, and I was the twenty-fifth.[64]

By the end of 1935 the circumstances in Brooklyn had reached "fatalistic" proportions. Since Wilbert Robinson's club lost to Cleveland in the 1920 World Series, only four Brooklyn teams had made it into the first division, none since 1932. With Stengel's position tenuous at best and the front office in a state of flux, the Dodgers were left groping for whatever measures they might take to shore up their position. Generally, such steps included the acquisition of new talent, preferably in mass. As Lopez was one of the only players of value left on the Brooklyn roster by 1935, it stood to reason that his name would be circulated in trade rumors. Lopez, however, had been assured by Stengel that his spot on the roster was safe and as such felt secure. He shouldn't have. Lopez told Donald Honig that during the winter of 1935 he went to New York on some business and while having drinks in his hotel room one afternoon with some friends, Stengel came by and — as he was prone to do — took over the conversation. Before anyone realized it, the time was nearing nine o'clock, so Lopez suggested they all go and get something to eat. After dinner Lopez, Stengel, and some other members of the party returned to Lopez's room, where Stengel continued to regale them until two o'clock in the morning, when Lopez's other friends left. After the others had gone, Stengel, who had become uncharacteristically quiet, told Lopez that the club was hurting financially and a trade was going to have to be made. "It's either you or

Mungo," Stengel said, "and I would like to keep Mungo because he is younger and brings people to the park." Lopez, seeing how much it bothered Stengel, who must have had it on his mind the whole day, told the manager not to feel bad about it and that if a trade had to be made then go ahead and make it. Stengel then gratefully promised his catcher that when a deal was struck, he would make sure that it was with a contending club. Soon after Lopez returned to Tampa, he heard the news that he had been traded to the Boston Braves, losers of a league-record 115 games that season. Upon running into Stengel the following spring, the exiled Lopez thanked him for sending him to Boston rather than the American Association.[65]

The Dodgers shipped Lopez, Cuccinello, and pitchers Ray Benge and Bobby Reis to Boston in exchange for Ed Brandt and Randy Moore. Bob Quinn, Brooklyn's former business manager, now in Boston, was seeking to strengthen his club up the middle and in one stroke had done so. The trade, however, was terrible for Brooklyn. Moore, a veteran outfielder coming off a .275 season, played in only fifty-five games for Brooklyn before being sent to the Cardinals, where he washed out of baseball (and went into the oil business). "Lefty" Brandt, credited with giving up the only major-league hit Manuel Onis ever collected, must have been the pitcher that Stengel felt the Dodgers needed. However, he lasted one season with the team, posting a dubious mark of 11–13 and was promptly shipped to Pittsburgh, where he won another sixteen games before retiring.

Having spent the first five years of his major-league career in Brooklyn, Lopez now found himself traveling with his pal Cuccinello to new environs and challenges. Only twenty-seven years old, Lopez hoped to ascend to a new level of baseball performance and leadership. Yet in spite of his youth, the wear and tear of eleven professional seasons, employed primarily from a crouched position, were beginning to take their toll. What awaited Lopez in Boston were the results of such toil and more frustration of a familiar kind.

Respect and
Durability

The 1936 Boston "Bees," as the "Beantown" National League club was then known, finished thirty-three victories and two places better than their 1935 predecessor. They wound up sixth. The trade for Lopez and Cuccinello was credited in a history of the Braves as one of the best trades the club ever made.[1] Lopez played parts of the next five seasons in Boston. For the first time in his career, however, he began to suffer injuries and watched his batting average slide. One of the reasons his average may have declined was the poor conditions where Boston was forced to play, at the chilly "Bee Hive," formerly known as Braves Field. Lopez:

> I think that Braves Field was the worst ball park to hit in. There was no question about it. No question! It blew in, the background was bad, the infield was soaked all of the time, everything was against the hitter. It was a good place to catch because you could play a ball game in an hour and twenty minutes. You'd be out of there. We'd have 2–1, 3–1 ballgames and that was it.... The wind there was terrible. I was always getting my fingers broken because of the way the wind blew in, causing the pitches to break down on the batter.[2]

The New England weather often forced Lopez and the Braves to play in wet, windy conditions. On September 21, 1938, the Braves played the better part of a doubleheader against St. Louis in a hurricane that became one of the great natural disasters in New England history. Lopez:

It was blowing I guess forty-five or fifty miles per hour while we were playing. We tried to get the umpire to call it. You know how hurricane weather is, cloudy and the wind blowing. We knew that it was coming. The umpire [Beans Reardon] says "no, it was announced that we are going to play a double-header and we got to make an attempt to play a second game, that's the league rule. But, if it gets any worse then I will call it." Well during the game a pop fly was hit to right center and Cuccinello was hollering for it and by God I ended up catching the ball by the dugout and I caught it foul. He finally did call it on account of inclement weather. It blew over a hundred miles an hour that day after he called it and before we even got downtown. Commonwealth Avenue is a beautiful street with sidewalks and a walkway in the middle and a one way that way and this and there are big Elm trees on both sides and the wind was toppling those trees just like match sticks.[3]

In 1937 the "Bees buzzed up another notch to fifth place" paced by the old-young arms of their two thirty-something rookie pitchers, Jim Turner and Lou Fette. Rarely will you find a fifth-place team with two twenty-game winners on it, and the fact that both pitchers were rookies who had kicked around baseball for some time makes it all the more

Lopez with the Boston Braves. (Courtesy Al Lopez.)

unique. The thirty-four-year-old Turner, who worked off seasons as a milkman, was almost returned to the minors after spring training, except that a more highly touted rookie pitcher, Vic Frasier, grew homesick. Frasier was sent home and Turner remained to win twenty games, losing just seven. He was only the third rookie to lead the majors in earned-run average, for which he won the Nick Flatley Trophy as Boston's outstanding player. Fette, who had won twenty-five games for St. Paul, in the American Association, and had cost Boston about $30,000, was a fixture from the start. He won twenty games and lost ten. Neither Turner nor Fette was a strikeout pitcher, both relying on good control. They kept the ball low, so that enemy batters hit it on the ground, which was kept damp and slow by Bill McKechnie, the manager. Having Lopez behind the plate also made it easier to work the bottom half of the strike zone. Lopez remembers both Turner and Fette as control pitchers who threw with their heads as well as their arms. These were to be the salad days for Fette and Turner, however, as neither hurler again enjoyed the kind of success he found during the 1937 season. Fette failed to post another winning season and was out of baseball by 1940. Turner never again notched winning numbers, but he did pitch in moderate amounts, some in relief, through 1945.[4]

The Chicago Cubs were thought to be the league's strongest team heading into the 1937 season, with the Cardinals and Pirates close behind. Charlie Grimm, the Cubs manager, predicted a tight race, with Pittsburgh winning it, followed by the Cardinals and the Cubs. Others argued that as many as six teams could vie for the National League pennant with only Philadelphia and Boston left out of the loop. Edward Burns, who covered the Cubs for the *Chicago Tribune*, noted that everything coming from the spring camps indicated that Boston had "an excellent chance" of supplanting Philadelphia in the cellar and as such, he picked the Bees to come in last.[5] Burt Whitman, however, of the *Boston Herald*, saw the Bees as finishing no worse than fifth, or possibly fourth, provided their pitching came through. "And," he added, "should [rookie] Vince DiMaggio [brother of Joe and Dom] ... continue hitting as he did on the way North from the St. Pete training camp, there's no telling where Bill McKechnie's team may finish."[6]

Edward Burns's prediction looked to be more accurate after the Bees' doubleheader loss to the crosstown Red Sox, 7–5 and 10–8, in the city's annual preseason finale. It proved even more prophetic two days later when the Philadelphia Phillies swept into town to open the season and claimed both ends of the "Patriots' day" doubleheader, 2–1 in eleven innings and 1–0. An eleventh-inning home run by Phillies rookie Morrie Arnovich broke up the first game's pitching duel between Guy Bush of Boston and Phillies right-hander Sylvester Johnson. Johnson held the Bees to four hits while Philadelphia collected eight hits off Bush. Johnson was replaced by Wayne LaMaster in the ninth inning after Boston put two men on. LaMaster, however, pitched his way out of the jam, allowing no hits the rest of the way. In the afternoon affair, Philadelphia hurler Bucky Walters celebrated his twenty-seventh birthday, turning in a four-hit shutout performance against Boston's Danny MacFayden. Only in one inning, the fourth, did the Bees advance a runner beyond first base. Eddie Mayo and Vince DiMaggio opened the frame with successive singles, but Frank McGowan hit into the first of three double plays turned in by the Phillies, and Tony Cuccinello ended the inning by striking out. The Phillies got their run in the fourth when, with one out, Bill Atwood reached first on an error by Rabbit Warstler, took third on Leo Norris's single, and scored when Cuccinello juggled Tom Scharein's slow grounder. Adding injury to insult, Wally Berger, Boston's center fielder, fractured a finger during warmups for the second game and was forced out of the lineup.[7]

The day after dropping the opening twin bill, Boston eked out an exhibition win over Holy Cross. With Lopez on the bench, Cuccinello and Elbie Fletcher both homered in the sixth, powering the Bees past the "Purple," 6–5.[8] Boston then traveled to New York to take on the Giants in their home opener. Facing them in game one was Carl Hubbell, the Giants ace. Hubbell, "uncoiling his long lean left arm," picked up where he had left off the season before (winning a career-high 26 games), limiting Boston to three hits, in a 3–0 shutout performance. Except for a streak of wildness in the eighth inning, when he filled the bases with walks, Hubbell remained in control throughout. The win, coming in "raw, cold weather," was Hubbell's seventeenth consecutive National League victory. The next day, Mel Ott's two home runs proved enough for the Giants as they bested the Bees again, 3–0. In the contest, pitcher Johnny Lanning was effective for Boston, but the Bees' light hitting did him in. The Bees had now gone thirty-four consecutive innings without scoring a run. For his part, Lopez picked up a hit, his first of the year, in three at bats. Boston's scoreless and losing streaks came to an end the following day against the Giants, and they won 3–1. With two outs in the top of the ninth, Boston's Elbie Fletcher banged a two-run double that fell just beyond the reach of Mel Ott's glove in right field, scoring Gene Moore from third and Lopez from first. The hit ruined an otherwise fine pitching performance by Giants' 6'4" rookie southpaw, Cliff Melton. Melton fanned thirteen Boston batters in the best strikeout performance of the new season.[9]

Moving to Brooklyn, the Bees uncoiled a rookie hurler of their own in the form of Lou Fette. Fette, who as noted had won twenty-five games the previous year at St. Paul, won his debut, 9–5. Burleigh Grimes, the Dodgers manager, was tossed out of the game for arguing with umpire Larry Goetz over the latter's ruling that Bees outfielder Gene Moore had held up on what Grimes thought should have been a third strike. The ejection marked the second day in a row that the volatile Grimes had been sent to the showers after disputing an umpire's call. Two days later the Phillies beat Boston again, this time, 7–4. It was Philadelphia's fourth win in six starts, while the Bees continued their early-season slumber.[10]

The Bees rebounded the next day against the Phillies, winning 6–4, on Tony Cuccinello's eleventh-inning homer. The blast, coming with Rabbit Warstler on first and one out, was Cuccinello's fifth consecutive hit of the day and the fifteenth overall for the Bees. Guy Bush, the "Mississippi Mudcat," entered the game in the eighth behind Ira Hutchinson and Bob Smith, getting the win for Boston, his second of the season. The victory was the Bees' third of the year, leaving them in sixth place with a three and five mark. It was also reported that Bob Feller, Cleveland's prized flame-throwing eighteen year old, was suffering from arm trouble. Club physician E. B. Castle explained that Feller had torn several fibers just below the elbow and would be out indefinitely. Feller, who had a tutor with him throughout spring training, planned on using the time to return home and take his high school final exams.[11]

On May 1, the *Chicago Tribune* ran an editorial cartoon on its front page depicting a moving van filled with destitute people, driving over a mountain of money toward a city labeled "lower standard of living." The van was inscribed "Moving Day, May 1, 1937. Hundreds of Thousands of unfortunate families compelled to move to cheaper quarters." Franklin Roosevelt's "New Deal" and its "mountain of government spending" was labeled by the *Tribune*, an outspoken New Deal antagonist, as the inflationary culprit, escalating the "prices of everything." The *Tribune*'s broadside came just weeks after the president announced a $250 million budget "slash," $100 million of which came from the federal relief dole, in order to prevent the need for new taxes. With the New Deal in retreat, Boston forged ahead, rapping out fourteen hits in a 10–2 win over the Phillies.

Vince DiMaggio led the charge, belting a two-run homer in the seventh, while Lopez went two for three. Jim Turner got the win for the Bees, allowing six hits and going the distance. The win pushed Boston into fifth place with a four and five record.[12]

Boston's problem to this point in the season was a noticeable lack of hitting. The team's batting ranked last in the National League, averaging a meager .214; Lopez was only four for twenty-eight or .142. In their first significant home stand of the season, however, they found their batting eye, winning two of their next three against the Giants. In the first game, Boston bunched five hits and three runs off Clyde Castleman in the second inning to nose New York 3–2. Danny McFayden held the Giants scoreless into the fifth and limited them to six hits for his first victory of the year. The next day, before 24,000 at the Bee Hive, Cliff Melton scattered four Boston hits en route to a quick 3–1 Giants decision. It was noted that the "cold, high wind, failed to bother Melton who fanned nine batters." The Bees came back the following day, winning 3–1, and evening their record at six and six. All Boston's scoring came in the fourth inning against the Giants' Hal Schumacher. Rabbit Warstler led off with a single, moved to third on Gene Moore's single, and scored on Tony Cuccinello's double. DiMaggio then "crashed a line drive off third baseman Lou Chiozza's glove for two bases," scoring Moore and Cuccinello. Billy Weir, Boston's sophomore hurler out of the University of New Hampshire, earned his first win of the season, allowing only six New York hits.[13]

The Bees kept their hot home streak alive the following day, routing the Cardinals 8–1. The win, moving Boston into the first division (4th place at 7–6), came at the expense of St. Louis hurler Lon Warneke, who gave up eleven of Boston's sixteen hits before being relieved by Nate Andrews with none out in the fifth. Lou Fette got the win, shutting down the Cardinals on three hits in nine innings. Lopez, batting in the eighth hole, was two for five. The first-division air proved a little too thin for the Bees. On the next day, the Cardinals sent Dizzy Dean out to face them. Dean, certainly one of the National League's dominant pitchers, scattered six Boston hits while striking out eleven and winning 13–1. The contest was over in the first inning when Ducky Medwick belted a grand slam off Boston's Jim Turner, who could not buy a ground ball. Three other homers followed Medwick's, boosting the Cardinals to the victory. The final game of the series was washed out as rain and cold weather moved into Boston.[14]

That weekend, War Admiral, a son of the great Man o' War, was named an early eight-to-five favorite to win the 63d running of the Kentucky

Derby. With Jack Dempsey and "Cactus Jack" Garner on hand, the three-year-old colt ran "like his sire," setting the pace from start to finish and winning in a time of two minutes and three seconds. "It was just a gallop," said jockey Charley Kurtsinger on his way to the winner's circle. The Bees handled the weekend with less aplomb, losing to Cincinnati 5–3, sitting out another game on account of cold weather, and falling to Pittsburgh, 6–3. In spite of their mediocre 7–9 record, however, Boston managed to remain in the first division, tied for fourth place. The team's on-again off-again standard continued right through the heart of the season.[15]

Lopez remained out of the Bees lineup through much of August and into September while recovering from a broken finger. With his catcher in the clubhouse, Bill McKechnie was forced to go with third-year backstop Ray Mueller. Mueller, filling in sixty-four games that season, batted a credible .251, including 26 much-needed RBIs. With two rookie hurlers fronting Boston's staff, one might think that Lopez's veteran savvy would be missed more than it was. But Turner and Fette were seasoned rookies and despite Lopez's absence, the low-ball artists continued to roll. In mid-August, with Mueller behind the plate, Lou Fette garnered his fourteenth win of the year against four losses, besting Waite Hoyt and Brooklyn 5–2. Fette fanned eight batters and allowed six hits in going the distance. He was aided in the eighth inning by a pair of Cookie Lavagetto errors, followed by Gene Moore's triple and Vince DiMaggio's home run, giving the Bees three runs and breaking open a two-all tie.[16]

A month later, with Lopez back in the lineup at least part-time, Jim Turner kept pace with Fette, baffling Chicago's batters in a 7–0 shutout performance. Turner quelled the Cubs with a "barrage of whitewash" for his eighteenth win. The support came when Elbie Fletcher led off the second inning against the Cubs' Bill Lee with a double to right, followed by walks to Bobby Reis and Tommy Thevenow, loading the bases. Lopez then grounded into a double play, but not before allowing Fletcher to score the game's first run. In the third inning, Debs Garms singled to center, followed by Eddie Mayo, who did likewise. Gene Moore then dropped a single in front of Tuck Stainback in center, scoring Garms and forcing the removal of Lee. With Charlie Root now in for the Cubs, Cuccinello singled, scoring Mayo, but was then forced out at second on Fletcher's grounder to shortstop. On the hit ball, a double play was foiled when Cubs second baseman Billy Herman threw wildly to first, allowing Moore to score from second. Root subsequently retired Reis and Thevenow in succession. In the seventh inning, Roy Parmelee came in for Chicago and immediately gave up a long Cuccinello double, followed by Fletcher's single and Reis's double, scoring Cuccinello. With two men on, Thevenow grounded out and Lopez was intentionally walked to load the bases. Parmelee was then lifted for Clyde Shoun, who "stopped the parade" by fanning Turner and getting Garms to fly out. The Bees finished their scoring in the ninth when Thevenow walked, was sacrificed to second by a Lopez bunt, and scored on Garms's triple to right. Garms scored when Shoun, backing up third on the throw, let the ball roll into the dugout.[17]

Lou Fette was thwarted the next day in his own attempt for win number eighteen, losing to the Cardinals 2–0. The Bees struck back the following day, however, scoring seven times in the first three innings and winning 8–7. After their initial scoring binge, Boston was held without a run until the tenth inning, when Elbie Fletcher singled and came home on Bobby Reis's double. Lopez, having rested the day before, went one for five at the plate. The two clubs split a doubleheader the next day as the season began to wind down. The only buzz created by the Bees in the campaign's last weeks was a dim possibility of spoiling the Giants' run for the pennant, but after losing two at New York to close out September, even that was beyond them, and the Giants won the title by three games over Chicago.[18]

After the season, Bill McKechnie, who had led the team for eight years, opted to take over the Cincinnati Reds, forcing Bees club president Bob Quinn to find a new manager. Having traveled to Boston from Brooklyn, Quinn was quite familiar with the managerial abilities of Casey Stengel. Quinn also knew that Stengel, having been replaced by Burleigh Grimes in Brooklyn, had sat out the 1937 season, albeit while paid handsomely, and wanted to return. After speaking with Stengel, it became apparent that Quinn might find not only a new manager for his team, but also a new investor for his club. Having made a "nice bundle" in the Texas oilfields, Stengel and Edna, his wife, agreed to invest $43,000 in the Boston franchise. Recognizing that his new venture required a manager, Stengel agreed to take on those duties as well.[19]

Injuries again hampered Lopez in 1938, when for the first time since his durable career began, he caught fewer than 100 games. Appearing in only seventy-one outings, Lopez struggled to piece together a .267 batting average on sixty-three hits. The primary culprit was a severe thumb injury to his throwing hand that sidelined the catcher for a good portion of the season. Lopez laughingly recalls the injury:

It was just like you take a chicken joint and pop it like that [straight back], it was the same thing. As soon as it hit it, it gets numb, it doesn't hurt, no pain on it. I put my hand behind my back and took my catcher's mask off and was reaching to take the chest protector off when here comes Stengel from the dugout. "What's wrong, Al?" Casey asked. "I think I got a busted thumb, Casey," I said. Casey says, "Let me see it." I said, "I don't want to see it, Casey." He says, "Let me see it." So I had to show it to him and he puked right there on the spot. It was so bad that they wanted to carry me off the field and I said, "I can walk!" I didn't want to look at it, so finally we walked in the dugout and they call a doctor from the stands and he says, "Take him in the clubhouse. Carry him in the clubhouse," and I said, "I can walk." So I walked into the clubhouse and went in the trainers' room and still I didn't look at it. I turned my head and he took all the gauze he could and wrapped it, my whole hand, to keep the dust off it and he says to call the club doctor, O'Brien, and O'Brien says to bring me to the hospital real quick. So they brought me to the hospital, I went in uniform, two guys drove me, they wanted to take an ambulance but I said that I didn't need an ambulance, "Just drive me over there." I figured they would put a couple of stitches on it and I would be back. We went over there and as soon as Dr. O'Brien cut the gauze off he says, "Get the operating room ready." My God, I stayed in the hospital three days. I was on the disabled list about six weeks, but as soon as it was over I went back out there catching. I was lucky because this Dr. O'Brien took my thumb and bent it over as far as he could so that it would grow like a claw and I would be able to still throw the ball if it ever grew stiff. I thought that was pretty good. He put a metal splint on it, not wooden, because it was more flexible. I had a little more play in it then than I do now.[20]

It was his ability to overcome this kind of adversity and his continued sense of leadership that was earning Lopez respect throughout baseball. Lopez came back the following year to have one of his busiest seasons, batting .252 over 131 games. The 1939 Bees, however, reminded Stengel and Lopez of their dubious past in Brooklyn. One outing, ironically against the Dodgers, particularly served to drive this point home. In the contest, Lopez came to bat with the game tied in the thirteenth inning, two outs, and Otto Huber, a pinch runner representing the winning run, on second. Going the other way, Lopez poked an outside pitch into right field for a clean hit and what appeared to be a sure run. However, on his way to the plate Huber tripped over third base, falling flat on his face. Instead of scoring, Huber was lucky to get back to third base ahead of the throw coming in from right field. When the inning was over, Huber was left standing on third and the game continued to a twenty-three-inning tie. After the game Stengel screamed at Huber, "What were you wearing, bedroom slippers?"[21]

During that season in Boston, Lopez also saw something he never forgot, involving the changing of the guard, so to speak, in baseball. He later talked about it with Donald Honig:

> I was a teammate of Al Simmons' at Boston in 1939. He was one of the greatest right-handed hitters who ever lived, but on the decline at that time. The Braves had acquired Eddie Miller from the Yankees to play shortstop. For the Braves, who didn't have much money, it was a pretty big deal. They laid out some cash and gave up about four or five players for Eddie. And he was worth it, too. He was a good ballplayer. One day there was a fly ball hit into short left, and Miller and Simmons went for it. It was one of those situations where you just want to close your eyes because you can see the collision coming, and there's not a thing you can do about it. They ran into each other with a smack and went tumbling to the grass. Everybody went running out there to see how Miller was. He was the bright young ballplayer, the one they had the investment in. Hardly anybody paid any attention to Simmons. Well, Miller was all right, but Simmons had a hairline fracture above his ankle, and was out for quite awhile. One day he came into the clubhouse and sat down next to me. He had a wistful little smile. "You know something Al?" he said. "Ten years ago, when I was playing for Mr. Mack, if that collision had happened, they would have sent a goddamned kid shortstop nine hundred miles from Philadelphia for running into me." I'll never forget him saying that.[22]

After the season ended, on October 7, 1939, Lopez married Evelyn M. "Connie" Kearney of New York City. A year later they were blessed with the birth of their first and only child, Alfonso Ramón Lopez, Jr. Lopez first met the diminutive Connie at the Hollywood Club in New York City, where she worked as a dancer. Connie, however, having attended some Dodger games in the past, was vaguely familiar with the catcher upon meeting him. As the two saw more of each other, they began spending evenings dining and dancing about town, often accompanied by Tony Cuccinello and his wife. After Lopez was traded to Boston following the 1935 season, the couple continued to see each other, but the bi-city courtship left them exhausted. It did not take long for the hectic arrangement to grow tiresome, and so Connie, able to find work in Boston, followed Lopez and the two resumed a less frenetic pace. After they were married, Connie's Irish and German-Swedish background, coupled with Lopez's Spanish descent, gave their household a peculiar, albeit distinctly American, flavor. To liven the pot even more, Lopez, shortly after their wedding, took his young bride home to live in Ybor City, where, according to their son, she was somewhat out of her element. Al Lopez, Jr.:

> She was a New York City girl that was really used to the big city and when she married my father and they moved to Tampa, it was a one-horse town.... Ybor City was even smaller and culturally speaking, it was a lot smaller. But she was very outgoing, she got to know a lot of people, and because they were apart so much she was forced to be very independent. She had a tough job trying to raise a son, get along with everybody in the family, and then go up to wherever my dad was. We spent the Summer with my dad.[23]

As noted earlier, Lopez lived during the off season at the home of his mother (Modesto Lopez died in 1926) in Ybor City. When the baseball season began, Lopez moved north with the club, leaving his wife and son behind until the end of the school year, when they would join him. The cross-cultural makeup of that Ybor City household might have been difficult to blend were it not for the amicable personalities involved. Again, Al Lopez, Jr.:

> My mother was Irish, German, Swedish, and English, I believe. Coming to Ybor City where everyone was Italian, Spanish, or Cuban, it was complete culture shock, but she did alright. As a kid I'm not sure I would have noticed how well my mother and grandmother got along. They seemed to get along fine, even though there was a language barrier. My grandmother was a very quiet, elderly lady that always appeared to be the same, gray-haired, spoke only Spanish, didn't venture too far from the house except to go to the grocery store and stuff like that. She helped with the house chores, cooking, and so forth and

was an excellent cook. My mother never really learned how to talk Spanish, although they could converse, and my grandmother never really learned to talk English. But, like I said, they could converse back and forth and seemed to get along fine.[24]

As a new father, Lopez spent as much time as he could playing with his son but never pushed him into sports. Lopez opted rather, like many parents of immigrant and ethnic backgrounds, to impress upon his child the importance of education. "My father very much pushed education," said the younger Lopez:

> When I was a junior in college I had a chance to sign a professional baseball contract and he basically told me not to do it and I didn't. I waited to sign until after my senior year. We could afford for me to go to college. At that point in his life, I think he was looking at if he didn't play pro ball then he probably would quit school and go into the cigar factories and get a job.[25]

If there was any one principle that Lopez tried to impart to his son while raising him it was that he must accept and live within a code of right and wrong. Lopez strongly believed in this, insisting that one could live within such a standard and still enjoy himself. Lopez also stressed to his son the need to be kind to others. Al Lopez, Jr.:

> My dad felt that he should always go out of his way to be nice to people. I mean even to the extent where people were infringing upon his freedom or his happiness. Fans can get to be very demanding or very interruptive. Being around other baseball players you saw how they acted toward fans, sometimes not very nice, for whatever reason. My dad never did that. He always went out of his way to be nice to people. He always told me, 'If you can be nice to somebody, do it.... The more people that like you, the better off you're going to be.... Even if they're not being nice to you, be nice to them." This was my father's code.[26]

After beginning the 1940 season batting .294, Lopez was reluctantly dealt to Pittsburgh. The Braves, who had been hard up for cash, sold Lopez to the Pirates for a reported $40,000 (Lopez thinks they got more than

Streetcar advertising baseball in Tampa, ca. 1940. (Courtesy Florida State Archives.)

that) and catcher Ray Berres. This was the second time Lopez found himself traded by Stengel, his friend, and the second time that he had "exchanged places" with Ray Berres. Because of Stengel, however, Lopez had once again felt certain it would not happen. Lopez:

> Stengel and I were having a talk. He said, "We can't make the payroll unless we sell somebody pretty soon. You and Eddie Miller are the only ones we can get money for, so we'll sell Miller." So I told Miller, the shortstop, and he didn't believe me. Finally I bet him a $100 suit of clothes that he was on the way out. I lost the bet.[27]

Arthur Sampson of the *Boston Herald* reported that selling Lopez "was the same as tapping blood out of Bob Quinn's heart." This was clear from the manner in which the seventy-year-old executive called reporters in to break the news. Sampson wrote that as the reporters gathered, Quinn had his back turned away from the door while Stengel stared sadly out the window. Nobody spoke until all the seats were taken, with standing room only remaining. "The silence was deathly." Suddenly, Quinn faced the reporters and mournfully said

> Well, fellows, I've just sold Lopez to Pittsburgh for Berres and a sum of money. It was the hardest job I've ever done in my 50 years of baseball.... I've never seen a better catcher in the half century I've been connected with the game. I've never had a better boy in my employ.... There are instances where you can release a player from your organization without feeling badly about the loss of his services. In the case of Lopez, how-ever, I never would have considered a deal for him if it hadn't been forced upon me.... When the fans refuse to come to your ballpark ... there is only one way to continue to operate. There was only one road left open to us and we had to take it. I've just told Al, however, that he'll never have to want for a job as long as I'm alive and still in baseball. He's the sort of fellow that can work for me any time.[28]

When Quinn was through, Stengel spoke in the same mournful tone as his boss. "I feel the same way about Lopez as Mr. Quinn does," he said. "I've never met a finer character in baseball. Al has played for me for sev-eral years, first in Brooklyn and more recently here. We've become very close friends. I'm certainly going to miss him." That the manager was upset about the deal was obvious. Sampson noted that as Stengel passed a refreshment stand after the conference, Duffy Lewis asked him if he wanted anything and he replied, "I don't know Duffy, is there anything left?" Fortunately for Stengel, Lopez had spent a great deal of time work-ing with Phil Masi and Stan Andrews, the young catchers who now had the job to share, along with Berres, the receiving load. "Lopez has helped both of them get a good start," remarked Stengel. "Al is one of the most unselfish players I've ever known. He has worked as hard as a coach bring-ing those youngsters along."[29] Lopez had also spent a good deal of time working with Berres, when the latter first came up to Brooklyn in 1934. "Lopez was very helpful," remarked Berres. "He taught me things such as what was expected of a big leaguer. I was involved both times Lopez was traded, but I never took his place. We exchanged places."[30]

Lopez became the bulwark of the Pittsburgh Pirates World War II–era teams through 1946. He posted impressive numbers in games caught, receiving more than 100 contests in each of his first four seasons with the team, and earned a second All-Star trip in 1941. The teams he played on, however, proved little more successful than those in Brooklyn and Boston. Furthermore, World War II began taking its toll on rosters across the league and Pittsburgh was no exception. In only one season, 1944, did Lopez's Pirates finish above fourth, finishing a distant wartime second.

The 1941 season, Lopez's second in Pittsburgh, proved to be the last in which baseball was largely unaffected by the "Total War" effort of World War II. The United States had begun drafting young men into the service in 1940, anticipating a need for manpower while it waged a naval quasi-war against German U-boats in the North Atlantic. Honoring their call to duty, many of baseball's top players, Lopez among them, reported for registration with their local draft boards. At the time there was concern that should the U.S. be drawn more thoroughly into the war, baseball would be forced to close its doors. Clark Griffith, however, became the game's unofficial lobbyist, extracting promises from government leaders that in the event of war, baseball would be spared. Baseball, argued Griffith, with its unifying qualities, should be carried on despite any mistaken notions of frivolity. Displaying the wartime value of which he spoke, Griffith and the other baseball owners began conducting benefit all-star games, donating baseball equipment to the armed forces and holding scrap-metal and blood drives.[31]

Shortly after the Japanese attack on Pearl Harbor, Griffith and others, anxious over how to proceed with the coming season, sought official word from the federal government on whether the game would be allowed to continue. Although commissioner Kenesaw Mountain Landis refused to argue the game's cause in person, he did sit down on January 14, 1942, and draft a note to Franklin D. Roosevelt. In it he informed the president that baseball was about to adopt schedules, sign players, make vast commitments, and go to training camps. He then asked what baseball should do, all the while assuring the chief executive that baseball was ready and willing to proceed with whatever instructions he conveyed. President Roosevelt replied two days later in what became known as the "Green Light" letter. Citing its role as a morale booster and expressing his personal view that the game should continue, Roosevelt gave baseball the go-ahead but left the final decision with the club owners. At the same time, however, he stressed that there would be no special exemptions and that individual players would have to take their chances in the draft like everyone else.[32]

Many active players had already done so. Bob Feller was en route to the December 1941 winter baseball meetings when he heard the radio flash reporting the attack on Pearl Harbor. Although Feller had been classified

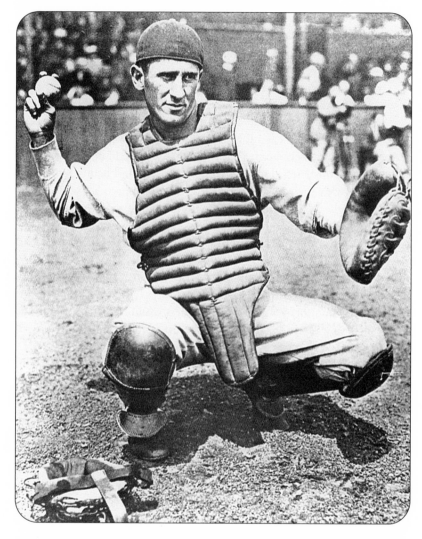

Lopez with the Pittsburgh Pirates, ca. 1941. (Courtesy National Baseball Library, Cooperstown, New York.)

available for immediate service, he could have avoided enlistment on the grounds of his father's terminal illness. Feller, as the only son, would legally have been allotted 2-C farmer status, which meant that he could have stayed home and run the family farm. He chose to enlist. Hank Greenberg, who was released from the service on December 5, 1941, after having been drafted earlier that year, was on his way to Detroit to begin

July 21, 1941, New York: Lopez tags Dodger Harold Reese, putting him out at home. Umpire Barr calls the play. (Courtesy UPI/Corbis-Bettmann.)

training for the 1942 season. Upon hearing of Pearl Harbor, he promptly turned around and re-upped. Present and future notables such as Ted Williams, Cecil Travis, Warren Spahn, Monte Irvin, and Enos Slaughter gradually followed suit, with many seeing combat action.[33]

Those players not joining the service were men who had for one reason or another been exempted as unfit for military duty. Lopez, then thirty-three years old, with a wife, young child, and aging mother to support, was among this group. According to Lopez, the health of his son was a major factor in the decision of the draft board. Al Lopez, Jr., was quite ill at the time and his parents feared they might lose him. The board also considered the welfare of Lopez's mother, Faustina, then sixty-seven years old and dependent solely upon her son for support. Lopez's exemption, however, was lifted after the 1944 season, as Adolf Hitler's "last-ditch" offensive in the Ardennes evolved into the Battle of the Bulge. The estimated 80,000 American casualties (killed, wounded, missing, and taken prisoner) reported amid the "Autumn Mist" created some concern that more U.S. soldiers would be needed before the move into Germany. Sick child and aging mother aside, Lopez began preparing for the call that he now suspected would come. However, by early January, with Hitler's forces "limping back toward the Reich," his objectives thwarted, the need for more recruits became less urgent and Lopez's exemption was restored.[34]

Even with Lopez in the lineup, the Pirates were not expected to finish as high as they did in 1944. St. Louis, led by pitchers Max Lanier and Mort Cooper and defending National League batting champion Stan Musial, was thought to be the cream of the crop. Musial, heading into only his third full season, had already compiled batting averages of .315 and .357. The Pirates, like most of their counterparts, were said to look "thin all the way around." Rip Sewell topped a pitching staff that also included Fritz Ostermueller and the promising left-hander Elwin "Preacher" Roe, who like Van Lingle Mungo before him, benefited from Lopez's defense. Aside from Lopez, the Pirates' veteran line-up included former Boston team-mate Vince DiMaggio, Babe Dahlgren, Frankie Gustine, and Pete Coscarart. Frankie Frisch, the former Cardinals pilot who took over for Pie Traynor in 1940, was manager.[35]

Vince DiMaggio, having failed the promise of his magical name in Boston, had come to Pittsburgh in a 1940 trade for Johnny Rizzo, eventually spending five seasons with the club. Frank Gustine, a multifaceted performer, had debuted with the Pirates in 1940 as well. Named to three All-Star teams, the fiery Gustine batted a lifetime .265. His competitive spirit was said to be infectious, making him one of the Pirates' most popular players. Pete Coscarart, along with pitcher Luke Hamlin, catcher Babe Phelps, and outfielder Jim Wasdell, came to Pittsburgh from Brooklyn after the 1941 season in a trade for shortstop Arky Vaughan. Although Coscarart started four seasons for the Pirates, he never hit above .264. Dahlgren, the onetime heir to Lou Gehrig's first-base position in the Bronx, arrived in Pittsburgh the year before, batting a respectable .287 with five homers and fifty-six RBIs.[36]

These "thin" Pirates began the season traveling to St. Louis for a two-game series against the favored Cardinals. Amid news that 5,000 Allied war planes were pounding Germany's *Festung Europa*— Fortress Europe — Max Lanier held the Pirates on the carpet, allowing two hits in the 2–0 shutout victory. The next day, St. Louis pushed two runs across in the seventh, snapping a three-all tie to win 5–3. Leaving St. Louis with two losses was not how Frankie Frisch, the famed "Fordham Flash," had hoped to begin the season. But if the Pirates could get wins against their other lesser-endowed National League counterparts, they might have a chance to sneak up on the Cardinals later in the season. By July, the Bucs, despite batting a major-league low .238, were winning their share of contests and proving to do what Frisch had hoped, holding firm in second place, eight games behind St. Louis. Like Harry Truman, then a dark horse vice presidential hopeful, they had "lost a few furlongs, but were still very much in the running."[37]

Piling up victories against other also-rans might keep one in a race, but does not, in and of itself, capture a flag. For Pittsburgh to challenge, it was going to have to beat St. Louis and hope that others did likewise. Yet, by early August, experts were noting that only a "total collapse" on the part of the Redbirds could prevent their winning a third straight championship. For instance, should St. Louis win only 30 and lose 29 of its remaining games for a .508 percentage, finishing at 99–55, the Pirates would have to play at a .766 clip, or 49–15, to beat them. This of course, would be some turnaround, considering that the two-time defending champions had played better than .700 baseball all season while Pittsburgh had come nowhere near that mark.[38]

In early August, the Pirates found a chance to close some ground on the Cardinals when the league leaders came into Pittsburgh's Forbes Field for a two-game set. In the first game, the Cardinals' Max Lanier went to the mound against Pittsburgh's Truett Banks "Rip" Sewell. Sewell, a veteran hurler, had labored in the minor leagues until the age of thirty-one. Desperate for pitching, the Pirates brought him up in 1938. Throwing his novel "eephus" pitch, a blooper ball, he performed well, particularly during the war years of 1943–44, winning twenty-one games in both seasons.[39] On this day, however, Lanier proved the more effective and the Cardinals won 8–4. It was Lanier's twelfth win of the year, giving him the league lead in strikeouts as well. Lopez, one of Lanier's victims, went a quiet zero for four. The next day the Cardinals finished the sweep, pounding three of Frisch's hurlers for eighteen hits in a 15–2 shellacking. St. Louis's Danny Litwhiler, who had been riding the bench because of a slump, collected four hits, including a three-run homer. With the losses, Pittsburgh fell to third place, nineteen games behind St. Louis and three and a half in back of Cincinnati.[40]

The Pirates still trailed St. Louis by a healthy margin a week later, but they had somehow managed to close the gap to within a game and a half of the Reds in second. A needed mid-August victory over the Giants, giving Pittsburgh four out of five against New York on the season, ignited Pirates hitters, providing a lift through the "dog days," that remained until season's end. The win also improved the Pirates' team batting average to .253, fifth in the league and the highest it had been all season. Lopez, however, while providing his usual strong defense, was batting a meager .226 in 226 plate appearances.[41]

The season rolled into September as George Patton's armored division raced across Belgium, closing to within twenty miles of the German border. At Pittsburgh, the Cardinals were making their own dash for the cup, needing eleven wins to claim it, but the resurgent Pirates stood in their way. On September 2, Bob Elliott, the Bucs' best clutch hitter, drove a run-scoring single to center, giving Pittsburgh its third straight win over the Cardinals, this time 5–4. "Speedy" Jimmy Russell set up the winning marker with a double. The drive kicked off the right-field wall, almost knocking Stan Musial over as he moved to keep it in the park. Cardinals manager Billy Southworth then ordered pitcher Ted Wilks to walk Jack Barrett. Elliott followed, driving the ball past second baseman Emil Verban into center, scoring Russell. Elliott's field day also included a double in the second, from which he scored on a passed ball, a home run in the third, his eighth, and another single in the eighth inning. The wins moved Pittsburgh to within fourteen and a half games of the now "slumping" Cardinals, but with the season drawing to a close, little real chance of catching them remained.[42]

By September 19, the Cardinals needed one more win for the pennant to be theirs. This was in spite of their woeful five-and-fifteen September pace. A combination of weak pitching, weak hitting, and poor fielding were the causes of the slump. When St. Louis entered its tailspin, they were twenty games ahead of Pittsburgh. Cardinals pitchers yielded ninety runs in the twenty games, an average of 4.5 an outing. They allowed 166 hits over the same span, allowing the opposition a collective batting mark of .253. Against this, Cardinals batters hit only .233, with 158 hits in 679 trips to the plate. They scored 57 runs, or 2.85 a game. Meanwhile, the fielders, not to be left outdone, committed twenty-three errors, more than one a game. Seven of the losses came by one run, while two of the club's five wins came by one run and two were shutouts. Finally, in the stretch, the Cardinals lost three series, tied one, and won one. They dropped eight straight games to the Pirates and six of nine to the Cubs, and they won two of three from the Reds. Had the Cardinals begun this slump in early August rather than September, the Pirates, based on the earlier noted projections, might have had a chance to catch them, but they did not. Two days later, St. Louis clinched their third consecutive National League pennant; the Pirates finished in second, a distant thirteen games behind.[43]

After placing fourth the following season, talk in the Pittsburgh clubhouse turned to unions and labor activity in 1946. Robert Francis Murphy, a Harvard-educated Boston lawyer who had once worked for the National Labor Relations Board, was attempting to organize major-league players into something he called the American Baseball Guild. Murphy was convinced that the rival Mexican League, then competing with major-league baseball for many of its performers, would be unable to lure American players if the owners would establish basic reforms in their business. So he pledged his guild to seek those reforms, bringing about "a square deal to the players, the men who make possible big dividends and high salaries for stockholders and the club executives."[44]

Murphy's platform included a minimum salary of $7,500, impartial arbitration of salary disputes and "other conditions of employment," 50 percent of a sale price to the player, freedom of contract, and the banishment of the unfair ten-day release clause. Murphy also argued that the reserve clause had to be modified. He simply doubted the necessity of restricting players' services to one club when an estimated 95 percent of them would be sold or traded anyway. While admitting that many of the higher-salaried players in the league might find the guild unnecessary, Murphy insisted that they needed the guild's protection as much as anyone.[45] "Let me give you an example," said Murphy. "Jimmy Foxx led the American League in practically every hitting department in 1932 and won the most valuable player award. For his efforts he received a $6,000 cut in salary. This would not have happened if he were part of the present baseball guild and had it bargaining for him."[46]

Recognizing the strong influence of labor in the steel city, Murphy centered much of his early attention on the Pirates, thinking that if he were successful there, other players would follow. Murphy met with the team at the Kenmore Hotel during their first trip into Boston that season, coming away optimistic that the guild's inaugural chapter had "found a home." By June, Murphy had received commitments from many on the Pirates roster to join him, particularly veterans like Lee Handley, Bob Elliott, and Jimmy Russell. Russell, who had a relative who had been injured in a mine accident, was particularly receptive, as was reserve catcher Hank Camelli, who had harbored lifelong pro-union sympathies.[47]

While Murphy was addressing the players in Boston, Lopez, who had recently joined the club after suffering a broken finger, and pitcher Fritz Ostermueller took the position that ten to twelve other clubs should first join the guild before any walkouts were planned, not just the Pirates. Lopez's position did not arise because he was pro management or against labor, but rather because the Pirates, standing alone, would be working against the percentages. In business, as on the diamond, Lopez believed in having the numbers on his side. Aside from that, Lopez had always thought himself a union man and would have walked out had a team vote called for it. Lopez's pro-union sympathies dated to his father's involvement in the cigar industry union in Tampa. Modesto Lopez had been "staunchly" pro labor, and as a member of the Cigar Makers International Union (CMIU), was blackballed by the Ybor City cigar manufacturers after a 1910 cigar workers strike (a strike the cigar workers lost because of pressure exerted by the pro business vigilante "Citizens Committee") because he had acted as a union spotter during the six-month work stoppage. It was the job of the spotter to watch the picket line, reporting any worker who went across, and Modesto did so. Because of this, he was forced to take a job two hundred miles away in a cigar factory near Quincy, Florida, for five to six months while his family remained behind in Tampa. While eventually returning to Ybor City, Modesto Lopez remained an active union supporter until his death in 1926 and passed this on to his son.[48]

Murphy, after securing what he believed to be a majority of the club, wrote Pittsburgh's management requesting an election at the earliest possible convenience to determine whether the players wanted the guild to be their collective bargaining representative. When Pittsburgh's ownership proposed that the guild defer the election until after the season, Murphy "flatly rejected" it as unreasonable and moved toward his last option, asking the players to strike. Club president William Benswanger, the son-in-law of Barney Dreyfuss, the late owner, then began vigorous action against the guild, appealing to the players' loyalties. It was also known that Benswanger was selling the team, and this raised some doubt in the minds of certain players, such as Lopez, who did not wish to harm Benswanger's investment.[49]

After initially setting a June 5 deadline for a strike vote, Murphy and the players agreed to postpone it for two days. However, they hinted strongly that a strike would occur if the elections were not permitted. Murphy and the players also received support from the city and CIO leaders, who promised to honor the strike if one occurred. President Harry Truman, responding to reports that he might seize control of the Pirates if they walked out, laughingly remarked that if he, a native Missourian, took over all the ballplayers who went on strike, then he would have two "damn good teams in St. Louis."[50]

Harvey Boyle, sports editor of the *Pittsburgh Post Gazette*, urged the players to go slow when contemplating a strike, for fear of alienating the fans. "There can be little doubt," wrote Boyle, "that talk of a strike so early in the organization plans left a bad taste in the mouths of fans, regardless of where their sympathies ordinarily lie.... [Players] would do well to consider in any decisions they make that fans, too, have a stake in the proceedings."[51]

On the morning of June 7, Al Abrams of the *Post Gazette* published several comments by unnamed Pirates giving some indication of the range of sympathies running among the club. "If we fail now," said one player, "the baseball guild will collapse. That's why I think the players shouldn't back down." "No sir," said a contented Pirate, "I don't belong to the guild. I don't want any part of it. I'm pretty satisfied with conditions the way they are." Another was unsure of what might happen. "I can't tell you whether we'll strike or not tomorrow night. We voted that we would in case the Guild isn't recognized. That's all I know." For one of the players, the final decision about a strike rested at home. "My wife called me on the long distance telephone. This strike business has her all worried. She doesn't want me to strike. She's boss."[52]

When the players arrived at the clubhouse on June 7, Benswanger was there to greet them. It was the first visit Benswanger had paid to the clubhouse since 1934. After again appealing to their personal loyalty, he left, leaving it up to the players to decide. Such an approach proved to be a good tactic for the owner. As noted above, many of the Pirates players, including Lopez, sympathized with the man and did not wish to harm his investment. "No one on the ball club can say a word about the treatment given them by Bill Benswanger," commented one of the unnamed Pirates that morning. "He's been fine to me and everyone else I've talked to on the team." When Murphy tried to get into the clubhouse, at what he said was the players' "insistence," hoping to offer his own "last words of advice," he was stopped by club lawyers, security officers, and manager Frankie Frisch. Chagrined, Murphy was then photographed by the *Post Gazette* standing outside the clubhouse, blocked by a sign reading, "For Players Only, KEEP OUT, that means you."[53]

With 16,884 anxious fans awaiting the outcome, the players deliberated in a "stormy session behind barred doors." They first decided that a two-thirds vote would be required to strike. While Murphy considered 90 percent of the club to be on his side, he had not counted on the real fact that many of these players were hesitant to place their jobs at risk. The fear of losing their jobs was great and became evident in the voting. Lopez, based on his father's experiences, realized more than most how a strike could affect one's family. Furthermore, the Benswanger sympathy factor had to be considered. As Murphy might have expected, few of the Pirates players wanted to harm Benswanger's personal investment. Lee Handley, a guild supporter, later admitted to such reservations because of the high regard in which he held Benswanger. Lopez and Fritz Ostermueller conveyed these same concerns to many of the other players, especially the younger ones like Ralph Kiner, advising them to stay out of it. The final tally, taken by written ballot, was 20–16 in favor of a strike, a majority yes, but not a two-thirds vote. While Lopez no doubt would have walked out had the two-thirds vote been obtained, it is clear from his statements that he preferred to wait and give either Benswanger a chance to reform club policy or to allow other teams to join the guild.[54]

Exactly twenty-five minutes after the Pirates had been due on the field for batting practice, field director Robert Rice opened the door of the dressing room and with the players "jostling" behind him, announced: "No strike." The players then "silently, almost grimly" filed onto the field. Murphy, puffing on a cigar in the shadows of the stadium runway, plaintively called, "Good luck," after several of the players. He later issued a statement that read in part, "As to the future plans of the guild, the mere fact that the guild members of the Pirates did not choose to utilize an economic weapon at this time does not in any way indicate that we shall not continue our fight in Pittsburgh.... Events of the last few days have proved conclusively that an overwhelming majority of the Pittsburgh players do desire to be represented by the Guild." Benswanger, upon hearing of the players' decision, declared: "I'm glad they went on the field.... I predicted it.... I think they showed good common sense. It was for the good of the game and in the public interest."[55]

Two days later, Murphy announced his intentions to file charges of unfair labor practices against the Pirates organization with the National Labor Relations Board. The eventual complaint alleged that the club, through its officials, "attempted to dissuade players from dealing through the American Baseball Guild, their chosen representative, for the purposes of collective bargaining." While the NLRB dismissed Murphy's complaint, the Pennsylvania Labor Relations Board ultimately sided with him, rejecting the Pirates' claim that a professional baseball club not only had an antitrust exemption, but a "quasi-religious status" outside the jurisdiction of the state. They then granted another election to Murphy, this one scheduled for August 21.[56]

Two days before the new election was to be held, the *Post Gazette* reported that Murphy had been in Chicago "conversing" with Pirates players at the team hotel regarding their vote. Frank E. McKinney, the new majority owner of the club having taken over for Benswanger, expressed surprise, stating, "I thought this was to be an election free of interference or coercion." McKinney need not have worried. With "the militancy of June" having long since passed and Murphy's influence diminished, there was little chance that the Pirates players would opt to strike, and they did not. In a vote registering 15–3 against, the guild's attempt to unionize the Pittsburgh Pirates collapsed amid an atmosphere of relative indifference. The only excitement generated on this election day came from a group of "bobby-soxers" clustered for hours in the halls of the Arrott Building (the downtown Pittsburgh headquarters of the Pennsylvania Labor Relations Board), hoping to catch a glimpse of Bing Crosby, one of Pittsburgh's new minority owners. "When is Bing Crosby going to vote?" one of them asked. Crosby, a member and former president of Actor's Equity, an entertainment union, now positioned along the opposite end of the bargaining table, no doubt opted to stay away. So did many of the Pirates players. Only nineteen of the thirty-one players eligible to cast ballots participated in the election, with Lopez, Billy Cox, Al Gionfriddo, Frank Gustine, and others abstaining, and one, Leroy Jarvis, challenged. Murphy, admitting that the vote came as little surprise to him, acknowledged that the loss constituted a setback, at least in Pittsburgh. The vote proved, however, to be more than a mere setback. In short order, Robert Murphy and the American Baseball Guild, lacking the support of a viable base from which to launch their salvos, faded from the scene.[57]

During the 1946 season, Lopez's last in Pittsburgh, an incident involving the catcher also occurred that, although no fault of his, proved embarrassing to the Pirates management and himself. Club executives had been considering firing Frankie Frisch as manager and the *Post Gazette*, conducting a fan opinion poll, asked its readers to suggest whether to keep him or who should replace him. The overwhelming majority named Lopez, who polled 1,306 of the approximately 4,000 votes tallied compared to

293 for Frisch.[58] The fan poll left Lopez feeling awkward because he knew that the Pirates had already decided to hire Billy Herman as manager. Because of this, Lopez requested a trade, thinking that it might ease the team's transition to the new manager. He told his bosses, "I think it is the best thing for the club to get me off and give Herman a chance.... It's no use having me here." The Pirates reluctantly obliged, trading him to Cleveland during the off season for Gene Woodling.[59]

In 1947, Lopez's last year as a big-league ballplayer, the aging catcher performed primarily as a backup for the Indians. In limited plate appearances, he hit .262, one point higher than his career average. While .261 is respectable, Lopez believes his career offensive statistics might have been higher if not for the rigors of donning the "tools of ignorance." He explains:

> There is no question about it. You know, catchers might hit another ten or fifteen points higher if they were playing other positions. I'm not looking for alibis. I think that you just get run down, you're catching doubleheaders in St. Louis and Cincinnati and it's 110° or 112° on the field when you're playing day games. We played all day games. It eats you up.[60]

By the time Lopez's playing career ended, the durable receiver had been eaten up more times than any catcher in baseball history, with 1,918 games caught. (Bob Boone surpassed this mark in 1988.) He also held the record for National League catchers with 1,861. Lopez further tied the National League record for most games caught without a passed ball (114 games in 1941) and led all National League catchers in assists three times [1932, 1933, 1936] and fielding percentage three times [1940, 1943, 1944].

After the season, Bill Veeck, who owned the Cleveland Indians, and Lou Boudreau, his player-manager, had a brief falling out. Veeck was upset over Boudreau's handling of the team that year and, according to Lopez, became interested in having Lopez take over as manager. During the World Series, Lopez, who was in New York shopping for a coaching job, was called by Veeck to discuss the matter. Upon finding out that Lopez was still without work, the owner asked him not to do anything before hearing from Veeck first. The whole process reminded Lopez of Pittsburgh and it made him uncomfortable. He told Veeck so. "I don't want the job. I was there [Cleveland] one year as a player and I don't want people thinking I was after the job, that I might have been undermining Lou." Lopez then told Veeck that he would prefer to get his start somewhere else and gain some experience, and that if Veeck still wanted him, he would be available. Veeck agreed, and Lopez, none the worse for his refusal, continued seeking employment.[61]

Although he played for losing teams the better part of his career, Lopez never lost his enthusiasm for baseball nor his desire to win. However, with no hope of playing for a pennant winner and having rejected Veeck's job offer, Lopez was determined to find a job managing or coaching somewhere. When the Pirates, who owned the Indianapolis club in the American Association, called with a chance to manage there for 1948, Lopez readily accepted.

Gentlemen, Start
Your Engines

Bill Veeck once declared that if Al Lopez had a weakness as a manager it was that he was too decent. He not only behaved like a gentleman, but according to baseball writer Leonard Koppett, "induced, by his presence, decent behavior in others." Koppett went further, referring to Lopez as the "human equivalent" of what took place when Houston's Astrodome opened as the first indoor ballpark. Koppett:

> Under a roof, moving among theater-type seats with and under good lighting, the customers tended to avoid littering the floor with peanut shells and hot dog wrappers and empty cups the way they did automatically in outdoor stadiums. It just didn't feel right in a theaterlike setting.... Lopez had the same effect: He was so serene, in good times and bad, that you didn't feel comfortable raising your own voice.[1]

This sense of serenity, however, did not preclude Lopez's winning ballgames. In fact, Lopez's success inspired others to consider him a living refutation of Leo Durocher's postulate, "Nice guys finish last."

His managing style, according to Veeck, was "completely relaxed." "In that calm cool way of his, he squeezed every possible drop of talent out of his team."[2] Toward that aim, Lopez believed that a quiet, professional demeanor was a necessity. If an individual was not performing up to what was expected, Lopez would take him out of the lineup. He felt that scolding or shouting at players only embarrassed them and hurt their confidence and he never advocated clubhouse meetings or fines. "What's the sense of lecturing or fining players?" he once said.

> They're adults. If they won't play our way, let them play their own way, someplace else. Pep talks are O.K. in football when you have to get a club up for only a handful of games, but you can't get a club up for 162. Most of the players don't listen to what you say in a meeting anyway ... and [i]f you're going to start fining for missing signs — bunts, steals — you've got a tight ballplayer.[3]

Tom Saffell, who played for Lopez at Indianapolis and now presides over the Gulf Coast League in Florida, recalls that Lopez enjoyed great rapport with the players. "Hell," said Saffell, "he was a player at Indianapolis for a while ... and if you did something wrong, he didn't jump all over you, he was very constructive with his criticism ... he was the best manager that I ever played for."[4] Jack Cassini, a teammate of Saffell's at Indianapolis, echoes the former's sentiments. "Lopez was a great manager, I really liked him. He was always three innings ahead of the other guy. Oftentimes we didn't know what he was doing, but then about the seventh or eighth inning it began to make sense."[5] Ted Beard, also at Indianapolis, described Lopez as an "expert at pulling the unexpected."[6]

Lopez traditionally had three rules he insisted that his players obey: "Outfielders must always throw to the cutoff man rather than to a specific base; no player should ever hesitate rounding first on a single when a teammate is trying to score from second; and everybody must keep the curfew."[7] Al Rosen recalled Lopez telling his players, "Look, if I put your name in the lineup, I expect 100 percent effort. If you can't give that to me, all you have to do is tell me that you're not able to play that day."[8] This calm approach differed greatly from the "whip-cracking style" of John McGraw and others and adapted well to the emerging awareness post–World War II players had gained regarding their individual rights.[9]

Lopez's composed, taciturn facade, however, masked a tumult that gripped him during a season, particularly after a loss. Al Lopez, Jr., recalls that while his father might not have returned home after a contest talking about it, "the game didn't stay at the ballpark." "He was very intent on baseball," said Lopez, Jr. "It wasn't just his job, it was his life. When they won, everything was jovial and everything progressed normally. When they lost, he was very quiet and was not very outgoing."[10] During the season Lopez also suffered from chronic insomnia and after night games regularly read westerns or detective novels before dozing off around four in the morning. The tension was so hard on his stomach that doctors warned him to avoid raw foods and ice cream at night. Lopez took the game seriously, hating to lose — and those around him knew it. "There's only one thing worse than losing a game," said Bob Lemon, "and that's watching Al sit there in the clubhouse and stare at his toes after you've lost one."[11]

A religious man, Lopez never thought it fair to appeal for divine help to win ball games. "If I pray and the other guy prays, what's the Lord going to do?" he asked.[12] Lopez believed that a manager could best contribute two things to a club. He could inspire his players and he could do a good job of handling the pitchers. "The manager has to be up every day," said Lopez, "keeping those guys in the best frame of mind, keep them from getting down on themselves, and he has to keep the pitchers fresh and strong."[13]

Lopez personified these traits throughout his tenure as a manager. Passion for the game, heart, respect, diligence, performance — these are the qualities that made up the man and that Lopez brought with him to Indianapolis for the start of the 1948 season. As noted earlier, the Indianapolis Indians were the top farm club of the Pittsburgh Pirates.[14] Lopez spent three highly successful years in Indiana, winning 100 games and the regular-season pennant his maiden year, 1948, and following it with two regular season second-place finishes. In 1949 his Indians won the American Association's Shaughnessy playoff, topping Minneapolis and upstart Milwaukee, before besting the Montreal Royals of the International League in the Little World Series.

Lopez was introduced to his new club during spring training for the 1948 season, at Victoria, Texas. As with most upper-minor-league organizations, the Indians' roster depended largely on whom their parent club left behind at the end of its own training session. This question was still being asked in the Indianapolis press as late as the third week of March. Harold Harrison, sports editor for the *Indianapolis Star*, reported that the Indians were counting heavily on Pittsburgh for infielders and pitchers. He noted that Les Fleming would be the man at first base, with Jack Cassini looking sure at either second or third. From there on, however, help would have to come from above. "The Tribal hopes" were that Pete Castiglione, the Indians' shortstop the year before, would return and that either Danny Murtaugh or Monty Basgall, both infielders, would come with him. With Cassini, Saffell, and Beard also on board, Lopez had speed to burn and the tools required to play his preferred brand of inside baseball.[15]

Pitching was Lopez's biggest concern. Among his potential hurlers were Johnny Hutchings, Jim Bagby, Frank Stare, Bob Malloy, and Bill Sweigar. Also thrown into the mix was veteran moundsman Frank "Red" Barrett. Barrett, beginning his second year in Indianapolis, had traveled baseball's bush trail since 1935, visiting Columbus, Georgia; Albany, Georgia; Mobile, Alabama; Rochester, New York; Columbus, Ohio; and Houston, Texas. He had also spent time in the big leagues with the St. Louis Cardinals, Boston Red Sox, and Boston Braves. Having arguably seen it all, this veteran recognized early the abilities his new manager possessed. "You could see," recalled Barrett, "that [Lopez] was going to be a great manager."[16]

As for the catching duties, it was noted in the local press that Lopez himself "is our number one man." Lopez, however, sought from the outset to quell rumors that he would carry the bulk of the receiving load, adding that he figured to catch only about fifty or sixty games. Earl Turner, a young backstop who had trained with Indianapolis on three prior occasions, was thought to be the best guess for the supplementary spot. If there were any doubts among his young players about Lopez's ability to respond as a backstop when called upon, they were dispelled in late March, when the manager connected for a two-run homer in an exhibition contest against San Antonio. His blast, coupled with Les Fleming's three-run shot, powered the Indians to a 6–5 win.[17]

At Indianapolis that season, Lopez also acquired the services of his longtime teammate, roommate, and friend Tony Cuccinello, as coach. Before getting the call, Cuccinello had been in Tampa serving as manager of the Smokers, then in the Florida International League. According to Lopez, he had always been "the type of player you could win a pennant with … a good solid ballplayer." Lopez hoped that his infectiously personable friend might pass along these "solid" qualities to the younger players.[18]

As a coach, Cuccinello was everything Lopez thought he might be; knowledgeable, affable, and well liked. Jack Cassini fondly recalls how Cuccinello once gave him a new glove because he did not like the look of the one the infielder was using. "I held onto that glove for years," said Cassini.[19] Bitsy Mott, a member of the 1947 Tampa Smokers, also thought highly of Cuccinello.

> Tony Cuccinello was Tampa's manager in 1947 and I loved it. He was the greatest guy to play for. He could have been a manager all of his life but didn't want the responsibility. He stuck with Al Lopez and ended up having a good career with him as a coach. I'll tell you this, some people have said that Cuccinello stayed in the big leagues so long as a coach simply because he and Al were friends. That is a bunch of bull. I look at it the other way around. Al was such a success because he had Tony Cuccinello at his right hand. If you will look at the record you will find that Al never went anywhere without Tony. I admire Al Lopez, me and him are good friends, but Tony Cuccinello was something else. He was one of the best managers I ever played for.[20]

Ted Beard also viewed Cuccinello as a tremendous asset to Lopez and thought he was the best third-base coach whom he had ever seen. "He played it aggressive," said Beard. "Once when I was with Pittsburgh, [Cuccinello] sent two of his runners home on me and I threw them both out. He knew that I had a good arm, but he had to test me; play aggressive. If I make a mistake, they score."[21]

With March slowing to a close, Lopez and the Indians wound up their four-week spring camp in Victoria by handing Houston's Dixie Series champions a sound 10–4 beating. The win was the eleventh of the spring for the Indians, five coming against American Association rivals, with three defeats. It was also the first time that season that the Indians had gone through a game without committing an error. In the contest, rookie Frank Stare became the first Indians pitcher to throw more than five innings, going six, while "blazing" Jack Cassini collected three consecutive infield singles to steal the show. After the game the team headed for home via a circuitous route that took them through New Orleans, Mobile, Birmingham, Memphis, and Little Rock. With exhibition games scheduled at every stop, the trip lasted about two weeks.[22]

When the team arrived in New Orleans for their two-game set with the Pelicans of the Southern Association, they were met with news that the expected help from Pittsburgh was on its way. Pitcher Stan Ferek and catcher Earl Turner had been optioned to Indianapolis and were en route to New Orleans "by automobile." Ferek, a "spectacled lefthander," had been used primarily in relief with the Indians the year before. Turner had spent 1947 with Albany of the Eastern League, batting .305 with 46 RBIs. Later that week the team was surprised by another development, this time

Tony Cuccinello, Tampa Smokers manager, 1947. (Courtesy Florida State Archives.)

the rumored retirement of club president Ownie Bush. Bush, however, dismissed the reports, alluding to the fact that similar rumors involving him had surfaced before with nothing coming of them.[23]

Upon arriving in Indianapolis, the Indians, winners of seventeen games in the warm South, were met with rain and "bleak" conditions. To make matters worse, a number of players had not yet arrived, having either traveled separately by car or been given permission to visit relatives along the way. Some of the players who had arrived with the team were ailing and not available for practice. This, however, did not prevent Lopez from scheduling a "brisk drill" on their first full day in town. Before leaving Union Station, Lopez announced that he would have his team in uniform by 11 a.m. the next day, weather permitting, for practice. He added that the drill would be a long one to make up for the time lost on the train ride home. The manager had good reason for immediately pointing his charges toward the diamond. The following day, the New York Yankees were coming to town to play an exhibition game, and it was well understood that Lopez wanted to "pin a licking" on his old pal Casey Stengel. Furthermore, the season opener against defending champion Kansas City was less than a week away and Lopez had yet to decide on his pitching rotation.[24]

Against the Yankees, Indianapolis fans received a preview "to warm their hearts," their team playing well but falling 3–2. Bob Malloy, Stan Ferek, and Bill Sweiger held "the famed Bronx Bombers" to six hits, but the Indians' offense failed to muster enough support to take advantage. With Kansas City next on the agenda, the *Star* unveiled the Indians' "new look" lineup, consisting of a manager and eight starters who had not been with the club in 1947. The one returning regular was Pete Castiglione, who had been optioned back to Indianapolis as they had hoped. Lopez was also listed by the paper as the probable starting catcher, although as mentioned earlier, he had other ideas. He fully intended to catch Turner, as his job was to prepare such prospects for their possible call-up to the majors. Illustrating, with Americana flair, the collective anticipation of the home opener, L. Strauss & Company, "The Man's Store," ran a poem in the *Star*, playing on Lopez's name with the title "Hellopez!" and greeting the season as one might an old friend.[25]

The season began amid "circus pomp" before more than 10,000 fans, serenaded by promenading trios with accompanying vocals and accordions. Billed as "Harlan's Hawaiians," the groups moved through the grandstand before game time and between innings, playing popular "old-time" tunes while eliciting a big hand from the crowd. Then there was the "spirited martial music" of Tex Campbell's band, which keyed up both spectators and players, consequently making it difficult on the umpires when the game started. Mayor Al Feeney and Governor Ralph E. Gates were the "ringmasters" of the festivities, satisfying both Democrats and Republicans and bringing a sense of political harmony to the affair. Lopez gave his official hello at Victory Field, along with the team's other newcomers, being introduced to the fans by Bob Kirby, chairman of the Indianapolis Chamber of Commerce athletic committee. Evelyn Germaine, a former soloist with the Indianapolis Symphony Orchestra, then led the crowded bleachers in a "melodious" rendition of the "Star-Spangled Banner" and the game began. Farwell Rhodes, Jr., of the *Star* reported that it may have been difficult for the uninitiated to follow the game's progress because of the crowd's "rowdier spectators." Typical, it seems, was the "blast from a matronly, gray-haired lady who yanked her pince-nez glasses off, jumped up from her seat and howled at one of the umpires: 'Kill the cross-eyed baboon — he wouldn't know a strike if he saw one!'"[26]

The baseball writers who covered American Association games had

predicted that Indianapolis would fare no better than fourth in the standings, with the Milwaukee Brewers and the Kansas City Blues favored to
lead the pack. Frank Lane, American Association president, argued that
while the writers had been fairly accurate with their predictions in the
past, they had undersold the Toledo Mudhens when predicting their last-
place finish. Similar sympathies might have risen from the new manager
in Indianapolis, who had no intention of allowing his club to slip to the
bottom of his league's first division. Lopez's Indians split the first two
games of the season against the Blues before turning their sights on Minneapolis, where they "blasted" everything in sight, winning 15–1. By the
end of the next week, following a 10–8 decision over Milwaukee, the Indians were firmly atop the league standings at nine and three. The need for
more effective pitching, however, was cited as the team's weakness.
Through the first month of the season, not one of Lopez's hurlers was able
to limit the opposition to less than a hit an inning. Stan Ferek, expected
to be the best of the staff, failed to last longer than four and a third innings
in his first two outings, yielding sixteen hits. The lone bright spot was Jim
Bagby, who had won each of his three starts, although even he needed help
in one of them.

Bagby was the type of veteran hurler that Lopez wanted on his staff.
In ten seasons of big-league action, Bagby posted respectable numbers,
winning ninety-seven games. His best years were with Cleveland in 1942
and 1943, when he won seventeen games in each. In 1941 Bagby had teamed
with Al Smith to help stop Joe DiMaggio's record hitting streak at fifty-
six consecutive games. But now he was looking simply to hang around
long enough for injuries to take their toll in the majors, necessitating his
recall. Bagby's father, Jim, Sr., had also pitched in the major leagues. The
senior Bagby debuted briefly with Cincinnati in 1912 before returning to
the majors at Cleveland in 1916. In that season, Bagby broke an even sixteen and sixteen but improved the following year, winning twenty-three
games. His best year came in 1920, when hurling for Tris Speaker and the
World Series champion Indians, he posted an incredible mark of thirty-
one and twelve.

The Tribe's pitching woes haunted them through much of May and
resulted in the team sinking as low as third place in the standings. However, showing the resilience of "Citation," the brilliant three-year-old colt
then on his way to horse racing's triple crown, Indianapolis hurlers
rebounded, pitching the club back into first by sweeping a twin bill from
St. Paul 9–1 and 5–4. The double victory, coupled with Columbus's 10–9

triumph over Minneapolis, hoisted the Tribe into the top spot by four percentage points. By Memorial Day, their lead stood at one and a half games over Columbus, and it grew to five two weeks later. Only Mauri Rose, who had just won his second consecutive Indianapolis 500, averaging 119.813 miles per hour, was outpacing the Tribe's momentum. And with thirty-nine C-54 "Skymasters" delivering "vittles" to potentially starving American servicemen and German civilians in West Berlin, the Indians displayed a hunger of their own, devouring their American Association competition. In the process, they "laced" defending champs Kansas City 13–7 to close out June, establishing a seven-game lead, and they never looked back. When the dust of the 1948 campaign had settled, Lopez and his Indians, like Harry Truman in that year of upsets, had given the pundits hell, capturing the American Association pennant with 100 wins to their credit.[27]

In September, Lopez was rewarded by the club for its success with a two-year contract estimated at $20,000, a figure said to have been better than that received by some major-league managers. Much of the team management's impetus for doing so, no doubt, came from the increased attendance figures that season at Victory Field, reaching an all-time high of 494,547 in 77 games. The Tribe's high times, however, came to an abrupt end when the Indians were "unceremoniously dumped" from the Shaughnessy playoff by the St. Paul Saints, who had finished third in the regular season standings.[28]

Jack Cassini insists that in spite of the postseason swoon, the 1948 Indianapolis squad was possibly the best Triple-A team ever put together. Cassini:

> From the time we broke camp that spring in Victoria, Texas, we didn't let up all season long. Pete Castiglione at shortstop, Les Fleming at first, Culley Rickard in right, veteran ballplayers who stayed on us younger ones to always play hard. Castiglione was a great player; fantastic arm, great range, the kind of shortstop that Lopez always had with him. The team itself, with speed, offense, and great defense, was a reflection of the things Lopez liked in a club. Except the pitching, Lopez always had pitching in the majors. At Indianapolis, we would just outscore them. We had three guys at the top of the order, Beard, Saffell and myself, who each scored over 100 runs in 1948. We would get on base, then Fleming and Rickard would drive us in. And, as I've said, we had Al Lopez managing us

and that counted for plenty. I don't know what happened in the playoffs that year. I mean, we won the pennant, but in a short series, anything can happen.[29]

With many of his regulars returning in 1949, Lopez justifiably felt that his team's chances of making another run at the crown were good. The only significant change in the club's makeup was the naming of Don Gutteridge as Lopez's assistant in the absence of Cuccinello, who had moved on to Cincinnati. In spite of his title, however, Gutteridge was forced into regular action for the Indians at second base when the expected contenders for the position failed to emerge.[30]

No American Association club had won consecutive titles since Milwaukee had strung three together in the war years of 1943, 1944, and 1945. Bill Meyer, then manager of the Pirates, had been the last skipper to run up consecutive championships, winning two with Kansas City in 1939 and 1940. For Lopez's Indians to win again, they were going to have to show more offense than they had mustered that spring in New Orleans. In their final seven exhibition outings played in the Crescent City, four of which the Indians won, the Tribe displayed a woeful batting eye, hitting an anemic .198. With a lack of offense, pitching, as usual, would be at a premium for Lopez.[31]

Upon leaving New Orleans a surprising eleven of fifteen overall, the team took their relatively unused bats and traveled north in the same winding fashion as the year before. They were set to arrive in Indianapolis near the middle of April. While in Little Rock, Lopez's pitching staff was "augmented" by the arrival of Forrest "Woody" Main, a 6'3½" two-hundred-pound right-hander who had been with the Pirates. In Pittsburgh, Main had been used primarily as a reliever, but Billy Meyer asked Lopez to give him a "thorough test as a starter" and Lopez was happy to oblige. "That's all right with me," Main declared. "I'd like to get a change from that bullpen work." Main was expected to join veteran big leaguer Mel Queen, also with Pittsburgh the year before, and Junior Walsh in forming the heart of the Tribe's rotation. Lopez hoped to find another starter or two from the trio of Jack Hallett, Edson Bahr, and Paul Erickson, all of whom had seen major-league action, and Joe Muir, a rookie southpaw.[32]

In spite of Lopez's optimism, American Association baseball writers once again failed to pick his team first in their preseason poll. The scribes judged St. Paul, who had bested the Indians in the playoffs the year before, as the team to beat, with the Tribe picked for second slot. Kansas City, who garnered the second-most first-place votes in the poll, but was thought fifth-best overall, was slated as Indianapolis's opponent in the opener. Lopez named right-hander Mel Queen to face the Blues, with a combination of veterans and youngsters penciled in behind him. Paul Hinrichs, a $40,000 bonus "twirler" who had trained with the Yankees that spring, was named Kansas City's starter. Among the newcomers whom Lopez expected to contribute were Dale Coogan, with only six months of professional experience, but who had made a great impression on Lopez, at first; Jack Conway, a fine shortstop who had hit .315 for Minneapolis the year before only to be sold by the New York Giants, who held his option; and Clyde Kluttz, a veteran catcher who had spent the previous season in Pittsburgh.[33]

In the opener, played before a chilly, late-arriving, but record-breaking crowd of 12,343, Mel Queen "was a King," tossing a five-hitter en route to a 8–2 victory over the Blues. Queen, who proved to be the stalwart of Lopez's staff that season, going 22–9 with a 2.57 ERA, held Kansas City at bay with near-perfect control, allowing just two hits over the first five frames. The Tribe's offense also emerged, scoring six runs in the bottom of the first off the highly touted Hinrichs. Hinrichs found trouble from the start when he walked leadoff man Bill Plate. Jack Conway then rolled to shortstop, but Joe Muffoletto, the aptly named (at least on that night) Blues second baseman, missed the bag, placing runners on first and second. When Muffoletto "muffed" the following Dale Coogan grounder, the sacks were filled. A walk to Culley Rickard next forced in a run and Saffell's single, which Muffoletto stopped near the grass, scored Conway. Coogan then came home when Gutteridge forced Saffell at second. With one out and men on first and third, Clyde Kluttz doubled into the left-field corner, bringing home two more runs and signaling an end for Hinrichs, who was replaced by Art Bonham. Bonham promptly gave up a single to Queen that scored Kluttz before settling down to get out of the inning. The Indians scored twice more, once in the sixth and another in the eighth to preserve the win. The next day the Indians completed the opening series sweep by scoring four in the seventh and winning 5–1. Don Gutteridge, playing second as he had the day before, tabbed two more hits to strengthen his grip on the position.[34]

The following afternoon, fans awaiting buses to take them to Victory Field for the Indians game with Minneapolis were forced flat to the sidewalk, "crowded into store entrances," and pushed into the East fountain basin on Monument Circle when more than twenty bullets "flashed" in a gun battle between the FBI and Public Enemy Number One, Clyde Milton Johnson. Johnson, who was wanted for a $43,000 Memphis, Tennessee, bank holdup, was seriously wounded in the melee after an agent fired into him at point-blank range. Once at Victory Field, the Indians "flashed" a few bullets of their own, taking the Millers to task 9–5. The victory was the third in a row for the Tribe, giving Lopez the kind of start he had hoped for. The two clubs finished up the next day with the Millers winning 10–2. In the loss, their first of the season, the Indians stranded eleven runners on base.[35]

Mel Queen was at it again the following evening, winning his second for Indianapolis, this time 5–1, over the Brewers. The "big punch" for the Indians came on Dale Coogan's first-inning two-run blast, his first homer of the year. After the game Lopez received news that Earl Turner was being returned to the club. Turner was optioned to Indianapolis by Pittsburgh on twenty-four-hour recall because Clyde Kluttz, the Indians' starting catcher, had broken his wrist two days before against Minneapolis and would miss several weeks. Turner was expected to arrive in time for an afternoon doubleheader with Milwaukee.[36]

Even with Turner in the lineup, the Indians took a downward spin for the remainder of April. The skid began when they dropped the aforementioned double dip against Milwaukee, 4–0 and 6–5, leaving St. Paul alone in first. They followed that with a ladies night loss, their third straight, to the Saints at Victory Field on April 25. When rain forced the postponement of the following day's game with St. Paul, it cost the club the chance to close ground, leaving them in fourth place. After besting Kansas City two days later 13–6, in their first road game of the year, the Indians dropped one to the Blues 6–5 on an unearned run that came back to bite them. Through it all, Lopez's only bright spots were Turner, who had belted two homers since arriving, and "Devastating" Dale Coogan, "the kid from Keokuk," who collected four hits against the Blues on April 28.[37]

A week later, with the Tribe in third place, five games behind St. Paul and Milwaukee, Lopez received the infield help he had been looking for when Jack Cassini was optioned back to the club. In spite of the fine play being turned at second by Gutteridge, it was Cassini, "whose speed and daring so typified the pennant-winning club of 1948," that Lopez wanted most at the position. That evening, the Indians returned home and beat the Columbus Red Birds 7–6 in ten innings. It was their first extra-innings contest of the year. The winning rally came against Ira Hutchinson, the Red Birds' "veteran relief hurler." In the tenth, Hutchinson walked Saffell, allowed Conway to sacrifice him to second, and then intentionally walked Coogan to set up the possible double play. Jack Crimian was then called upon by the Birds to face Indians outfielder Frank Kalin, who already had three hits, a walk, and sacrifice in five appearances. Kalin, working the count to two and two, rapped an ill-fated Crimian curve between short and third, scoring Saffell with the winning run.[38]

As spring turned to summer, the Indians were still in third place but trailed league-leading St. Paul by just two games and the Brewers by a game and a half. These standings followed a doubleheader at Milwaukee in which the Indians had the opportunity to make up ground on the Brewers, but instead they came away with a split. After having lost the first game 8–3, the Indians fought back on the arm of rookie Joe Muir, winning 5–1. Going into the contest, there was some question, especially in the mind of Lopez, about whether the young Muir had the makings of a starter. Muir, who spent the entire season pitching better on the road, "justified" Lopez's faith, going the distance and allowing a scant four hits, only one of which came after the fourth inning. It was Muir's strongest performance to date, improving his record to three and five and serving clear notice about what might be expected from the young southpaw in the season's second half. At the plate, the Indians made the most of their seven hits, two coming off the bat of recently acquired outfielder Froilan "Nanny" Fernández. Fernández, a veteran of three big-league campaigns, proved to be a huge addition to Lopez's lineup, batting .312 with 21 homers and 35 doubles. With the speed of Beard, Saffell, and Cassini in front of him, Fernández also drove in 128 runs that season. The year's performance won Fernández, nicknamed "Nanny" by his older sisters, both the team and the league's Most Valuable Player honors.[39]

The next morning it was reported that beginning on June 16, WFBM-TV in Indianapolis would televise all Indians night home games. In announcing the thirty-six game package, Frank McKinney, vice president of the Indians, and Harry M. Bitner, manager of the station, expressed their hope to "keep up the interest [in the Indians] generated by the 500-mile race telecast." "We'll try it out this season," said McKinney, "and see what happens." No plans were made beyond the year, however. It was also noted that the games would be televised through the use of at least two cameras "mounted atop the grandstand," so that the fans at home could receive the best possible view. That night, Fernández and Conway continued their assault on Milwaukee pitching, each belting a homer, and the Indians won 3–2. The win kept the Tribe within two games of St. Paul and moved them just half a game in back of Milwaukee with one more game to play in the series. If Lopez hoped to reel in the Brewers, this was the time.[40]

Extending pole in hand, Lopez's Indians rapped out fifteen hits against Milwaukee, including two homers and three triples, on their way to an 8–4 victory. The important early-season win moved Indianapolis into second place, one game behind the Saints. Mel Queen was again the Tribe's ace, going eight and two-thirds for his eighth win of the season, while Conway and Fernández homered for the third straight night.[41]

While in Minneapolis the following week, Lopez's club was dealt a blow when Pittsburgh released outright Culley Rickard, the Indians' leading hitter, to San Francisco of the Pacific Coast League. The release of the popular Rickard, part of a deal designed to bring "24-year-old sensation" Dino Restelli to Pittsburgh, came as a complete surprise to Lopez, who had already placed Rickard in his lineup that night. There was also some speculation that Bobby Rhawn, recently acquired by Pittsburgh from the Giants, might be sent down to fill the vacancy at third left by Rickard and to provide some additional pop. Until a replacement could be found, however, Nanny Fernández was forced to fill in. That evening in Rickard's absence, Tom Saffell "turned in one of the greatest swatting performances ever given by a Tribe outfielder," powering the Indians past the Millers 10–6. In five at-bats, Saffell connected for three homers, a double, and a single. According to Saffell, the double almost went out of the park as well, hitting near the top of the short right-field fence at Nicollet Field in Minneapolis. He also drove in five RBIs and scored five runs. It was the second time that season that Saffell had collected multiple homers at Nicollet Field, the other coming on May 3 when he sent two into the stands. Conway and Fernández also contributed their usual positive numbers, Conway a homer, his eighth, and Fernández three hits.[42]

The Millers had recently improved their roster by acquiring the services of veteran Negro League performers Ray Dandridge and Dave Barnhill, the first blacks to play in Minneapolis. "Hooks" Dandridge, at thirty-six, possessed a strong arm and was still sure-handed in the field at either third or second. But it was his bat that impressed the most. Dandridge "raked" Triple-A pitching that season for a .362 average and followed the next year by winning the American Association's Most Valuable Player Award. Barnhill, then thirty-five (although the *Star* listed him as twenty-six), arguably could have been a big-league pitching star except that some considered him "too little, too black, and too old." But in his day, insisted Cool Papa Bell, he "had smoke."[43] "He threw just as hard as anybody," confirmed Buck Leonard. The smallish Barnhill won seven games for Minneapolis in 1949 but came back to win eleven the next season, leading the Millers to their first pennant in fifteen years.[44] In relief against the Indians during Saffell's big outing, Barnhill allowed four singles in five innings of work while Dandridge got two hits, including his first American Association home run.[45]

Saffell and Fernández began the next night where each had left off, the former banging out two homers, giving him five in two games, while Fernández tagged another pair. In all, nine home runs were sent out of the yard in the 10–7 come-from-behind, Indians victory. It was the Tribe's tenth win in its last fourteen road outings. Coupled with St. Paul's 16–4 loss the following evening at Kansas City, it moved the Indians into first place, half a game in front of the Saints.[46]

Throughout the remainder of June, Indianapolis hovered in or near first place, never more than a game or so from the top. On June 14 the club was bolstered by the return of Les Fleming, the slugging first baseman who had spent the early part of the year in Pittsburgh. Lopez hoped that the return of Fleming would bring the added power that his club would surely need if it were to repeat as league champs. He also looked to insert Fleming into the cleanup spot immediately upon his arrival. While Fleming's numbers dipped to fourteen home runs and sixty-nine RBIs in 1949, he proved a vital cog offensively for Lopez down the stretch.[47]

The day after Fleming arrived, the Indians received another lift, obtaining swift outfielder Jerry Scala from the Chicago White Sox. A week before, Scala had been released by Chicago to Oakland in the Pacific Coast League. Rather than report, however, and without notifying Chicago team officials, Scala returned to his home in Bayonne, New Jersey, to visit his ailing mother. Upon being suspended without pay, "the fiery Italian" notified the Chicago offices that his mother's condition had improved, whereupon he was summarily ordered to report to Indianapolis as part of another deal. Saddened by the unusual turn of events were the "proud citizens of Bayonne," who had planned on presenting their favorite son with a new automobile before the Yankees–White Sox game on June 13. When they learned that Scala would not be present in the Bronx, the "Scala Night" affair was reluctantly called off and all contributions for the car were returned.[48]

Fleming and Scala were both joining a team that had just won eleven of eighteen on the road, or .611 away from their home park, and that was beginning a twenty-one-game home stand. Bob Stranahan of the *Star* acknowledged as much, asserting that Lopez's charges were playing "plenty good enough to keep them in the thick of the pennant fight." After a rain-out on June 16, however, the club slowed its pace, splitting a doubleheader with Columbus and dropping a 5–3 decision to surging Louisville before tagging the Colonels with twin losses, 4–0 and 4–3. On June 21 Mel Queen collected his tenth win, shutting out Kansas City 1–0, but then watched his team lose the second game 5–3. In the ensuing forty-eight hours, the two clubs faced off twice more, the Blues winning 7–6 and Indianapolis 2–1. The Tribe then ended the month with another split, this time against the Saints, 5–2 and 4–13. Because St. Paul's "apostles" were playing in the same generous fashion, the Indians held on, exiting June with a game and a half lead.[49]

The team's inconsistency continued through July, and by early August, after having opened up a three-and-a-half game lead, it began to hurt them. The downturn started on August 2, when the Indians, looking ahead to three games with St. Paul, were "whitewashed" by Milwaukee 7–0. While the Tribe won the series, their lead over the Saints dwindled by a game. Some of the Indians' problems were attributed to injuries. Both Dom Dallessandro, the team's leading hitter, and Earl Turner had missed action with various ailments. With the Saints "marching in," Lopez desperately needed them both back in the lineup.[50]

The team's injuries hardly seemed noticeable in game one as the Indians, relying on Mel Queen and all the offense they could muster, routed St. Paul 7–2. Queen, pitching on two days' rest, gave up eleven widely scattered hits in going the distance. He did not allow a run until the eighth, when St. Paul scored twice on two doubles and a single. It was the fifth time that season that Queen had bested the Saints and his sixteenth win overall. The Tribe, led by Clyde Kluttz and Les Fleming, scored runs in the second, third, fourth, and sixth innings respectively. They posted three in the climactic sixth when Kluttz singled, was advanced on a bunt by Queen who was safe at first, and scored on Beard's single to left. Cassini's grounder to short was then dropped by Buddy Hicks, loading the bases. Fernández next doubled to left, scoring the final two tallies.[51]

In game two, however, Edson Bahr, who had been sent by Indianapolis to the Saints earlier in the season, got the assignment and proved effective "with his slow stuff," allowing just six hits in the 5–3 St. Paul win. The "apostles" obtained ten hits and two runs off starter Bob Malloy, who was spelled in the eighth by Forrest Main. But it was errors that proved costly, helping St. Paul score three of their five runs. Bahr scored the game's first mark after singling to center in the third. He moved to second on Jim Pendleton's base hit to right and scored when Ted Beard bobbled Hank Schenz's subsequent "bingle." In the eighth, with Main pitching for Malloy, Wayne Belardi walked, stole second, and scored when Pendleton scooted a single past first. Pendleton, who wound up at second on the play, was ruled safe when Cassini dropped the throw in from Beard. Schenz then rolled one to Conway, but the shortstop's throw to first "popped" out of Fleming's glove, scoring Pendleton and Hicks, who had been passed intentionally. Had it not been for the "stretching" of Fleming at first, other errors would have also occurred. The mistakes surely wore on the frayed stomach of Lopez, whose teams typically played strong defense. "We made few mistakes and didn't give runs away," said Don Gutteridge. With the series rubber match a day away, the Indians' skipper urged them to relax and play focused.[52]

Junior Walsh faced St. Paul in the third game, but the right-hander was ineffective, giving up six passes during the 8–2 loss. Walsh, who was seeking his sixteenth win of the season, had trouble finding the plate and was also hindered by a soft defense that remained suspect. In spite of the performance, however, Walsh was called up by Pittsburgh the following day, making a noticeable gap in Lopez's pitching corps and one he would have to remedy. The game, played before 10,147, moved the Victory Field attendance for the year past the 330,000 mark, while the loss itself left the Tribe sobered, a mere game and a half in front.[53]

The Indians rallied the next day, besting Kansas City 7–6. Russ Peters belted a "tremendous" triple to far right-center with the bases full and none out in the bottom of the ninth to claim the win. Indianapolis had come to the plate for their last try in the ninth, trailing 6–4. Les Fleming started it by beating out a deep grounder to second. Royce Lint, running for Fleming, advanced to third on a "sizzler" to right by Dallessandro, and then Gutteridge pinch-ran for him. With men on the corners and no outs, Scala placed a perfect bunt down the third-base line to load the bases, bringing up Peters, whom Lopez had started at shortstop in place of Conway after the latter had begun the previous 114 outings. With Mel Queen due to start the next evening, the Tribe thus fulfilled their hopes of regaining some of their lead lost in recent days.[54]

The late-inning heroics enjoyed by Indianapolis the day before did not repeat for the Indians in their second game against Kansas City, this time won by the Blues in ten innings, 3–2. The loss, coupled with a St.

Paul victory, wiped out the Indians' "first place edge," leaving them dead-locked atop the standings. Even this position proved fleeting as the Blues, on "Sad Sunday," took two more from the now slumping Indians, 11–1 and 7–3. The losses proved decisive, dumping Indianapolis into second, a full two games behind the Saints. In taking the series three games to one Kansas City had captured a set from the Tribe for the first time all season. Lopez, hoping to regroup his club, named Bob Malloy to start the ladies night lead-in with Minneapolis the following evening and was not disappointed, his team winning 5–2. In the contest, Jack Cassini, benefiting from a board placed in front of a Sixteenth Street lightpole that had previously both-ered him at the plate, drove in three of the Indians' runs on five hits, two coming on his third homer of the season. The Tribe won again the next night, nipping Minneapolis in the tenth 4–3 on Dallesandro's bases-loaded single to right. With Indianapolis brooms at the ready, however, the Millers fought back, winning game three 8–6. In spite of taking the series, Indi-anapolis remained a daunting two games behind St. Paul.[55]

With a day off for travel, Lopez's squad went into St. Paul looking to reclaim the lead but came up missing, losing a "wild" affair 10–9. In spite of allowing thirteen hits, including two homers by Nanny Fernández, the Saints pushed three runs across off Forrest Main in the ninth to win it. St. Paul followed it up the next day, taking Lopez's men to task, this time 6–5. The rival clubs split their last two, Indianapolis winning the night-cap 6–3 after having lost that afternoon 7–2. The near-sweep separated the Saints and Indians further, providing St. Paul with a comfortable four-game advantage with little over a month to play.[56]

But the Tribe raced back! After allowing the Saints to enjoy their lead for the next week and a half, Lopez's crew got their engines started, stag-ing a "remarkable back-to-the-wall stand" and closing to within a game and a half on September 9 with three "tilts" remaining. Aware that St. Paul had dropped an afternoon affair at Kansas City earlier that day, the Indi-ans surged ahead of Louisville in the seventh inning of their contest to win 5–2. Royce Lint, on in relief of Elmer Riddle, struck the decisive blow when he sent a two-out single over the head of second baseman Chuck Harrington to score Jerry Scala, who had singled and advanced on a wild pitch. Before the contest, Lopez, Mel Queen, Earl Turner, and Nanny Fernández had received diamond rings for being named to the league's All-Star team. The presentations were made by Ted Sullivan, the Indians' business manager. Fernández had also received a government bond and other gifts for being selected his team's Most Valuable Player.[57]

The next evening, Lopez's resilient Tribesmen pummeled Toledo 11–4 while St. Paul lost at Milwaukee, to pull within half a game of first with only a final-day twin bill left to play. Before an inaugural men's night crowd of 13,473, the Indians sent twelve men to the plate in an eight-run third, including Les Fleming's "tremendous" 465-foot grand slam "over the bricks in center," to put the game out of reach. Two more victories and a St. Paul loss would earn for the Indians their second consecutive American Association pennant. With everything riding on the arms of his chosen starters, Lopez, not surprisingly, opted to go with Mel Queen and Royce Lint in the final two outings. The manager also announced that his team would be without the services of Jerry Scala, who had gone to Bayonne the day before upon receiving word that his mother had suffered a stroke. It was believed that Scala would be back in time for the postseason.[58]

The Tribe's "Indian summer" waned on its last tomorrow when in spite of beating Toledo twice, 2–1 and 6–4, they were nosed out by St. Paul, who won two at Milwaukee, thereby preserving their narrow half-game lead. It was the Saints' first pennant since 1938 and established them as the top seed going into the Shaughnessy playoff. In their final bid to overtake the "apostles," the Tribesmen were applauded by a standing-room-only crowd of 15,390, the biggest turnout of the year. While certainly disappointed at not winning the pennant, Lopez immediately sought to focus his club's attention on the task ahead, that being the playoffs. The year before, the Indians, perhaps amid the glory of their own championship, had not performed as they should have and were treated accordingly. This time Lopez was determined to see that his club remained in a baseball state of mind. Bob Stranahan of the *Star*, commenting on the local excitement surrounding the playoffs in 1949 compared to the year before, observed that the entire community seemed to be thrilled with the prospect of a postseason. In 1948, noted Stranahan, the playoffs proved unpopular, especially after the Indians were "dumped" by St. Paul. "The consensus then," he wrote, "was: 'Nuts. We're the champs. Why go through the playoffs?'" In 1949, however, after finishing a close second, the feeling was different. The talk in and around the community this time came from "the other side of the mouth," said Stranahan. The gist of it seemed to be, "We'll show 'em in the playoffs."[59]

The playoff format called for the pennant-winning Saints to host Milwaukee, who had recently given them so much trouble, while the Indians took on Minneapolis. Both series were slated as best-of-seven sets. Indianapolis had never won the overall championship in the thirteen years that the Shaughnessy playoff system had been in effect. In fact, pennant winners had captured the postseason crown only four times in thirteen attempts, the last coming in 1946 when Louisville bested Indianapolis four games to none. St. Paul had lost its own 1938 bid, four games to three.[60]

Lopez initially chose Joe Muir to start game one against Minneapolis, but a rainout caused him to adjust his rotation, going instead with the southpaw Chet Johnson. Johnson, who had been slated to pitch the second game, had come through "brilliantly" the previous Thursday against Columbus, and so Lopez opted to use him, followed by Queen in game two. The youthful Muir was shuttled to the bullpen with a possible start later in the playoffs. The series the Indians wanted from Minneapolis was not the one they received, being forced to slug it out for seven games after losing the first three at home in Victory Field. In game one Johnson was routed in the sixth inning, the Tribe falling 4–0. Jack Maguire, who had batted .343 on the year for the Millers, collected four hits, while league home-run champ Jack Harshman belted his fortieth.[61]

In the second game, the Millers "hammered" Mel Queen for nine hits and a 6–5 two-game advantage. Nanny Fernández belted two homers in successive turns at bats for the Indians while Dom Dallessandro hit one in the fourth, but it wasn't enough, the Millers moving ahead in the seventh to stay. Dave Barnhill yielded eight hits to the Tribe but retired them in order in six of the nine frames. It was a typical performance from Barnhill, who once pitched a shutout at St. Paul while allowing eleven hits.[62] "He was in trouble constantly and wormed his way out every time," Jack Harshman later told John Holway. Holway noted that some around the league, including Lopez, believed that Barnhill cut the ball in order to worm his way out of jams. Lopez:

> All of the sudden I see where Barnhill struck out 14 in St. Paul, goes some place else, strikes out about 15. Something wrong here some place. Now he's going to pitch against us. Turns around to the outfield. I called for the ball. Every time he turned around, I said, "Hey, watch what he's doing to that ball there!" I still don't know whether he was doing anything or not, but I think he was.

Barnhill also recalled the "stink" that Lopez made about him. Barnhill:

Yeah. Every time I took the ball and rubbed it up, Al Lopez would run out and hold up the game. They thought I was cutting it on my belt. But there's the umpire right there looking at me. Heath told me, "Dave, it looks like that's *worrying* 'em when you turn your back and rub up the ball. Continue on doing it." Al Lopez: "Hold it! Hold it! He scratched the ball!" Umpire said, "Now look here. If you walk out here one more time, hold up the game, I'm going to forfeit the game to Minneapolis." That's the only thing that stopped him from going out there.[63]

That same day Jerry Scala was placed under suspension by the club for refusing to return for the playoffs. Ownie Bush explained that Scala had been notified of his suspension by telegram and that Frank Lane, general manager of the Chicago White Sox, who held Scala's contract, had also been notified and was in accord. Indianapolis officials had been "irked" the week before when Scala refused an offer to fly home to visit his mother, opting instead to drive, thus making the trip two days longer. Among the team's top hitters with a .341 average, Scala informed the *Star* that he would not leave his mother's bedside as long as her critical condition persisted. "A baseball game," said Scala, "doesn't mean so much that I should go back to Indianapolis now." All this of course followed the twenty-three-year-old outfielder's earlier refusal to report to the Pacific Coast League and his late arrival upon being assigned to Indianapolis by Chicago. While Lopez, who lived with his own mother until her death, might have sympathized somewhat with Scala's dilemma, it is doubtful that he viewed the outfielder's refusal to report with any strong sense of empathy. With his team now down two games in the playoffs, Lopez needed Scala in the lineup and did not get him.[64]

The final contest against the Millers at Victory Field ended with the same loathsome result, the "skidding" Tribe falling 4–3 in twelve innings. Lopez and Tommy Heath sent nine pitchers to the hill that night with Bob Malloy, the fourth Indians hurler, working the twelfth inning. Malloy walked the first man he faced, Workman, who then moved over on Ray Dandridge's sacrifice. Bob Brady, who received an extra chance when Clyde Kluttz dropped his foul, then hit one between first and second with Fleming deflecting it into short right field, scoring Workman on the play to win it. Having lost for the third time, the Indians found themselves within a breath of elimination and facing the daunting task of winning four straight at Nicollet Field, where they were nine and two on the year.

However, as Max Greenwald noted in the *Star*, they had faced a similar "back-to-the-wall" scenario during the season's final week, coming away with seven consecutive wins. Hoping to rekindle the same fire, Lopez turned to Joe Muir in game four. The rookie had looked good hurling a two-inning relief stint in game two, holding the Millers hitless, and he had shown well on the road all year. He had also topped the "apostles" three times during the regular season, all coming at Minneapolis.[65]

Muir again confirmed Lopez's belief in him, allowing the Millers six hits on the way to a 16–2 thrashing. With "sterling" control, Muir stayed ahead of the batters most of the game, forcing the Millers to chase marginal pitches late in the count, resulting in a wealth of grounders. A seventeen-hit attack provided him with all the support he needed. The Indians, taking advantage of a strong wind blowing out to right, belted four homers, two by Jack Conway, who had four hits for the day, scoring each time. Every member of the Tribe had at least one hit, and all scored except Muir. Bill Ayres, who had won for the Millers in the opener, failed to last an inning under the onslaught of Frank Kalin's grand slam, Conway's first homer, and Fernández's triple.[66]

Taking them one at a time, Lopez's men survived game five by the narrowest of margins, nipping the Millers in the ninth inning 9–8. It was Les Fleming's second homer of the game that broke the eight-all tie in the top of the last to get the win. His first had come off Barnhill's initial offering to start the second. It was also the 35th homer hit by Indianapolis at Nicollet Field that season. The game's turning point came in the sixth inning after Don Mueller had "blasted a terrific homer," putting the Millers in front. Dandridge followed by beating out a slow roller toward third and moved to second on a fielder's choice to Cassini. Harshman was then walked intentionally to set up the double play, but Muir walked Bill Jennings, filling the bases with two outs. Dave Barnhill then came to the plate and "cracked" one into the left-field corner, scoring all three runners. But while advancing, Harshman failed to touch third base. His blunder nullified all three tallies and Barnhill's triple, as it was ruled a force play at third for the inning's final out. To many, the gaffe was obvious. Barnhill recalls that when Harshman missed the bag, people in the stands were yelling for him to go back and touch third. But by that time, he was in the dugout and the force-out was recorded. The forfeited runs proved to be the difference in forcing a sixth game.[67]

The Indians topped Minneapolis again the following night 7–6, evening things at three games all. In the process, the Tribe overcame a four-run deficit on homers by Kalin and Earl Turner. Jack Cassini's "timely hitting" also aided the cause. Royce Lint began the game on the hill for Indianapolis but gave way to Muir in the fifth, who came through again for Lopez, allowing only three scattered hits over the final five innings. Before the game began it was announced that the team's leading hitter, Dom Dallessandro, would miss the remainder of the season. After game five, the "stocky" veteran outfielder, who was batting a robust .342, had complained of chest and abdominal pains. Upon examination by team physicians, Dallessandro was advised to sit out the remaining games or at least until receiving a clearance from a doctor of his own choosing. He left the following day for his home in Reading, Pennsylvania, with his advanced career in jeopardy.[68]

With Milwaukee having already upset St. Paul and awaiting the winner, the Indians and Millers met in game seven to decide which team would oblige the Brewers on the next rung of battle. When it was over, the Indians, losers of three straight tilts on their home field, had downed the Millers 8–5, climaxing "the most remarkable comeback in American Association history." Lopez's bunch clinched the decision with a five-run barrage in the fourth, capped by Nanny Fernández's three-run homer. The Tribe again received stellar southpaw relief, this time from Royce Lint, who entered the game for Queen in the seventh with the sacks full and none out, but he slammed the door, allowing no hits the rest of the way. Roy Weatherly had four of the Indians' thirteen hits while Don Mueller led a ten-hit attack for St. Paul. Bob Stranahan, admitting that there were few who would have given Indianapolis a "plugged nickel for their chances" a week before, praised the "old men" for coming off the floor to survive. The 1949 club, he said, had "been up against all sorts of handicaps with injuries to key players and others being hauled out when they seemingly were needed most." But, Stranahan applauded, "the Indians apparently have thrived on adversity ... they didn't know when they were beaten."[69]

With the nation shaken by evidence that the Soviet Union had developed nuclear capabilities, Lopez calmly prepared his charges to face Milwaukee in round two of the Shaughnessy tournament. In another seven-game battle, the first three won by the Indians at Victory Field, the Tribe outlasted the Brewers four games to three to advance to the Little World Series. In game seven, Lopez again called on Queen, who hurled seven-hit baseball while banging his first homer of the year and two singles in the 9–5 win. Fleming added two doubles, one "a 400-foot smash which struck the scoreboard in right center," driving in two runs, and

Kalin also homered. It was the first time the Indians had won the Shaughnessy playoff in the event's fourteen seasons and marked the "first Hoosier entry" to qualify for the Little World Series in twenty-one years. In the series, set to open October 1, the Indians would face the Montreal Royals, the Dodgers' top farm club and winners of the International League's playoffs, having bested pennant-winning Buffalo and runner-up Rochester.[70]

Before the series began, the Indians had to decide how to cut up the $4,604 they earned for finishing as runners-up for the pennant. One player who was left completely off the payoff list was Jerry Scala, the outfielder who had been with the club before returning to his mother's bedside. Evidently the Tribe members did not approve of his action in returning home in the last days of the season when they were fighting "tooth and nail for the bunting." The players voted a division of twenty-six shares with the nineteen regulars, Lopez, Gutteridge, and popular team trainer "Hump" Pierce all receiving full amounts of $177.08. The team's share for defeating Minneapolis and Milwaukee came to another $6,096. In the Little World Series, the players stood to earn much more, since they shared in the gate receipts for the first four games just as was done in the major leagues. The winner's share in 1948 had amounted to nearly $1,000 per man.[71]

In both of the first two games of the series, played at Royals Stadium, the Indians came away 5–1 victors. Joe Muir and Royce Lint got the wins in the light-hitting affairs, allowing nine hits between them to shackle a lineup that included outfielder Sam Jethro and shortstop Bobby Morgan. Jethro, a former Negro League star, had stolen a league record eighty-nine bases and batted .326 that season. His 207 hits and 151 runs scored were all-time Montreal marks. Morgan had been voted the league's most valuable player after leading the league in hitting with a .337 average. He had also driven in 110 RBIs, but he had slowed noticeably late with only ten coming after mid-August. Other notable Royals included Al Gionfriddo, who had come to Montreal from Brooklyn after the 1947 World Series, and Chuck Connors, who went on to television stardom as "The Rifleman." After game two, Fernández, Lint, and Queen were all buoyed by the announcement that the Pirates had purchased their contracts for the 1950 season.[72]

The Royals fought back to win game three 3–1, but then they were faced with the prospect of needing three wins in four attempts at Victory Field. In the tightly played contest, Mel Queen and Chet Johnson held the Royals in check, allowing just three hits, but two of them combined with two errors and a walk in the fifth to give Montreal their runs. Poor hitting on both sides had been the rule to this point in the series, with Indianapolis batting an anemic .188 and Montreal worse at .133. Addressing the situation after game three, Lopez remarked that he was confident his team could and would hit better in the coming days. "I especially expect Fernández, Kalin and Roy Weatherly to snap out of it now that we are back in our own park," said Lopez. Neither Fernández nor Kalin had gotten a hit to that point in the series and Weatherly had only a single.[73]

Lopez's optimism aside, the Indians' bats failed to receive their wakeup call for game four. After an October 5 rainout provided both clubs with needed rest, play resumed in Indianapolis. Clarence Podbielan, a twenty-four-year-old Royals hurler, spoiled the Indians' home debut 7–1 to even the series. Podbielan, who stopped the Indians cold on two hits, one an infield single, retired them in order in seven of the nine frames. Both Tribe hits came in the fourth when Beard opened with a walk, Cassini singled to center, and Fleming walked to load the bases. Weatherly then beat out a single that was knocked down by Rocky Bridges at second, scoring Beard, but Kalin followed with a double-play grounder, killing the rally. A series of disputes also marked the Indians fourth after home-plate umpire Pat Padden called a balk on Podbielan and waved Beard home. However, Augie Donatelli, the crew chief at first, ruled that Podbielan was not in the legal pitching position when he stepped off the rubber and ordered Beard back to third. The Royals then protested Donatelli's decision at first when he called Weatherly safe on his single. During the wrangling, Cassini charged home from third to score but was ordered back to third by Padden. This brought Lopez out of the dugout to argue the call, but to no avail. The undersized Victory Field crowd of 10,123 bettered the average for the games played in Montreal. It also boosted the players' share in gate receipts for the first four games to $42,110.95.[74]

As it had with Minneapolis, game five proved to be the turning point in this series, producing "as stormy a finish as ever seen at Victory Field." In the hotly disputed contest, won by Indianapolis 5–4, Roy Weatherly came to bat in the bottom of the tenth with two outs and Fernández on first, belting one to the right-field wall. Fernández, determined to score, was off with the crack of the bat, streaking around the bases headed for home. As the ball was relayed from the outfield, catcher Toby Atwell straddled home plate and blocked Fernández from scoring. In fact, Montreal would rightly argue that Fernández never made it to the plate. Upon taking the throw, Atwell quickly applied the tag, but Augie Donatelli "immediately" called Fernández safe. Donatelli, who had already signed to work in the American League the following season, ruled that Atwell had illegally blocked the plate without first having possession of the ball. Royals manager Clay Hopper and the entire Montreal squad surrounded Donatelli in a furious protest, forcing Pat Padden to come in from third, squeezing in front of his smaller colleague, who quickly retreated to the dressing room.[75] Fernández, who does remember being tagged short of the plate, recalls that while on first he had told Chuck Connors that he was going to score on anything hit to the outfield. Fernández:

> We were all tired as hell. Well, Weatherly hit that ball and I take off, I don't hesitate at third and go all the way around. I can't remember if they tried to hold me at third or not, I just ran. The throw comes in to the plate and has me by three or four feet, but the catcher, who had the plate blocked, didn't have possession of the ball while doing it and so Donatelli called me safe. Clay Hopper, Montreal's manager, came running out of the dugout mad as anything, he was a hothead, arguing the call, but we just walked off the field; we'd won.[76]

Jack Cassini, who can still picture Fernández "stuck in the mud at home," insists that the Royals were mad about that call long after the series ended. Cassini:

> Chuck Connors, the "Rifleman," was the first baseman for Montreal. I saw him years later at an oldtimers baseball function and he was still mad about that play. He said, "You dirty bum, you stole the game!" Clay Hopper and the Royals were mad as hell, but we just got out of there.[77]

    It was the type of play that can steal the wind from a team, and it did that to the Montreal Royals. The next day the Indians, behind seventeen hits and another strong performance by Royce Lint, routed the Royals 12–2, capturing Indianapolis's first "fall classic" since 1928. Clarence Podbielan, who had pitched two-hit ball for Montreal four days earlier, and Clyde King were the victims of the Tribe's revived attack. Fernández led the way with four hits, while Conway added three and Earl Turner homered. For their efforts, the Indians knocked down an extra $336 per man as their winning share of the series loot.[78]

"Nice going gang ... you did it," a reserved Lopez told his team after the game. Bob Stranahan, somewhat surprised by the manager's composure, observed that for a guy whose club had just won the top prize in minor-league baseball, Lopez seemed very quiet, "subdued you might say." He attributed it to Lopez's "uneasy stomach," and the uncertainty over "what the future held." Lopez's name had been linked in recent weeks with several big-league managerial jobs. What Stranahan failed to grasp amid the revelry, however, was that for Lopez, a postgame celebration belonged to the players and as he would in later years at Cleveland and Chicago, he deferred the spotlight to them. With delight teeming through the Indians clubhouse, a *Star* photographer captured Lopez sitting beside "Podner," the Tribe's "good luck" pigeon mascot. It seems that the company of a pigeon amidst the well-deserved gaiety suited the contented skipper just fine.[79]

Three days later the speculation over Lopez's immediate future ended when it was announced that he would return to pilot the Indians in 1950. "That's a fine bunch in Indianapolis," Lopez said while on a visit in Pittsburgh. "The fans are swell and the boys I worked with were great. We had good seasons the two years I have been there and I can see no reason to make a change." Whether Lopez wanted change or not, he was going to face it in the coming season. Aside from the players whose options had already been purchased by the Pirates, thirty-two-year-old Frank Kalin announced his retirement and Jack Cassini was traded to Brooklyn. It would indeed be a new core group of players that Lopez would work with in 1950. Outfielder Gus Bell, a youngster who had joined the Indians during the latter part of the season, nineteen-year-old pitcher Bob Friend, and infielders Monty Basgall and Ed Bockman were expected to be among those challenging for playing time.[80]

One change that Lopez did not have to face was that of his assistant coach. The next spring, "with the same energy and 'let's go and get 'em chatter that marked his baseball career, Don Gutteridge began his second season with the team. As he had the year before, the thirty-six-year-old was ready to get in the lineup and "hustle with the best of them," if forced to. The Indians coach had learned much of what he knew about the game while playing for Frankie Frisch in St. Louis. The running game emphasized by Frisch on the Cardinals congealed nicely with that preferred by Lopez, as did Gutteridge's must-win attitude. Gutteridge, who could often be heard clamoring it's "a great day to work," summarized his coaching philosophy this way: "In ten seasons in the big leagues I've been out of that first division only once. So you can see I don't like to be with losers."[81]

Lopez and Gutteridge proved to work very well together, both at Indianapolis and later in Chicago. "With Al," said Gutteridge, "what you saw was what you got." What struck the coach most about Lopez at Indianapolis, aside from the latter's ability to stay ahead of the opposition, was the skill he displayed in evaluating talent. "Guys that no one else saw anything in, Al might find something useful," he remarked. "At Indianapolis, Joe Muir, no one thought he had anything, but Al stuck with him and he did a great job for us. And Les Fleming, people thought that he was washed up, but Al put him at first and he killed the ball."[82]

Lopez also showed early in his third season at Indianapolis that he had lost none of the competitive fire that typified his first two campaigns. While in Little Rock, during the team's annual spring migration North, Lopez was ejected from an exhibition outing and escorted from the premises by a policeman. In the game's seventh inning, with runners on first and third with two outs, Gus Bell was called out on strikes after working the count full. The outfielder, who immediately turned to argue the call with umpire Bill Malesky, was promptly given the thumb, bringing Lopez and Gutteridge into the fray. After a heated exchange took place, both Lopez and Gutteridge, who had entered the game for Monty Basgall at second, were similarly shown the exit by Malesky. But when an irate Lopez failed to leave the premises as quickly as the umpire thought he should have, Malesky called for the assistance of a police officer stationed in the stands to usher him out.[83]

In spite of Frank McKinney's pledge that the 1950 Indians would be stronger than the 1949 club,[84] it never fully materialized. While the team played well early on and were in fact tied for first place on July 4, the traditional harbinger of final standings,[85] they eventually slowed, finishing four games behind Minneapolis. In the Shaughnessy playoff, the Tribe quickly swept St. Paul but then lost in seven to the Columbus Red Birds, who had bested Minneapolis earlier. The final game, played at Victory Field, ended when Columbus first baseman Mo Mozzali touched Royce Lint for a round trip in the top of the thirteenth to win it 3–2.[86]

While disappointed with the loss, Lopez could be proud of his team's having again exhibited its trademark "never-say-die" spirit. And with a pennant, two second-place finishes, a Little World Series victory, and a combined 277–182 (.603) record to his credit, it was becoming clear that he understood what it took to win ballgames and to be a successful manager. While such skills were appreciated in Indianapolis, they were valued even more by Indians of a different sort. Because of this, after the season, with a new regime taking over in Cleveland, Al Lopez received the callup he had been waiting for, a return to the major leagues.

El Señor

In November 1949 Bill Veeck and his partners sold the Cleveland Indians to a syndicate of local businessmen headed by an insurance executive named Ellis Ryan. Hank Greenberg, who had held a minority interest in the club for over a year and had most recently been its farm director, was installed by Ryan as the new general manager. Having little regard for the leadership qualities of the incumbent Cleveland manager, Lou Boudreau, Greenberg sought someone "he could work with." Lopez was that someone, and after the 1950 season Greenberg hired him to take over in Cleveland.[1]

Greenberg recalled thinking that the decision to replace Boudreau with Lopez would be unpopular because of the length of time Boudreau had spent in Cleveland and the player-manager's overwhelming popularity. Also, the press had already reported that Boudreau was going to be re-signed for another season and might feel slighted when their sources proved incorrect. On the night of Lopez's signing, Greenberg secretly flew his new manager into Cleveland and took him to the "Wigwam," Cleveland Stadium's dining room for the press and employees of the club. Greenberg recalled:

> Reporters had come from the surrounding cities and were gathered around conversing when out walked Al Lopez from the men's room into the huge dining room. I said, "Gentleman, here's your next manager of the Cleveland Indians, Mr. Al Lopez." Well, you could have knocked the writers over with a feather. They felt they had been outsmarted even though it

was they who had gone out on the limb to announce Boudreau
as our manager.... Fortunately for me, Al Lopez had played
for the Cleveland Indians in 1947 and was a veteran ballplayer
with a great personality and great disposition. He had been
friends with all the writers and they had enormous respect for
him. So while they disliked me for having pulled a fast one on
them, they still respected my decision. They heaped praise on
the choice of Lopez becoming the new manager but took their
embarrassment out on me for getting rid of a great hero in Lou
Boudreau.[2]

Thus, amid some controversy, did Lopez arrive in Cleveland.

Robert Moskin once compared the life of a big-league manager to
that of a lion tamer. "Danger can come from any quarter," wrote Moskin.
"Victory and defeat hang on fractions of inches and split-second decisions. He dare not wait one pitch too long to lift a pitcher. He must order
a steal at exactly the right instant. Moving a fielder three feet as the count
on the batter changes may save or lose the ball game. Every play and every
pitch is a crisis."[3]

Lopez spent six "crisis"-filled seasons in Cleveland, and during that
time the Indians never won fewer than 88 out of 154 games. Under Lou
Boudreau, the Indians, having captured a World Series title in 1948, had
sagged badly into fourth place by 1950. In the Lopez-led six years that followed, they finished second five times and captured the pennant in 1954.
Lopez had always believed that a manager had to adapt his style to the
material presented. In Cleveland the material was powerful but lacked
quickness. He recalls, "I didn't have too much speed on the [Cleveland]
club. We usually only stole around thirty bases, but we did have guys who
could hit the ball out of the park; Vic Wertz, Al Rosen, and Larry Doby.
So our game was to hold the other side with our good pitching and wait
for somebody to sock one out."[4] This Cleveland squad combined pitching and power hitting in a manner that few teams have ever equaled. The
pitching rotation of Bob Lemon, Early Wynn, Mike Garcia, Bob Feller,
and Art Houtteman composed what many consider the best starting rotation in major-league history. The fact that four of the club's hurlers
(Lemon, Feller, Wynn, and Hal Newhouser) are now in the Hall of Fame
supports the claim. Add to this the above-mentioned power hitters, Bobby
Avila at second, versatile players like Al Smith, and defensive whiz catcher
Jim Hegan and the Indians posed a formidable lineup.

Lopez's greatest asset as a manager was his ability to handle pitchers.

Bob Lemon, the ace of Cleveland's staff, had once been a third baseman and then an outfielder. However, in 1947, when Lopez was a player with the Indians, Cleveland coach Bill McKechnie asked him to spend some time with Lemon to help him make the switch to pitching. "Bill, the only thing with him is control," said Lopez. "If he can get the ball over the plate, he'll be all right."[5] Bob Feller, in his autobiography, wrote that Lemon had what baseball people consider "a live arm," one with the strength to throw hard and to put movement on the ball, but he needed help. Feller:

> Lopez told him to concentrate on two pitches, his curve and sinker, and to work hard at throwing them for strikes. Lopez was teaching him what every pitcher learns early in his career, that pitching is like real estate, the three most important things are location, location and location.... Lopez told Lemon to keep throwing the curve and sinker and to not even look to Al behind the plate for any signals. The instruction was right on the money, and when Lemon cashed in with three straight 20 win seasons right after that, you had to think that Lopez, who helped Lemon so much although he had no experience as a coach or manager, was destined for greater things.[6]

Lopez believed that Lemon should have had a long pitching career but that it was cut short on account of the way he threw the sinker, his best pitch. "He came up with chips in his elbow. It was the way he threw the ball. He threw it in a manner where it jerked the hell out of your arm and caused the chips."[7] Tony Cuccinello thought that over the years Lopez developed an almost "subcutaneous sensitivity to pitchers and their frailties." Cuccinello: "Many times I've seen him start a relief pitcher warming up in the bullpen when the starter seemed to be going along fine, then all of the sudden—bang! bang! bang!—a couple of hits and the starter is out of there."[8]

If there was one pitcher that Lopez had to use kid gloves with, it was the volatile but extremely effective Early Wynn. The brash Wynn was reputed to have been the only pitcher in the league who would knock Ted Williams down with a pitch. He was also known to throw at teammates during batting practice. While he enjoyed pitching batting practice, Wynn refused to use the defensive screen that served to shield the pitcher from line drives. Any careless batter who slipped up and sent one up the middle near Wynn was certain to be leveled on the next pitch. He

June 23, 1951, New York: Lopez stamps his foot as he argues heatedly with umpire
Bill Grieve on a decision in the third inning of an Indians-Yankees matchup. Both
Bob Lemon and Bob Avila came home on a wild pitch, and Grieve ruled that Avila
had to go back to third. (Courtesy UPI/Corbis-Battmann.)

was, however, quite protective of teammates, and if an opposing pitcher
decided to knock one of them down, Wynn would respond in kind at the
earliest possible convenience. Lopez laughingly recalls his relationship
with Wynn, remembering that the pitcher was not as ornery as the press
depicted him. Lopez:

Early was a real competitor. Won twenty some-odd games every year. How could you not like him? But he was a competitor and you know, this one time, he was arguing with an umpire and I went out there to take him out. I had a rule that even if you were pitching like a dog, I am going to go out there in a nice way and ask you for the ball, pat you on the back and you could go in. If you had something to argue about, wait until we get back in the clubhouse. When I go out there it's not to show you up so don't show me up. So this one day Early was arguing with the umpire when I came out there and he threw the ball at me hitting me in the stomach. It was more of a flip, toss, but the press played it up. I said give me the goddammed ball and don't be throwing it at me. After the game he came and apologized to me. I said, Early, I know how you feel but

Early Wynn, center, being congratulated on his twenty-third victory of the 1952 season. Gathered around him from left to right are Bob Lemon, Bobby Avila, Larry Doby, Hank Simpson, Dale Mitchell (grasping Wynn's shoulders), Luke Easter, and Mike Garcia. (Courtesy Cleveland Public Library Photograph Collection.)

the people upstairs, the fans and media, they see that and think you're mad at me. I told him don't get mad at me, get mad at the guys who are hitting.[9]

Lopez tells another story about Wynn:

One day Early had been having a bad day and I had gone out to talk with him. If you went out to talk with your pitcher, then the second time he had to come out. Well, Early was in trouble and arguing with the umpire and he sees me coming and just lets the umpire have it. The umpire told him that if he kept it up that he would be gone. Early said, "What do you think Lopez is coming out here for, to bring me a ham sandwich?"[10]

When Lopez's starters tired, he turned to his youthful bullpen duo of left-hander Don Mossi and right-hander Ray Narleski. The two hurlers joined the Indians in 1954, but Lopez already had five starters, so he moved them both into relief roles. While Don Mossi was considered a good-looking prospect, it was Narleski whom Lopez preferred in the ninth inning of a close contest. Narleski threw the best fastball on the staff and used the hard stuff to save thirteen games in 1954, two more than the entire Cleveland staff had saved the year before.[11]

However talented the Indians may have been, only one team could win the American League pennant, and since 1949 that team had been the New York Yankees. Led by Casey Stengel, who had come to New York in 1949, the Yankees, whose exceptional scouting system continually produced performers who took the measure of their American League counterparts, won pennants in all but two years from 1949 until 1964. In 1958 Marshall Smith poked fun at the doggedness with which Lopez pursued Stengel and the Yankees. Smith:

For as long as most people can remember, a Yanqui desperado named Casey Stengel has been shooting up the American League and getting away with the swag. Catching him seems almost impossible. Not only does he know all the tricks and the short cuts, but his equipment is superb. He has powerful guns capable of firing accurate, murderous shots that make an enemy helpless. He also has the horses, the finest, strongest, swiftest horses that money can buy. If any of his guns fails to shoot straight, he has others cached away in carefully protected arsenals. If any of his magnificent horses gives out, he has others hidden in the canebrakes, waiting for his whistle. With all his limitless resources and daring, the Yanqui should feel completely safe from pursuit…. But he does not. Every time he looks over his shoulder he sees the same relentless, inescapable figure…. He is always there, always following. This pursuer is not a glamorous hero but a doleful, threadbare man wearing a big sombrero…. Alfonso Ramón Lopez never gives up.[12]

Lopez's Cleveland Indians were the American League bridesmaids in 1951, 1952, and 1953, winning 93, 93, and 92 games respectively. His first team in 1951 almost won the pennant. Feller, Wynn, and Garcia each won twenty games and were buoyed by an Indians offense that led the league in home runs. Hank Greenberg felt that this club should have won the pennant, but the Yankees, with better all around depth, captured it by five games. The Yankees clipped Cleveland again the following year, this time by two games. Even Lopez was discouraged after his club finished second for a third consecutive year, 1953. With his insomnia growing worse and criticisms growing louder, he confided to Greenberg that perhaps it was time for a change. Greenberg, however, "would not hear of it." With the Indians winning ninety games a year, Greenberg felt it ridiculous to even consider changing managers. Lopez reluctantly agreed, saying, "If you want me back, I'll be back."[13] The following spring Greenberg responded publicly to suggestions that there was, perhaps, trouble between him and Lopez at the end of the 1953 season. "Who brought Lopez to Cleveland?" he asked. "And I let a very popular fellow [Lou Boudreau] go to do it. I told Al Lopez I wanted him back and that was all there was to it. Lopez works for me."[14]

Al Lopez, Jr., recalls the intense pressure his father faced to win in Cleveland:

> There was a lot of pressure. But I don't know that it was something that was bad pressure. Those were the heydays of the Cleveland Indians. I mean, those were great teams. … the city of Cleveland was just consumed by the Indians. The Cleveland Browns were world champions, but they took a back seat to the Indians. Everything in that town revolved around baseball and my father was at the heart of it.[15]

Cleveland third baseman Al Rosen put together a tremendous season in 1953, leading the league both with his 43 home runs and with his 145 runs batted in. He just missed winning the triple crown by finishing a percentage point behind Mickey Vernon of Washington, with a .336 batting average to Vernon's .337. Lopez describes Rosen as a great fellow and a nice guy to have had on the team. He recalls that the 1953 batting race came down to the last game of the season, and in one particular at-bat, Rosen missed first base and was called out by the umpire. The lost hit proved to be the difference. "The umpire said that he didn't hit first base … if he had hit the bag, he would have been called safe," said Lopez.[16]

Most managers would not have considered Lopez's first three years in Cleveland a bad start. But for Lopez second place was just that and made him even more determined to beat the Yankees. He believed that the 1954 acquisition of outfielder Dave Philley, who had come over in a deal with the Philadelphia Athletics after batting .303 the previous year, and "a bumper crop of Indian rookies" might do the trick. It was the addition of Philley that had the Indians skipper especially optimistic. "He's a good ballplayer in all departments," said Lopez. "Philley can run, hit and field and he's a great hustler." At a luncheon before the Cleveland Advertising Club, Lopez called young players such as infielder Rudy Regalado and pitchers Don Mossi and Ray Narleski "the best since I've been in Cleveland," and predicted that they would "pay off." "I'm hoping to finish one notch higher," concluded Lopez. Bob Feller, representing the players before the admen, echoed Lopez's optimism, but he guardedly pointed out that getting "the right man in the right spot may take a Houdini." "I'm glad that Al Lopez has the job and not me," said Feller.[17]

Casey Stengel, who felt nothing but contempt for the rest of the American League after winning five straight championships, was every bit as confident that his Yankees would take home another crown and made no secret about it. "If I don't win the pennant this year," remarked a boastful Stengel, "they oughta commence firing the manager." When informed by a reporter that Lopez was predicting a Cleveland pennant, Stengel replied, "Did the Mexican say that? Well, you tell the Señor, unless my team gets hit by a truck and my brain rots, he ain't gonna win because the Yankees are." This was in spite of the fact that his club was absorbing its "worst Spring effort in years," losing nineteen of twenty-seven outings.[18]

Lopez and the Indians were "squarely on the spot" in 1954. Many thought that Cleveland could not win the big one and saw it as looking like a champion until the chips were down. Of course, given the fact that the big one is usually the one you lost, such a judgment is often suspect.

Regardless, Gordon Cobbledick suggested the widely held belief that 1954 was the year that the Indians would have to prove themselves. Cobbledick and fellow *Plain Dealer* reporter Harry Jones then picked the Yankees to repeat, arguing that Cleveland's newcomers indeed had to make a contribution even to keep things close.[19]

Lopez announced on April 8 that Early Wynn would start the first game of the season at Chicago against White Sox left-handed ace Billy Pierce. His reason for giving Wynn the nod over Bob Lemon was the fact that Lemon had spent a good portion of the spring away from the club, having been called home when his father had a heart attack. Lopez also noted that Lemon, an effective hitter, suffered a disadvantage against lefties that switch-hitters such as Wynn did not face. It was the second opening-day showdown between Wynn and Pierce, who had squared off against one another in 1952 with Wynn getting the decision. Lopez also indicated that Lemon would go to the mound in the second game of the two-game set, with Houtteman, Feller, or Mike Garcia, who was having an abysmal spring, to follow in the home opener.[20]

In Chicago, before 31,025 fans in shirtsleeves, the largest opening-day audience in Comiskey Park history, Early Wynn went the distance, outclassing Billy Pierce, who left after the seventh, en route to an 8–2 victory. The Indians, paced by Bobby Avila's double and three singles, pounded out two home runs, a pair of doubles, a triple, and ten singles in the unseasonable 70° Chicago warmth. Wynn, the Tribe's best pitcher during the spring, going 3–0 over seven outings, dominated the affair after Jim Hegan's triple in the sixth gave him a 6–2 lead. The White Sox managed only two hits after that. Gordon Cobbledick, expressing faint optimism, wrote that the win proved little except that the Indians were "vastly better" than Chicago "on this day" and could "probably" beat them four games out of every seven.[21]

The following day was much the same, with Cleveland's batters rapping out fourteen hits while Bob Lemon stymied the Chicago opposition, limiting them to three hits — one during the final eight frames — and winning 6–3. Lemon's performance was compared favorably to his one-hitter against the same Sox in Cleveland the previous season. With twenty-nine hits over the two-game series and terrific pitching, Cleveland was serving notice of the potent one-two formula it intended to use during the coming campaign.[22]

The Indians then headed for Cleveland and an opening-day shot at the Detroit Tigers before a crowd predicted to be in excess of 50,000.

Lopez, who decided, as expected, to stick primarily with his big-three pitching rotation of Wynn, Lemon, and Garcia, announced that it would be Mike Garcia who would get the call in the home opener. Some criticized the choice of Garcia over Bob Feller, particularly after Feller had finished the spring strongly, a rarity for him, blanking the Giants over five innings on April 4. Meanwhile Garcia had struggled noticeably, going one and four over seven contests with an 11.35 ERA. Lopez, however, recognizing the "Big Bear's" penchant for coming along slowly in the spring, disregarded the numbers and penciled in the right-hander to take the mound against the Tigers.

In the opener, the two teams took the field but were forced back inside after eight innings complete for a one-hour-and-thirty-minute rain delay. The lights had to be turned on after the delay, a first for a Cleveland home opener, to finish the contest, a 3–2 Detroit victory. For the first seven stanzas, it was a pleasant afternoon with the sky bright and the field dry. Taking their cue from the balmy conditions, the Indians scored a run in the first inning to take the early lead. The Tigers fought back in the fourth, tying the count, but saw it eclipsed in the sixth when Al Rosen launched his first homer of the year into the left-field stands. An inning later the skies grew dark and as Harry Jones of the *Plain Dealer* noted, "the darkness spelled doom for the Indians." After two Detroit batters had been retired in the top of the eighth, with the rain falling at this point, the Tigers tied the score on a single, a stolen base, and another single by Jim Delsing, who had three of the nine hits off Garcia that day. After a brief Cleveland rally was "spiked" in the bottom of the inning, play was halted. It was noted that during the delay, rain came down so hard that it seemed impossible to finish the contest, and more than half the crowd left. But at 6:28 p.m. the order was given to resume play, and Garcia, whom the long delay obviously affected, let the game slip away after walking the first two men he faced. When Al Kaline failed to move Ray Boone over, forcing him at third, Bill Tuttle singled to deep short, filling the bases. Matt Batts then followed with a slow roller toward shortstop that Rosen, playing back at third with the slow-footed Batts at the plate, failed to cut off, allowing Walt Dropo to cross the plate with what turned out to be the winning run.[23]

The Indians welcomed Chicago into Cleveland the following day and came away the doormat, losing 8–1. The White Sox, having lost their first three decisions, chased Art Houtteman with five runs in the top of the first inning, while Bob Keegan, an ex-Yankee prospect, held the Tribe to four hits. In spite of the loss, Lopez did find the play of rookie hurlers Dick Tomanek, José Santiago, Don Mossi, and Ray Narleski to be a "cheering note." "The youngsters looked just as good as they did all through spring training," said Lopez. Tomanek, who had been with Indianapolis the previous season, hurt his arm in the third inning and was forced to leave the game. The injury proved to be a bad break for Tomanek, who because of it lost his position in the bullpen to the recently signed veteran Hal Newhouser. Tomanek did not pitch for Cleveland again that season.[24]

After the game, Lopez also was forced to defend the play of newly acquired outfielder Dave Philley, who had been struggling at the plate. "A fellow couldn't try any harder than Philley has been," said Lopez. "Of course there will be a limit to how far we can go if he doesn't hit, but I'm confident he'll start soon." The Cleveland press, however, lacked Lopez's patience and understanding. Both Cobbledick and James Doyle of the *Plain Dealer* hinted at taking Philley out of the lineup, with Cobbledick arguing for the insertion in Philley's place of Dale Mitchell, who, according to Cobbledick, could do "with his eyes shut and one hand tied behind his back what Philley is straining all his physical resources to do" — hit the baseball.[25] With Lopez sticking with Philley the next day, Chicago scored five runs in the fifth inning on homers by Jim Rivera and Minnie Minoso, winning 6–2.[26]

While Philley struggled, the Tribe's two most productive hitters at this early stage in the season were, surprisingly, Bill Glynn with an "astounding" .667 mark and Bob Avila, at .476. Both Glynn and Avila credited their success to the personal attention given by veteran infielder Hank Majeski, "one of the club's most valuable men." Collectively the triumvirate was known as the "three musketeers," for whenever you saw one of them outside the ballpark, the others were generally close behind. It was the ancient Majeski, then thirty-seven, who after spending twenty years in professional baseball, had taken the others under his wing, providing encouragement or advice when they needed it. "I don't know what I'd do without him," Glynn admitted to Harry Jones of the *Plain Dealer*. "He kept me going last year when I wasn't doing so well.... And this Spring when I wasn't playing much and things looked pretty hopeless, Hank would tell me to keep swinging.... He keeps me awake." Avila, who roomed with Majeski, called it the best break he ever received. "Hank talks to me all the time, tells me what I do wrong. He's a good fellow. Real smart baseball man, too. I learn a lot from him." No one was more aware of Majeski's importance than Lopez, who like Majeski had played the role of mentor/veteran to a number of younger players during his own career and recognized the value of having such players in the clubhouse. "Hank is the kind of guy you like to have on a ball club," said Lopez. "He likes to work with kids and they listen to him because they respect him. He hasn't only helped Avila and Glynn. He has helped other players, too." Tom Korczowski, a rookie shortstop, agreed, commenting that few expected him to remain on the final roster, but because Majeski kept working with him and helping him, he did. "I'll never forget him for it," declared Korczowski.[27]

The lost home stand against Chicago continued a woeful stretch that saw the Indians drop six of seven after their first two victories. On April 25, however, Dave Philley, oblivious to the naysayers, delivered a two-run homer in the top of the tenth, sealing a 10–9 victory at Detroit. The victory sparked the Tribe, who won their next two, closing out the month with a six and six record. By the time they had swept Washington in a three-game series, culminating with a 5–4 victory on May 15, the Indians had moved into second place, a game behind the pace-setting White Sox, with a 16–10 record.[28]

The May 15 win over the Senators came after the Indians had fallen behind 4–3 heading into the last of the eighth. Bob Avila, however, tied the score with a leadoff home run over the left-field fence off Frank Shea. Dave Philley, continuing tough in the clutch, followed with a double. Al Rosen then sacrificed Philley over and Larry Doby singled him in with what turned out to be the winning tally. After witnessing the affair, Lopez commented that this Cleveland bunch was the "come from behindest" squad he had ever had. "No," said Lopez, "I can't remember any team I've had here pull games out of the fire like this one's been doing.... They're hard on the nerves, but I'm not complaining."[29]

Lopez's club continued to give its skipper little to complain about, stringing together nine consecutive victories by May 22. The ninth win came when Al Smith, making the most of his chance as a starter, singled with two out and two on in the tenth inning to edge Baltimore 4–3. It had only been a couple of weeks earlier that Smith, a twenty-six-year-old rookie whose baseball fortunes were at a "low ebb," had been preparing himself for a return ticket to the minors. But when Rudy Regalado was injured in late April, Smith, normally an outfielder, was moved to third base and showed Lopez enough to warrant keeping him in the lineup even after Regalado returned. Lopez merely shifted Smith to left field in place of Wally Westlake, and "Fuzzy"—as Smith was known—did not disappoint. His game-winning hit climaxed a day in which he went two for two, with three walks. "Smith's play has been a big factor in the winning streak," declared Lopez. "He has speed, a good eye and a good arm." Gordon Cobbledick described Smith as one who had been "cleverly disguised as a villain a few weeks back, [but] has been unmasked as a valued undercover member of the sheriff's staff." In fact, according to Cobbledick, Lopez's entire squad was showing a "never-say-die spirit" that few, including himself, believed that it possessed. Maybe it cannot last, surmised Cobbledick, but "a team imbued with the spirit these new Indians have shown is going to require a lot of beating and I haven't seen another club that looks capable of administering it."[30]

Cleveland extended its streak by two a day later, sweeping the Orioles 14–3 and 2–1. Art Houtteman, getting the start for the Indians in the second contest, helped his own cause by walloping a double to left-center with two outs in the twelfth inning, scoring George Strickland. Houtteman's double settled a tense pitching duel with Baltimore's Bob Turley, who had hurled shutout ball until Al Rosen homered in the ninth, knotting things at one all. The win was sweet revenge for Houtteman, who had suffered a 2–1 loss in ten innings against Turley in Baltimore exactly two weeks earlier. It also came on the heels of the 14–3 "walkaway" in which the Indians recorded sixteen hits in support of Bob Feller, who garnered his first victory of the season and the 250th of his career. The pair of wins placed Cleveland solidly in front of their American League rivals, two and a half games ahead of Chicago and three and a half in front of New York.[31]

The win streak, Cleveland's longest in three years, came to an end two days later when the Indians, "long overdue for an off-night, gave one away" 4–2 at Chicago. Two errors, one by Bob Lemon and the other by Regalado at third, led to a pair of unearned Chicago runs and the margin of victory. While the errors in fact proved the difference, it was also Cleveland's inability to hit Billy Pierce and Virgil Trucks that played a deciding role. Pierce, posting only his third victory of the season, went as far as the eighth before being relieved by Trucks with the bases loaded and two outs. Trucks, "rescuing" the White Sox, quickly gathered the third out and subsequently retired the side in the ninth to end it. Cleveland fell to the White Sox again the next day when Chicago's Cass Michaels sent a bases-loaded, one-out single over Larry Doby's head in the bottom of the ninth inning to rally for the win, 5–4. Lopez had recognized that with the bases loaded and only one out, a long fly ball would score the deciding run anyway. So he ordered Doby and the other outfielders in, hoping, if possible, to catch the go-ahead run at the plate.[32]

While the loss pulled Chicago to within a half a game of the Indians in first place, Lopez held to the belief that New York and not the White Sox was the team to beat. With this in mind, Lopez mapped out his pitching rotation for the coming week looking toward the Indians' forthcoming visit to Yankee Stadium. He announced that the "Big Three" of Wynn, Lemon, and Garcia would face Detroit in a series beginning in Cleveland on May 28. Art Houtteman and Bob Feller were then slated to go against Chicago the following Monday, allowing Lopez to come back with Wynn, Lemon, and Garcia in New York. "Call it a tentative schedule," said Lopez. "You never know what might come up." Harry Jones noted in the *Plain Dealer* that given the two recent losses to Chicago, Lopez's decision might seem a risky venture. But on closer inspection, Jones pointed out that Houtteman and Feller both had achieved notable success against the White Sox, while Wynn, Lemon, and Garcia were equally hard on the Yanks. Since June 14 of the previous season, no Indians pitcher other than the "Big Three" had started a game for Cleveland against New York, and in that period they had garnered fourteen wins in twenty attempts.[33]

Lopez's scheduling paid immediate dividends, as the "Big Three" swept through the Tigers lineup, winning all three games, allowing one unearned run in the process. In the first game, a brisk one-hour, forty-seven-minute encounter, Wynn held Detroit to two hits and no runs, winning 3–0. Larry Doby collected three hits in the affair while Rosen belted his thirteenth homer. Bob Lemon followed the next day in similar fashion, blanking the Tigers 7–0, winning his seventh. On Memorial Day, Mike Garcia rounded out the series with a four-hitter that bested Detroit 4–1. Garcia's win was the fourteenth consecutive home victory for Cleveland, giving them a one-and-a-half-game lead over Chicago, who was next up on the bill, and three games over New York.[34]

The White Sox rolled into Cleveland the following day looking to regain first place by disposing of the Indians in their doubleheader matchup. The best they could earn, however, was a split, thereby missing a chance that would not come again. Chicago won the opener 6–4 when Minnie Minoso's two-run blast off Bob Feller snapped a 3–3 deadlock, treating "Rapid Robert" to his first loss of the year. In the nightcap, Minoso attempted to simulate his earlier heroics by doubling in a run off Art Houtteman in the fifth and scoring himself one batter later on Carl Sawatski's single, to notch a 3–2 lead. But the Indians, again displaying their "never-say-die spirit," came roaring back to tie it in the sixth on singles from Regalado, Strickland, and Houtteman. With the score still tied 3–3 in the top of the ninth, Jim Hegan launched a leadoff homer over the left-field fence, putting the Tribe ahead for good. Two more Cleveland runs followed on a single by Smith, a double by Avila, and a sacrifice fly by Doby, securing the 6–3 win and maintaining the Indians' tenuous one-game lead.[35]

The Indians totaled twenty-four hits in the two games, four of them by Bobby Avila, the league's leading hitter, who raised his average to .388, a forty-two-point rise since May 10. During the sixteen-game stretch, Avila "rapped the horsehide," going .432 at the plate. Avila credited much of the improvement in his work to Mickey Grasso, the veteran catcher obtained from Washington in a deal the previous winter, who had been on the disabled list since the spring with an injured ankle. "I swing the bat, but Mickey here tells me what to expect," said Avila. "We talk things over before the games. He tells me who I can pull the ball on and when I should just meet that pitch." Lopez believed it was Avila's hard work in Mexico that off season that brought him around, both at the plate and in the field. "Bobby told me this Spring he really bore down during Winter baseball and I think it is reflected in his hitting and fielding," Lopez said. When asked what he thought his chances were of batting .400 for the season, Avila grinningly responded, "If I hit .400 or even .375 I run for President of Mexico.... Maybe I hit .400 in the Mexican league, but not up here."[36]

With the Indians preparing to travel to New York for the start of a three-game set, Hank Greenberg presented Lopez with additional power and bench strength for his lineup in the form of twenty-nine-year-old Vic Wertz. Wertz, a seven-year veteran, was brought over from Baltimore in exchange for pitcher Bob Chakales and was immediately slated by Lopez for use as a pinch hitter and for "emergency duty" in the outfield or at first base. "I think Vic can do us a lot of good," said Lopez. "He's going to be good insurance in case anything happens to our other outfielders." When told that Wertz had been hitting only .202 in Baltimore, Lopez expressed little concern. "He's a better hitter than that," Lopez said. "This fellow has been a real good ball player and we're hoping that once he gets over here with us, he'll start to go again and help us a lot."[37]

Of course, not everyone within the Cleveland community was thrilled with the exchange. One unnamed Cleveland player was reported to have commented that "Wertz sure won't hurt us — unless we have to use him."

Gordon Cobbledick, the self-proclaimed "big old spoil-sport," wrote that the Indians had traded away a talented hurler to plug a nonexistent hole in the outfield. "Why sacrifice a promising young pitcher to obtain a player who hasn't been able to help the pitiful Baltimore Orioles?" he asked. Cobbledick argued that the Wertz deal would have helped the team more a year or two earlier, before the acquisition of Dave Philley. But with the outfield solidified since Philley's arrival and Wertz penciled in as a reserve, Cobbledick believed that Chakales had more long-term value, especially given the advancing age of the "Big Three." To give up young hurlers like Chakales, said Cobbledick, "is to invite disaster."[38]

With Lopez's "tentative" pitching arrangement having paid dividends to this point, Early Wynn, as expected, was penciled into the starter's role for the first game of the important June series at New York. But it was not the same Wynn who had performed so strongly against the Yankees over the course of the past year who took the hill for Cleveland. On this day, New York scored seven runs on six hits in the first inning off Wynn and Don Mossi, giving their ace Allie Reynolds a seemingly insurmountable lead. But these Indians, as noted by Harry Jones, were "the team of destiny." After New York had tallied all their runs in the first, five Cleveland hurlers held the Yankees hitless the rest of the way and the Indians managed a come-from-behind 8–7 victory in ten innings. Mossi blanked the Yankees in the second inning, Ray Narleski in the third, Bob Hopper in the fourth and fifth, Mike Garcia (slated to start game three of the series) in the seventh and eighth, and Hal Newhouser, who got credit for the win, in the ninth and tenth. New York's seven-run lead had dwindled to 7–6 as early as the fourth inning, the tribe scoring three in the third on Larry Doby's "king sized" 430-foot homer off Reynolds and three more in the fourth. The score remained 7–6 into the ninth when Avila, swinging at the second pitch offered by Johnny Sain, who had just come in for a tired Reynolds, sent one into the left-field seats to knot the contest at seven all. Al Smith, stepping to the plate in the top of the tenth, "duplicated the blow" to win it with another homer off Sain, who had been scored upon only once in fourteen previous appearances. The victory moved Cleveland a full two games ahead of Chicago and four in front of New York.

The next day the Yankees, playing without Yogi Berra or Gene Woodling, and with shortstop Phil Rizzuto ailing from a pulled thigh muscle, shook off the infirmary blues long enough to "halt the Tribe" 2–1. The Indians, with eleven hits in the contest, hurt their own chances by stranding nine runners on base against Ed Lopat, while Yankee Joe Collins's eighth-inning homer provided the crafty Lopat all the cushion he needed. In game three, New York "repelled" the Indians again, this time 8–3. Whitey Ford, who had been beaten by Cleveland once that season and chased from the box on another occasion, was given the start by Stengel and did not disappoint, allowing seven scattered hits in the contest. Bobby Avila's being tossed from the game in the sixth inning for jostling umpire Bill Grieve did not help Cleveland's cause either. After suffering the two losses, Lopez saw his team's American League lead slashed to scant percentage points.

Throughout the next few weeks, the Indians' possession of first place became somewhat insecure as both Avila and Rosen were sidelined with injuries. Rosen, who had been on the injured list for much of the early season, was forced out with a fractured forefinger, while Avila fractured his right thumb and cut his right forefinger applying a tag to Hank Bauer during the series in New York. Gordon Cobbledick reasoned that regardless of the Indians' strong bench, stars like Rosen and Avila could not be replaced and that the club would be helpless and dispirited without them. Dave Philley, however, responding to the crisis, commented, "There is only one way to play this game. You gotta bleed and believe."

This statement was indicative of the confidence that the Indians maintained, despite the injuries, that they would win the pennant. In Philadelphia for a series with the Athletics, reserve outfielder Dale Mitchell asked a reporter how much he thought the Indians would win the pennant by. When the "aged cynic" responded that the Indians would not win it at all unless they got some infield help, Mitchell shook his head in violent disagreement and responded, "We'll win it, all right. The only question is how much we'll win it by. Two games — 10 games. But we'll win." The reporter, who had traveled the Cleveland beat since Tris Speaker roamed center field for them some thirty years earlier, could not remember the last time he had heard such an expression of confidence from an Indians player. "Destiny?" Mitchell scoffed. "Naw, I don't think we're a team of destiny.... I just think we're the best ball club in the league, with something to spare."[39]

The injuries forced Lopez to juggle his lineup more than at any other time since his arrival in Cleveland three years before. Yet no sense of panic ruffled the outward serenity in which Lopez conducted his daily affairs. It was in such crisis modes as these that Lopez, if not his stomach, felt most at home while managing. In fact, Lopez believed that these were just the scenarios that managers were hired to confront. He maintained, as mentioned earlier, that a manager's most important asset was his ability to handle the personnel, keeping them in the right frame of mind. At a time when Indians such as Dale Mitchell might have had every reason to question their chances of winning, Lopez's own quiet confidence inspired them to succeed. He was working to win ballgames, and so could they. In confronting the rash of injuries plaguing his team since the early part of the season, Lopez had made thirty different lineup or batting-order changes, exclusive of pitchers. The versatility of players such as Mitchell and Al Smith allowed him to shuffle his deck repeatedly in almost Stengel-like fashion. By July, Lopez had penciled no fewer than four players into every position except shortstop and center field, where he had used three. Harry Jones noted that all the tinkering had signaled a changed Lopez. "He is now far more willing to juggle the lineup and to experiment and you can hardly question the moves he has made," said Jones. Lopez's lineup shifts, however, represented no dramatic change in his managerial style, at least in a philosophical sense. He was merely confronting the challenge that he was hired to face — doing his job.[40]

By July 4 Lopez had his club back in rhythm and surging, the Indians having moved four and a half games in front of second-place New York and six over Chicago. A day earlier, the Indians, at full strength with Rosen and Avila in the lineup, had come from behind to edge the White Sox 5–4 in fifteen innings. The victory climaxed a three-game set that buried Chicago in third place, six games behind and marked an end to any serious threat they might have posed to Cleveland's pennant chances.[41]

As Chicago swooned, the now healthy Indians turned up the heat, going forty-seven and fourteen through July and August, followed by sixteen and seven in September. In the process, they continued their onslaught of second-division clubs, compiling a total of eighty-nine wins against twenty-one defeats while breaking even with New York and Chicago. With Stengel applying the whip, however, the proud Yankees refused to wilt, remaining within striking distance of the Indians into September. On September 12 the two teams faced off in a crucial late-season doubleheader in Cleveland with Stengel clinging to the hope that his charges might yet catch Lopez's "never-say-die" ball club. Stengel's optimism was dashed, however, as the Indians won both contests, going unchallenged the rest of the way. In the first game, played before 84,587 wild-eyed Cleveland fans, Rosen doubled home two runs off Allie Reynolds, giving Lemon all that was necessary for the 3–1 win. Early Wynn followed with a victory in game two, and a week later the Indians clinched the pennant. Aside from a championship, their strong pitching, Bobby Avila's .341 batting average, and Larry Doby's league-leading thirty-two homers won the Indians a record 111 games that season. The total wins bested the old American League mark of 110 set by the 1927 "Murderers' Row" New York Yankees. In appreciation, the city of Cleveland "showered" the team with a parade across Euclid Avenue in its downtown section. As the breezes off Lake Erie blew through "open convertibles filled with happy Indians," Lopez looked forward to the challenge of his first World Series.[42]

The second-place Yankees finished the season with an outstanding 103 wins, ironically the most ever for a club led by Casey Stengel. Years afterward, Stengel discussed his 1954 Yankees with Maury Allen, trying briefly to explain how a five-time defending World Champion could win 103 games and not capture the pennant. There really was no easy way for the "Old Professor" to figure it. In the end, Stengel begrudgingly concluded that the "Señor beat me and you could look it up."[43]

After losing seven straight World Series, the National League wanted nothing more than to end the American League's hold on the fall classic. The New York Giants, led by fiery Leo Durocher, had finished fifth in 1953. But in 1954 they were transformed into a pennant-winning club, buoyed by the return of Willie Mays from the army and the acquisition of southpaw Johnny Antonelli from the Braves. Mays belted forty-one home runs that season, led the league with a .345 average, and patrolled center field with an abandon that few could emulate or even try. Other contributors included Don Mueller, who batted .342, third baseman Hank Thompson, and veteran Negro League performer Monte Irvin, who combined with Thompson to belt forty-five home runs. Durocher believed that his club was stronger than the Giants' 1951 pennant winners and, in spite of the odds, was confident of his chances. Also, the Giants players, having beaten the Indians in thirteen of twenty-one exhibition games that spring in Arizona, had little doubt that they were the better team.[44]

Sal "the Barber" Maglie, whose colorful moniker came from his penchant for giving batters a close shave, started the opener for the Giants against Bob Lemon. Maglie fell quickly behind 2–0 in the first inning after he nicked Al Smith with a pitch, Avila singled, and Vic Wertz tripled them home. The Giants tied it up in the third on singles by Whitey Lockman and Alvin Dark, Don Mueller's forceout, a walk to Mays, and a single by Hank Thompson. The tight contest remained locked at two all into the eighth inning, when with Doby and Rosen on, Vic Wertz stepped to the plate against Giants reliever Don Liddle. Durocher, playing the

Al Lopez and Casey Stengel, ca. 1954. (Courtesy Al Lopez.)

percentages, thought it best to send the left-handed Liddle in to face Wertz, who had already singled three times against Maglie. But Wertz, showing the power that brought him to Cleveland, pounded Liddle's first pitch to the deepest region of the Polo Grounds, 460 feet away in right-center. No one in the park that day believed that Wertz's smash could be caught. The

The 1954 Cleveland Indians. Top row (left to right): Larry Doby, Early Wynn, Mike Garcia, Mickey Grasso, Hal Newhouser, Wally Westlake, Bob Hooper, Art Houtteman, George Strickland, Bob Lemon and Rudy Regalado. (Third Row): Traveling Secretary Spud Goldstein, Don Mossi, Bob Feller, Dave Philley, Hank Majeski, Al Rosen, Vic Wertz, Dale Mitchell, Jim Hegan, Trainer Wally Bock. (Second Row) Ray Narleski, Hal Naragon, Coach Tony Cuccinello, Manager Al Lopez, Coach Ralph Kress, Bill Lobe, Coach Mel Harder. (First Row): Al Smith, Dave Hoskins, Bill Glynn, Bob Avila, Dave Pope, Sam Dente, Batboy Harold Klug. (Courtesy Cleveland Public Library Photograph Collection.)

only question was whether it would fall in for a triple or an inside-the-park home run. The idea that anyone could get to it was beyond the realm of possibility. Yet Willie Mays, waiting in left-center field, broke on the ball with the sound of the bat, pounded his glove to indicate that he had it, and gave chase. With his back to the plate, Mays, sprinting full throttle, reeled the towering drive in, making a tremendous stab and catch, and then turned and while falling down, his hat flying off, threw a remarkable strike to Davey Williams at second to thwart the "stunned" Indians' rally. After the game, a dejected Lopez said, "Wertz hits the ball as far as anybody ever will, and it's just an out."[45]

In retrospect, Lopez recalls Mays's catch as great, "no question about it." But he thinks that Mays may have overrun it, rendering the play more difficult than it had to be. "He let it get over his head which is the most difficult kind to catch," said Lopez. "He made a great play, but he was coming from center field and then the ball just got over him and he had to catch up. Then he fell down on the ground while making the throw and that made the catch seem all the more sensational."[46] Mays, who later told Monte Irvin that he had it all the way, recalled that he saw it cleanly from the beginning:

> As soon as I picked it out of the sky, I knew I had to get toward center field. I turned and ran at full speed toward center with my back to the plate. But even as I was running, I realized I had to be in stride if I was going to catch it, so about 450 feet away from the plate I looked up over my left shoulder and could see the ball. I timed it perfectly and it dropped into my glove maybe 10 or 15 feet from the bleacher wall. At that same moment I wheeled and threw in one motion and fell to the ground. I must have looked like a corkscrew. I could feel my hat flying off, but I saw the ball heading straight to Davey Williams on second. Davey grabbed the relay and threw home. Doby had tagged up at second after the catch. That held Doby at third ... while Rosen had to get back to first very quickly.[47]

Following "the catch," Marv Grissom, a right-handed American League castoff, replaced Liddle and went the rest of the way for New York. With one out in the tenth, Mays walked for the second time and promptly stole second. Hank Thompson, who according to Lopez had a great series, drew an intentional pass, setting the stage for pinch hitter Dusty Rhodes, hitting in place of Irvin. Rhodes, batting a career-high .341 with fifteen homers, popped Lemon's first pitch into the right field corner of the stands for a 260-foot "Chinese homer" that secured the 5–2 victory. Avila, playing second, had thought the ball so shallow that he raced out to right field to make the play, only to watch as it fell into the bleachers.[48] Al Rosen, later discussing the relative importance assigned Rhodes's homer versus Mays's catch, told Jack Torry that "there's no doubt the game changed after Mays' catch.... The series changed right there. If we go ahead, you never have the opportunity for Rhodes to come up and do what he did."[49]

The second game pitted Johnny Antonelli for the Giants against twenty-three-game winner Early Wynn. The Indians got started with a bang when leadoff batter Al Smith hit Antonelli's first pitch for a home run. Antonelli, however, while yielding seven more hits and six walks, stopped every Indian threat thereafter. In the fifth, Wynn walked Mays

Lopez as manager of the Cleveland Indians, ca. 1954. (Courtesy National Baseball Library, Cooperstown, New York.)

and gave up a single to Thompson. Dusty Rhodes then followed, again batting for Irvin, and dropped a Texas League single into short center, scoring Mays with the tying run. After Davey Williams struck out, Wes Westrum walked. Antonelli then grounded to Avila, forcing Westrum at second, but Thompson scored the Giants' go-ahead run. Rhodes, who took over left field, iced the 3–1 victory with a powerful homer in the seventh, his second of the series. After the contest, Lopez's serene demeanor escaped him when a reporter persisted in asking what the turning point of the game was. "There wasn't any turning point," the restrained Lopez murmured. "There's got to be a turning point," the reporter insisted. "What was it?" "There wasn't any, I'm telling you," Lopez repeated, breaking out of his whisper. "Was the turning point when Doby couldn't catch that ball Rhodes hit?" the reporter kept on. "Now goddam," Lopez shouted. "What are you trying to do? Ask your questions and answer them, too? Goddam. What are you trying to do?"[50]

Lopez remembers game two as a heart-breaker and one that his team could not catch a break in. Lopez:

> First man up, Al Smith, hits a home run. I think, gee that's great. But we just, what's his name, Hegan hit a ball in the Polo Grounds that everybody thought was top tier. But the wind was blowing in that day and Monte Irvin ended up making the catch. Irvin told Hegan that the ball couldn't have missed the stands by an inch. It would have been a home run with three men on. Not an inch, he said. "I gave up on it, lost it." The upper tier in the Polo Grounds used to jut out toward the field and Irvin said that the ball was up near the stands and started coming out and came down barely missing the stands.[51]

Bob Feller claims that the loss of that second game put Lopez's back against the wall and might have changed his pitching strategy for the rest of the series. He argues that Lopez, rather than pitch Feller, who had gone 13–3 that season, in either the third or the fourth game, chose to pitch nineteen-game winner Mike Garcia in game three and come back with Lemon in the fourth. Regardless, Feller, who finished his World War II interrupted career with 266 wins and is considered one of the very best pitchers of all time, did not pitch an inning during that series. "I've never been quite sure why Lopez didn't use me in that series," Feller has said. Feller:

> I've never asked him myself, even though I have seen him a thousand times since. Leo Durocher, the Giants manager at the time, said that he has often wondered the same thing. Lopez never said anything about it [to me]. He could just tell me he thought that Lemon had a better chance to win in the fourth

game and I would accept that. To the best of my knowledge,
Al has never given his reason to anyone.[52]

Feller suspected that Lopez did not think he could win in the series. Feller:

> In those later years, Lopez seemed to think I was doing it with
> mirrors. He didn't seem convinced of my ability. He had trou-
> ble believing that I could get people out because I didn't have
> the blazing fastball anymore. It almost seemed that he couldn't
> wait to take me out if I gave up a couple of hits. He'd almost
> beat the ball back to the mound.[53]

Feller's hunch proved correct. When recently asked why Feller was not used
in the 1954 World Series, Lopez frankly replied that "He wasn't that good
of a pitcher anymore." Lopez believed that Feller's best days were behind
him and asserted that had he felt otherwise, he would have used Feller
more often than for him to go only 13–3 that season.[54]

Moving to Cleveland, the Giants, behind the four-hit pitching of
Reuben Gómez and Hoyt Wilhelm, drove Mike Garcia from the mound
and won 6–2. New York, well rested after having chartered a plane to
Cleveland while the Indians took a train, scored a run off Garcia in the
first inning on two singles and an error. They then chased Garcia with
three runs in the third. After two more singles and an intentional walk
loaded the bases in the fifth, Dusty Rhodes, who was enjoying a career
series, rapped a pinch single on the first offering to bring another run.
Davey Williams' perfect squeeze bunt in the sixth tallied the final score.

The Giants mopped up in game four, becoming only the second
National League club in history to sweep a World Series. Bob Lemon,
whom Lopez was pitching on three days' rest, was routed in the fifth
inning, and Hal Newhouser failed in relief as New York took a 7–0 lead
before coasting to the win, 7–4. Shortly after the series, a dismayed Lopez
described the Giants as a great team that would have beaten anybody.[55]

The 1954 World Series was, to that point, the most lucrative in history for the players, who shared in a record pool of $881,763.72. The
attendance of 251,507 also set a new record for a four-game series. The
loss for Cleveland, however, was devastating. The defeat transcended all
areas of Cleveland's game; it was a total team effort. The Indians' number three and four hitters, Larry Doby and Al Rosen, combined for an
anemic .194 batting average with 0 runs batted in, while the "Big Three,"
Lemon, Wynn, and Garcia, posted ERAs 6.75, 3.86, and 5.40, respectively.

Vic Wertz gave Lopez his only reason to smile, batting .500 and becoming the only Cleveland batsman to hit safely in all four games. This was in addition to the blast that Mays secured. On the series, Lopez later explained:

> We won 111 games that year. Still a record. We never had a real slump all year. There hasn't been any club that ever played ball that didn't have a slump during the season and I think that is what happened to us; we hit a slump at the World Series. I could feel the club was slacking a little bit toward the end of the year. Things were not going the way they should. We had a number of injuries; Rosen was hurt. The last three or four days of the season we had already clinched and that may have hurt us. I still think that on account of our pitching we were the best team, but the best team didn't win.[56]

Despite the loss, it was announced on October 3 that Lopez's hometown, Tampa, was planning a "rousing" welcome-home ovation to honor its favorite-major league son upon his arrival back in that city. Mayor Curtis Hixon proclaimed the day, October 6, as "Al Lopez Day," with a theme of "Al Lopez, world champion citizen of Tampa." Upon arriving, Lopez and his family were "accorded a hero's welcome." The celebration, a three-pronged event, began with the dedication of the city's new ballpark, Al Lopez Field. It continued with a parade that formed at the park, moving east through West Tampa, downtown Tampa, and Ybor City. While the parade meandered through each city section, various organizations paid homage to Lopez with speeches, gifts, and the "mammoth" cake presented at the West Tampa Public Library, colorfully adorned with "Welcome Home Al" and 111 candles, each representing a Cleveland victory that season. As the day's events concluded, Lopez and Connie, his wife, were found taking part in a big street dance on East Broadway between Fifteenth and Sixteenth streets complete with two bands and other entertainment.

During the parade, as thousands turned out, trucks, buses, and cars clogged cross streets at every intersection. A banner that was hung across Howard Avenue read "West Tampa Is Proud of You, Al." Traffic in downtown Tampa was practically brought to a standstill. Everywhere Lopez moved, from the time he stepped from his official car at Al Lopez Field, he was shaking hands with admirers, signing autographs, and acknowledging the plaudits of his hometown fans, many of whom slapped him on the back yelling, "We'll get them next year." Sharing honors with Lopez in the festivities were his wife, Connie; son, Al, Jr.; his mother, Faustina Vasquez Lopez; his sisters, Mary Rivera and Amelia Moran, and an aunt, Josefa Vasquez. Mayor Hixon, acknowledging the love and respect the community had for Lopez, joked, "I hope he doesn't decide to run [for mayor] against me." When it was all over and Lopez was asked what he had thought of the day, he smiled, pointed to his heart and said, "What can you say? It's just wonderful."[57]

Before leaving Cleveland for Tampa, Lopez had met with Hank Greenberg to discuss the coming season. Afterward, the G. M. announced that some changes would have to be made for the Tribe to make another run at the pennant in 1955. When confronted in Tampa with Greenberg's comments, Lopez calmly replied, "We do that every year. We take stock of what we have and decide where we will have to strengthen the team for the next season." Just what Greenberg had in mind with regard to strengthening the club, however, Lopez did not let on. "It's going to be a tough year," Lopez said. "After all you don't win 111 games every season and I don't think we will be that good next year. The Yankees have a great team and will be stronger in 1955. They are still the team to beat and from here on out all my baseball thoughts will be on how to beat them."[58]

This attitude was uncharacteristic of the usually optimistic Lopez. It was equally confusing, given the fact that his club had just won the American League crown in record fashion. But the Indians were a wounded club, suffering both physically and emotionally after losing a four-game sweep to the Giants. Jack Torry notes that "a pall hung over the team that autumn and winter ... [and] by the following spring, the team was still shaken." Rosen told Torry that he thought an "ominous feeling pervaded the clubhouse" because of the defeat and that it might have been time to trade some of the players. Greenberg and perhaps Lopez must have agreed. Rosen, the cornerstone of the previous year's "never-say-die" Cleveland clubhouse, held little hope that things could ever be the same. They were not.[59]

The remaining two years of Lopez's stay in Cleveland represented a "return to normalcy," with his teams placing second to the Yankees in 1955 and 1956. The 1955 club had the best shot at overtaking New York, but it came up three games short. As late as September of that year, Lopez, buoyed by the performances of Al Smith and his relief tandem of Narleski and Mossi, felt that his team still had a chance. "If we didn't have Smith," said Lopez, "I'd hate to look at our standing.... [T]hen there are the two young game-savers, Ray Narleski and Don Mossi, they're terrific." Smith was the Indians' most consistent performer that season. In spite of injuries and sickness, he never missed a game, nor did he complain. The versatile "Fuzzy" played parts of the season at all three outfield positions, third base, shortstop, and second base. "What more could any manager ask for?" remarked Lopez. Smith was also a great runner on the basepaths and excelled at the plate. He led the team in batting all season, consistently averaging around three hundred (.306 in 607 at-bats). He also led the team in home runs (22 on the year), until late in the season, when Larry Doby got hot and passed him. Smith was perhaps most valuable for the cohesive role he played in the clubhouse, always smiling and keeping his teammates relaxed and happy.[60]

Even the play of Smith, Narleski, and Mossi, however, could not prevent the Indians from mailing it in down the stretch, allowing New York to pull away. What had been a late-September mathematical chance at the pennant evaporated in a lapse that left many in Cleveland searching for answers they could not find. William "Sheep" Jackson, sports editor for the *Cleveland Call and Post,* the city's black weekly, wrote that he had "listened to fans on the buses, on the corners, in the restaurants, yes and even at the Marciano-Moore fight." Fans in Cleveland demanded to know what had happened to the Indians. "Did they yield to pressure?" they asked. "Did they choke?" Jackson did not think so, and he argued that the contention itself was "libelous." He believed the problem was that the Indians had been pressing all season long. Jackson:

> [T]hey have been pressing since the world series with the Giants in 1954. Every single player on the squad who played in the four games lost to the New York club have dreamed about it since last fall. They started out this season with the 1954 world series ringing in their ears.... The players heard about it all last winter. They were kidded about it all during the 1954 spring training period. Man oh man these fellows are only human. There is just so much that this old human body of ours can take.[61]

Aside from his club's "pressing," Lopez, thought by Jackson to be the "best manager in baseball," had to deal with injuries and sickness all season long. Vic Wertz was out for a month with a thumb injury. Then during the stretch run, he came down with polio. Bobby Avila, George Strickland, Larry Doby, Bob Lemon, and others all suffered injuries of one form or another. But in spite of their ailments, Cleveland remained in the hunt, and after breaking even with the Yankees in a September double-header, they found themselves returning home in first place. "Fans were jubilant.... But fate stepped in." The Indians lost three straight to Detroit, who were playing their best baseball of the season, and were knocked from contention. In his editorial column, "From the Sidelines," Jackson surmised that the team had simply worn out and then proceeded to question the fans for their lack of support throughout the season, particularly in the Detroit series.

> The fans booed several players unmercifully this year. It was entirely uncalled for. The players resented same. This did not help matters. We can remember the first game with Detroit. There was as much spirit in the crowd as you could find at a "WAKE." The fans were not yelling encouragement. Here was a team in first place. They needed moral support. They didn't get it from the home fans. Why?[62]

With the 1955 collapse emerged more talk of a winter "house cleaning." Jackson agreed that such was called for, "to a point."[63] Gordon Cobbledick was more emphatic, arguing that the team could not afford to enter the 1956 season with the "same dull, drab ball club."[64] At the top of Cleveland's wish list was Chico Carrasquel, the fleet Venezuelan Chicago White Sox shortstop, who was also being sought by the Yankees. Many observers felt Chicago would demand either Lemon, Wynn, or Garcia in such a deal. The White Sox, however, lacking power, were searching for a "long-distance hitter," and Larry Doby fit their bill. They agreed to send Carrasquel and center fielder Jim Busby, a good base runner, to Cleveland for Doby. The White Sox had sought to obtain Doby, whose name seemed to pop up in trade talks every winter, the prior season straight up for Carrasquel, but the Indians, coming off a pennant, had been unwilling then to do it. The addition of Busby to the mix as well as Doby's own diminishing numbers and advancing age now made the agreement possible. Lopez, who was pulled off a Tampa golf course and informed of the news, was said to have been so excited that he shot a round of 72, his best of the winter. While he hated to let Doby go, the Señor felt that the new players would open up Cleveland's increasingly predictable game. Lopez:

> Carrasquel is a good ball player ... and this way we not only get a shortstop who can hit, we also get a center fielder to fill

Doby's shoes. We'll have a lot more speed and that's something we needed badly. Busby is a very good base runner and Carrasquel runs pretty well, too. Both of them can hit and run.[65]

One happy Chicago fan differed with Lopez, wiring the *Plain Dealer* to comment that "there have been too many stretches in late seasons when he [Carrasquel] played ball strictly the South American way; full of zing one day, siesta the next." It was noted that perhaps Lopez could talk Carrasquel out of those siestas — "in Spanish." Doby, learning of the trade while in New Orleans on a barnstorming tour, remarked, "I have enjoyed playing for Cleveland. It is a wonderful organization. I hope I can fill the bill for Chicago and I think I can."[66]

In spite of the rhetoric coming out of both organizations, not everyone in Cleveland was happy with the trade. Gordon Cobbledick reported a phone call that Hank Greenberg had received from an irate Indians fan. The fan in question was an African-American woman, who according to Greenberg, "spoke with deep feelings." She said that she and many other "colored persons" believed the Indians had been unfair to trade Doby. She argued that while Doby may not have had one of his better seasons, neither had a good many of Cleveland's other players. Greenberg, she contended, should have sought to trade one of them. Greenberg, responding to Cobbledick, insisted that Doby was traded because he was still a good ballplayer, not as punishment. He then explained that in baseball, you cannot get something for nothing. "To get what he [Greenberg] believed the Indians needed he had to give up something of comparable value," wrote Cobbledick. "He had to give up one of his better ball players." The White Sox would not have traded Carrasquel and Busby for one of the other players. "Well," responded the fan, "the way you tell it, it doesn't sound so bad."[67]

The trade itself did little to alleviate the fan apathy noted by "Sheep" Jackson at the end of 1955. Cleveland fans, it seems, had simply grown tired of the second-place finishes. Their discontent was reflected in the large drop in attendance from 1.47 million in 1954, much of that coming late in the season, to 865,000 in 1956. Referring to Lopez's knack for coming in second, Casey Stengel reasoned, "The big knock you hear about Al is that he has an outstanding record of finishing second. One great ballplayer could make him recognized as a great manager." Hank Greenberg agreed, suggesting that "Lopez has finished second [so often] because he has had second place material." This is an interesting comment, given the fact that

Greenberg supplied Lopez with most of the material in question. Lopez gave his own opinion on the continual second place finishes. "I'm not a failure, but I don't feel that I have accomplished what I've wanted. I want to win. I keep saying that the Yankees can be had because I keep thinking they can, and I want my guys to believe they can win. I want to finish first!" What Lopez left unsaid was that, for the most part, his players had never measured up to New York's. At Cleveland, he had pitching and power but lacked speed and had an inconsistent defense. Later at Chicago, he greatly improved an undistinguished pitching staff, had speed and fielding, but never had power and the hitting was indifferent. Until he could match the overall strength and depth of New York's squad, he would remain "valiant," but futile, in his pursuit of the Yankees.[68]

With six seasons under his belt as the Indians' manager, Lopez, tiring of the criticism of Cleveland's fans and media alike, resigned. In doing so, he acknowledged that the team's followers were becoming weary of seeing their club finish second under him, and "so he left voluntarily," giving them a chance to finish sixth under someone else. The *Plain Dealer* acknowledged as much the next day when it wrote that in the eyes of many Cleveland spectators, Lopez "had failed to deliver." Gordon Cobbledick, however, while conceding that many of Cleveland's fans felt Lopez to be "something less than the best manager in the world," argued that he was certainly "far from the worst." The Chicago White Sox agreed, and promptly hired Lopez as manager. "He left one club that couldn't beat the Yankees," said a scribe, "to join another club that can't beat the Yankees."[69] But with the chase always an integral part of the game, Lopez could hope at least that his White Sox players would have the "Go-Go" to handle it.

"Go-Go" Lopez

Immediately upon arriving in Chicago, Lopez began tailoring the White Sox and his strategy to the vast acreage of Comiskey Park. In 1957 the field's dimensions were 352' down the foul lines, 375' in the power alleys, and 415' to center. Acknowledging that half the games were played at home and lacking bona fide power, Lopez opted for the inside brand of baseball that he preferred.[1] Smart and fast ballplayers are what Lopez desired the most. "I'm speed conscious," he said. "Speed and arm, these are the basics. I like a running club. You win games by scoring runs and speed is what gets them."[2] Along with speed and alertness, Lopez counted on veteran pitching and occasional power, if he could get it. Having virtually the antithesis of the club he won with in Cleveland in 1954, Lopez was out to prove that there was more than one way to win a pennant.

The Chicago White Sox under Lopez were a team whose entire success was built on the then "anachronistic theory" that baseball is played primarily with a ball and not a bat. They could not hit but they could squeeze an astounding number of runs out of their opponent's mistakes — walks, hit batsmen, dropped third strikes, passed balls, wild pitches, and balks mixed in with an occasional stolen base or sacrifice fly. A walk and a stolen base became known throughout the league as an Aparicio double.[3] Lopez's adroit use of Luis Aparicio, his shortstop, preceded the base-stealing revolution that spread throughout the majors by the 1960s.

The White Sox, under Paul Richards and then Marty Marion, had been contenders in each of the five prior seasons, finishing third in all of them. Lopez's 1957 White Sox changed that, winning ninety games and creeping up a notch to second place but remaining behind the Yankees as usual. For his efforts and that of his team, Lopez was named American League manager of the year in the Associated Press annual poll.[4]

After the 1957 season, Chicago, looking to bolster its pitching staff, sent Minnie Minoso and infielder Fred Hatfield to Cleveland for Early Wynn and Al Smith. Frank "Trader" Lane — both the new general manager in Cleveland (having replaced the fired Hank Greenberg) and the former Chicago G. M. who had brought Minoso to the Windy City in 1951—"powered" the deal. It was Chicago's second major transaction in a forty-eight-hour period. Two days earlier, the White Sox, having turned down a Larry Doby-for-Gene Woodling deal with Cleveland, sent Doby, left-hander Jack Harshman, and a minor leaguer to be named later to the Baltimore Orioles for twenty-four-year-old outfielder Tito Francona, hard-throwing right-hander Ray Moore, and veteran utility infielder and former batting champion Billy Goodman. Lopez enthused over both deals, particularly the acquisition of Wynn and Smith. "With Wynn and Moore, the White Sox have the best pitching staff in the league, if not in baseball," Lopez exulted. And when "I was at Cleveland, I was crazy about Smith. He's a better fielder than Minoso ... and will drive in from 80 to 85 runs a season." Lopez planned on using Moore, one of the league's fastest pitchers, in relief. The practice of moving veterans to the bullpen was one Lopez had picked up from his first big-league manager, Wilbert Robinson, who liked his pitchers "old and experienced."[5]

While Doby was not surprised that his trade to Baltimore had developed, he was "chagrined" that neither Chuck Comiskey, who traded him, nor Paul Richards, his new boss at Baltimore, took the time to inform him of it. Doby told the media that he learned of the trade when his eight-year-old daughter saw the story in the morning newspaper. "I had the family primed for it," said Doby. "I foresaw the likelihood of a deal. The Sox got me two years ago to win the pennant in Chicago and the team didn't win it. I guess that makes it my fault." Doby may have been correct in assuming this, as he and Jack Harshman had been labeled by the *Chicago Tribune* as the "two big disappointments" of the 1957 season.[6]

Regardless of the new acquisitions, the following season differed little from the previous one, as the "Pale Hose" eked out eighty-two victories in another runner-up campaign. The team did, however, improve during the course of the season, particularly from the midpoint on, creating some optimism for the next year. Toward the end of the season, Lopez announced that he would return to manage Chicago in 1959. There had been some speculation that he might retire because of his continued frustration over the Yankees' apparent invincibility. On announcing his decision to stay, Lopez responded to the rumors by remarking, "I wouldn't have taken the job if I didn't feel the club had a chance to win the pennant.... I'm not in this thing for the money. Fortunately, I'm pretty well fixed. But I love baseball and I think we have a good chance of winning this thing."[7]

Lopez's optimism was becoming a familiar tune to many baseball writers, and the majority of them, turning a deaf ear to it, chose the Yankees as American League favorites in their preseason polls. One skeptical Chicago bard went so far as to proclaim that if Lopez could win the pennant with this team he would not simply be manager of the year, but manager of all time.[8] Ignoring the naysayers, the 1959 White Sox, adhering strictly to the percentage techniques of their skipper, won the American League pennant for the first time in forty years. (The last had been won by the 1919 Chicago "Black Sox.") Lopez's "Go-Go" Sox achieved what few thought possible, leaving the baseball world dumbfounded in the process. During the preceding four decades, a period in which every other major-league team had won at least one pennant and the Yankees twenty-four, the White Sox had become more than a symbol for the hopeless; they embodied what columnist William Furlong characterized as a form of "self-flagellation." Furlong continued, describing the team as "a raffish array of peripatetic ballplayers who have moved from club to club with the mournful frequency of derelicts changing flophouses, if with somewhat greater style."[9]

But 1959 was different. The team earned its "Go-Go" moniker with a "jackrabbit" lineup that stole 113 bases, an astonishing number in those years and nearly three times the league average. It was built upon the Lopez-stressed fundamentals of speed, pitching, and defense, especially up the middle. The anchor of Lopez's pitching staff was the tough veteran Early Wynn, who won twenty-two games in 1959, his nineteenth big-league season. His supporting cast consisted of Bob Shaw, Billy Pierce, and Dick Donovan, with Gerry Staley and Turk Lown working out of the bullpen. The double-play combination of Aparicio at shortstop and Nellie Fox at second base was as sure-handed as any in the game. Each led the league at his position in putouts, assists, and fielding average. On offense, Aparicio stole 56 bases; Fox batted .306 and won the Most Valuable Player award.

Nellie Fox was another of those ballplayers that Lopez loved having on his team. But the perennial All-Star had not arrived in the majors with a "sure-thing" label attached. In fact, it took upper-level negotiations between two of the game's overlords before Fox was given an opportunity to prove himself. Lopez:

> Fox originally came up with the Athletics. In those days all of the owners were baseball men and knew each other. Connie Mack of the Philadelphia Athletics had brought Fox up from the minors. Mack had Fox playing first base, which was a mistake. Fox had no power, so Mr. Mack put him on waivers. Back then the waiver price for a ballplayer was $15,000 or something like that and Clark Griffith of Washington claimed him. So, Mr. Mack, doing Griffith what he thought was a favor, called him on the phone and said, "Mr. Griffith, I see where you claimed this young man Fox." Griffith [replied], "Mr. Mack, I need players. I'll claim a guy with one arm or one leg." Mack says, "Mr. Griffith, you are throwing your money away. He is not worth $15,000." So Griffith withdrew the waiver claim and Mack kept him. Well, Fox is on the Athletics and Chicago has got a guy by the name of Joe Tipton, this screwball catcher. Tipton is not getting along with the White Sox manager, Jack Onslow, so Chicago wants to get rid of him. They call Mack and Mr. Mack says, "I'll give you Fox for him." Chicago took him just like that and shipped Tipton the hell out of there, without even attempting to find out anything about Fox.... It turned out to be a great trade for the White Sox. By God, Fox came over there and between Joe Gordon helping him on his fielding [Fox was converted to second base], and making the double plays and stuff like that and Doc Cramer teaching him to use that thick handled heavy bat [which had been Cramer's model with the Athletics] to try and hit the ball all over, they made him a good ballplayer.[10]

Lopez's White Sox began showing in spring training that perhaps the 1959 club had the talent and depth to win a pennant. During the second week of April, Lopez, noting his team's improved depth, declared, "With players like Ray Boone, Don Mueller and Billy Goodman, we can go to our bench at any position now, without fear of getting hurt." With the Yankees once again expected to prevail, Lopez would need every drop of talent his players could provide. Chicago traveled to Detroit to open the 1959 campaign, coming away with three wins over the Tigers. During this series, the White Sox showed that they were ready to pick up where they had left off the year before. Forty-three men took part in the opener, one short of the American League record, but it was Nellie Fox's homer in the fourteenth inning that won it for Chicago, 9–7. The home run, Fox's first since September 19, 1957, was just one of his five hits. That day it was also announced that Fidel Castro, a noted baseball fan, had declined club president Bill Veeck's invitation to attend Chicago's home opener during the Cuban leader's upcoming visit to the United States. In spite of the rejection, Veeck's opening-day ceremonies later in the week promised to be festive. The following afternoon, under chilly 39° conditions, Chicago kept things hot as Early Wynn, "the old man of the White Sox pitching staff," breezed through nine innings, striking out six Tigers batters and giving up only seven hits, to record his 250th career victory. Sherm Lollar and Luis Aparicio, "the young Babe Ruth from Caracas," homered for Chicago. Norm Cash, the strapping son of a Justiceburg, Texas, cotton farmer and the White Sox' rookie first baseman, belted a two-run homer the next day, cementing the sweep.[11]

The capricious Veeck, long considered baseball's ultimate showman from his days with the St. Louis Browns, had come to Chicago earlier in the year after purchasing a majority interest in the club from Dorothy Rigney, daughter of the late White Sox owner, Charles A. Comiskey, for $2.5 million. Rigney and Chuck Comiskey, her brother, had been involved in a prolonged court dispute wherein Comiskey sought to block the sale of Rigney's shares to Veeck and/or to have Rigney transfer enough shares to himself so that he would become majority shareholder. At the time, Comiskey owned 1,041 shares, or 46 percent interest in the White Sox, compared to the 1,541 shares, or 54 percent, held by his sister. Comiskey's petition to prevent the transfer, however, was denied in late April, thereby allowing Rigney and Veeck to complete their deal. Within hours of the decision, the club's board of directors convened and, with Comiskey abstaining, named Veeck team president and Comiskey vice president.[12]

With Kansas City due in for the home opener, David Condon of the *Chicago Tribune* speculated about "what wonders" showman Veeck might have in store for White Sox fans. "There very likely will be music, a few fireworks, or some whatnot," said Condon. While "no midgets," such as Eddie Gaedel, Veeck's infamous gimmick during his St. Louis Browns days, were penciled into the lineup, it was suggested that "little guys" Aparicio and Fox might qualify. In discussing the team, fellow *Tribune* correspondent Richard Dozer noted that "unlike last season," Lopez had made no alterations in his batting order against Detroit, except for pitchers. This was considered a positive sign, given the manager's propensity for lineup shuffling in his search for consistency.[13]

On a day "as bright as a dollar," 19,303 fans turned out on Chicago's South side to greet their White Sox and the new season. Paced by thirty-two-year-old Billy Pierce's six-hit performance, the White Sox won their fourth consecutive game 2–0. Pierce, remarking how nice it was to now have four wins behind them, admitted to being nervous, especially after the starting time was delayed because of fireworks. After it began, however, he settled down, quickly earning the thirty-second shutout of his career. The final two innings of the contest went by so swiftly that beer vendors, instructed to start dispensing free refreshments to every patron in the seventh inning, did not have time to finish their task. The following afternoon, the White Sox rallied from nine runs down to the brink of victory, scoring seven runs in the eighth inning, before falling to Kansas City 10–8. The excitement of the contest was diminished somewhat when the game deteriorated into a "beanbrawl." Barry Latman started it after serving up a grand slam to his counterpart, Bob Grim, when he fired the next pitch into the side of Joe DeMaestri's head. DeMaestri, Kansas City's veteran infielder, was carried off the field on a stretcher and taken to Mercy Hospital for overnight observation. Kansas City's Russ Meyer then retaliated, pelting Nellie Fox on the right elbow and sending that veteran infielder to the clubhouse. Fox, however, was expected back the next day for his 519th consecutive starting assignment. In the series finale, Kansas City got a five-hit performance out of journeyman "feeder" Ned Garver and "trounced" Chicago, 6–0.[14]

With Fidel Castro declaring before the United Nations that "We're not Reds," and pledging to stand by his nation's alliance with the United States, Chicago beat Detroit 6–5. "Jungle" Jim Rivera's double in the eighth inning, following a Lopez protest of Ray Narleski's quick pitch to Al Smith, decided the issue. Norm Cash also added a home run for the winners, providing Detroit the impetus to later trade for him. After a 5–2 loss to Detroit the next day, the White Sox found themselves in third place, two games behind the front-running Indians.[15]

Just over a week later, the White Sox traveled to Cleveland for a two-game set and swept both, moving to within one game of first place. Lopez, calling upon Wynn and Pierce, "the only pitchers among his shaky staff of starters who had pitched complete games," got what he was looking for. Both responded with victories in spite of their team's questionable defense.

Pierce, retiring the first thirteen batters he faced, went nine innings, winning 5–2. He failed to yield a hit until the fifth inning and chased a shutout into the sixth. Pierce also helped himself at the plate, belting a two-run double in the second and tripling in the ninth to ignite another two-run burst. Wynn struck out eight but was hurt by three costly errors and needed the help of former Cardinal Gerry Staley en route to a 6–5 win. With the Yankees coming into Chicago to play two, the White Sox could not afford any more spotty hitting or poor fielding, both of which had hurt them to that point in the year. Regarding his team's emerging penchant for winning ugly, Lopez lamented, "We've won a few games we had no business winning, but of course we have given some away, too."[16]

The Yankees had been shaken the prior weekend when they were swept in three games by the Baltimore Orioles. Posting an unusual (for them) record of 6–7, Stengel's proud favorites lagged behind the league's leaders, dwelling amid the second division. Stengel noted that it was not any one player costing his ballclub, but rather a combination of "a lot of things" going wrong. Infielder Gil McDougald, who had missed ten days after being hit on the right hand by a pitch, was slated to return.[17]

The first game of the Chicago–New York series was rained out. The postponement proved to be a blessing of sorts for the White Sox, for a third of their roster, including Lopez, assistant coach Don Gutteridge — who had played and coached for Lopez in Indianapolis — and trainer Ed Froelich had fallen ill with upper respiratory infections. Reserve outfielder John Callison, the first to be affected by the "virus," became sick in Cleveland and was withheld from the lineup with a 102° temperature. The fact that so many of Chicago's personnel were affected prompted suspicion that it might have been food poisoning, but that was soon ruled out. "In sickness and in health," the White Sox met the Yankees the following day and "gulped a bitter pill," losing 5–2. With Lopez and six of his players bedridden in front of television sets, the remaining White Sox went mildly through the motions, giving the Yankees' Bob Turley his second win of the season. In the contest, Nellie Fox delivered four hits, but he could not overcome the eleven men Chicago left on base. The problem of scoring runs was posed again the following day, as Chicago stranded sixteen men on base. This time, however, Al Smith, who had heard nothing but boos all season because of his poor play, responded by driving Nellie Fox across with the winning tally in the eleventh inning to secure the 4–3 victory. Yankees reliever Ryne Duren endured a miserable performance that saw him walk six, including Fox in the final frame to set up Smith's go-ahead single. Billy Pierce, facing trouble throughout, held on for his third win of the year. Lopez, still down with the virus, was forced to sit this one out as well. But the victory solidified Chicago's second-place status, leaving them a game behind Cleveland.[18]

The following night, Early Wynn pitched a one-hit masterpiece and accounted for the game's only run, a homer in the eighth, powering Chicago past the Red Sox, 1–0. For seven innings Wynn dueled Boston's Tom Brewer on a scoreless basis, the only hit going to Pete Runnels in the first inning. Thereafter he slammed the door on the Red Sox with an assortment of breaking pitches, striking out fourteen batters. It was the second one-hit game of Wynn's career and his thirty-eighth shutout, second at the time among active pitchers. (Warren Spahn had forty-five.) Jim Rivera was lost to the team, however, fracturing a rib during the game, and was placed on the disabled list for three weeks.[19]

Seeking to fill the void created by Rivera's injury and to provide the offense with some additional pop, the White Sox traded left-hander Don Rudolph to Cincinnati for Del Ennis. Ennis, a former member of Philadelphia's 1950 pennant-winning "Whiz Kids," had led the National League in RBIs in 1950, when he drove in 126. To that point in his career, the thirty-three year old had belted 286 home runs and tallied almost 1,300 RBIs. Lopez hoped that he might be able to get the same kind of production from Ennis that he had gotten from Dave Philley while in Cleveland. In another deal, Veeck sent Ray Boone to Kansas City for "Suitcase" Harry Simpson. Boone, however, arguing that he would rather retire, balked at the trade and refused to report to the Athletics. The reasons cited for the refusal were his wish not to become "a pawn in a lot of trades" and that his knee was causing him a lot of pain. Boone's fear of becoming a "pawn" was certainly realistic. While he later did report to Kansas City, playing sixty-one games with them that season, they moved him along to Milwaukee, where he remained briefly before finishing his career with the Boston Red Sox. Simpson, who had played for Lopez in Cleveland and was used primarily at first base, did not figure as a regular starter for the White Sox. But it was thought that he might provide veteran stability at a position primarily manned by two rookies, Norm Cash and Ron Jackson. Both of these deals showed Veeck's determination to assist Lopez whenever he saw a possibility arise. His pattern of trading for veterans to fill gaps created during the season continued and paid nice dividends as the campaign wore on.[20]

With Del Ennis in the lineup batting fifth for Lopez, the White Sox's other offensive sources went on hiatus and the team lost four straight. Even Early Wynn could not pull them out of the brief spin, losing 6–4 to Washington on May 6. In spite of the losses, Lopez remained confident and ordered a limited workout for May 7, an off day in which all regulars were excused — except Jim Landis, who was one for his last twenty-two.

The layoff may have helped, for within a month, Lopez had his White Sox running in first place, one game in front of the surprising Orioles. The club itself, taking its lead from the light-hearted Bill Veeck, was playing extremely loose. Veeck's own antics served to lessen the tension in the clubhouse and kept the players from placing too much pressure on themselves. For instance, between games of a June 7 doubleheader versus the Red Sox, Veeck brought out six cows, two horses, and three donkeys for "dairy farm day" activities, which included a milking contest between the two clubs and Early Wynn's arriving on horseback as a masked stranger. A "balky Holstein," noted as having booted "Sox Hopes in Milking Duel," prevented Chicago from winning the contest when it twice kicked over the pail Nellie Fox was trying to fill. Fox gave up in disgust after his bucket was upset the second time. As a result, Ray Moore and Early Wynn gathered only seven and a half quarts of milk in the three-minute race, while Boston's Gary Geiger, Jim Busby, and Pete Runnels produced eight and a half quarts to win. Also included in the goings-on were several giveaways to the fans, including one hundred dozen eggs, one ton of salt blocks, one thousand ice cream bars, and one thousand pounds of fertilizer. Each fan also received a carton of chocolate milk. Chicago split these games with Boston, and after losing another game two days later to Washington, they were once again tied for first place with Baltimore, who had defeated Cleveland 7–3 before 46,601 excited Orioles fans.[21]

The lead shifted again the next evening as the Indians, powered by Rocky Colavito's four consecutive homers, dropped Baltimore 11–8, while the White Sox topped Washington 4–1. "Soaking wet in 90° heat," Early Wynn limited the Senators to five hits for his eighth win of the year. The contest marked only the second time in the last twenty games when the services of the bullpen were not required. Wynn struck out seven Senators, permitted only one runner beyond second, and "most important," held the "fearsome" Washington bats without a home run for the first time in seven engagements with the club that season. Wynn had the backing of ten White Sox hits, including a "cannon shot triple" by Al Smith in the first inning that drove in score number one, then flowered into the second score with the aid of a Senator's error. Billy Pierce matched Wynn stride for stride the following night, hurling a one-hitter on the way to a 3–1 victory. Jim Landis's two-run double in the ninth inning decided the issue. With the win, Chicago extended its lead to one and a half games over Cleveland, who had moved into second by defeating Baltimore again, this time 2–1.[22]

Through the midpoint of the tight 1959 pennant race, first place in the American League tended to be precarious at best, offering the extreme possibilities of front running one day and cellar dwelling the next. After jockeying for the league lead most of the season, Chicago surprisingly found itself in the second division after a doubleheader loss at Boston on June 20. The *Chicago Tribune* headlines cried, "Kerplunk! Sox hit second division; Lose 2." The losses came on the heels of three others and represented the White Sox' longest losing streak of the year. The culprit of course was again the team's lack of consistent hitting. In the two losses to Boston, Nellie Fox, the team's leading batter, went hitless in five attempts, while Luis Aparicio sat out most of the set with an ankle injury. In the meantime, Veeck was at it once again, trying to wrangle some offense to help his club. However, this time his attempts were stymied as possible deals for Minnie Minoso from Cleveland and Roy Sievers from Washington fell by the boards. "I'd have bet everything at even money we were going to make both deals," said Veeck. "I'm convinced that Cal Griffith could not make his deal, although he wanted to, because of outside pressure." What botched the Minoso trade was the fact that Minoso hit two home runs while the deal was in the works, leading "Trader" Lane to back off. "Trader" Veeck, however, was not dissuaded and vowed to continue seeking help.[23]

Through July and the first weeks of August the American League standings continued to fluctuate among the leaders, with Cleveland, Baltimore, and Chicago all making runs at the top spot. In the middle of the month, however, the White Sox surged ahead and sat alone atop the leader board, three and a half games in front of Cleveland. The lead was Chicago's biggest of the year to that point. The stretch culminated with a win 5–1 over Kansas City on August 14. In the contest, Sherm Lollar "rocketed two over the left field screen," that accounted for all but one of Chicago's runs. Bob Shaw, a third-year pitcher with five career wins coming into the season, gained his sixth consecutive triumph and twelfth victory of the year in fifteen decisions — the best winning percentage in the league. Shaw blanked the Athletics until the eighth inning, scattering five singles. Earl Torgeson and Billy Goodman also ran their hitting streaks to seven games, rapping out three hits between them. Equally important was Jim Landis's eighteenth stolen base, pushing the White Sox' yearly total to eighty-four.[24]

The following night, Jim Rivera missed a suicide squeeze sign in the ninth inning, choking a Chicago rally and providing Kansas City with a 2–1 win. The White Sox, with a "glorious" opportunity to move four and a half games in front of Cleveland, "fumbled the chance through Rivera's lapse." The ninth-inning "fiasco" began with the White Sox down a run and Sherm Lollar coming to the plate. Lollar, the home run hero of the previous day, was promptly plunked on the leg, and Rivera was sent in to run for him. John Romano followed with an easy bounder toward first, but Ray Boone threw the ball past Bud Daley, the pitcher covering first, allowing Rivera to race all the way to third as the tying run and Romano safe at first with none out. Bubba Phillips then popped out to Dick Williams at third, setting the stage with one down and men on the corners. This brought up Jim McAnany. Tony Cuccinello, coaching at third, called time out and jogged over to the dugout for a chat with Lopez. Cuccinello then went to the plate for a discussion with McAnany. Daley then came with the pitch and McAnany executed, bunting it just to the right of the mound. "But where was Jungle Jim?" After making a belated start to the plate, he had turned and fled back toward third. However, Frank House, Kansas City's catcher, was in hot pursuit and provided the toss to third in time to get the out. Aparicio then walked to load the bases and Lopez sent Earl Battey up to pinch-hit for pitcher Turk Lown. But the move proved futile, as Battey fanned, bringing the game to an end.[25]

Why would Lopez, managing a first-place team, risk laying down a suicide squeeze in the ninth inning of a tight contest? Why the gamble with two men on and one out? Did he lack confidence in his offense to the extent that he felt it necessary to manufacture runs in that fashion? Tony LaRussa explains that you take risks during a ballgame to create opportunity. The creation of opportunity, says LaRussa, is the "crucial concept" in baseball.[26] In spite of the White Sox being in first place by three and a half games, Lopez understood that his club was batting only .252, sixth in the league, and so he opted, as an aggressive manager would, to "find an edge" in that situation. As LaRussa points out, however, aggressive managing connotes moves that will fail if the other team executes their response perfectly. This Kansas City did. Left unsaid is that such moves will also fail if they are executed improperly, as with Rivera. In a game where failure is the norm rather than the exception, risks such as the one taken by Lopez often mean the difference between winning and losing. Championships are won and lost from the collective execution of a season's gambles. How Rivera's mistake might effect the year's cumulative wager and whether Lopez or his coaches might become less aggressive because of it remained to be felt.[27]

The next day, the White Sox, still smarting over the late game loss, fell to Kansas City again, this time 7–2. In the contest, Billy Pierce strained his lower back and the ligaments attached to his right hip, sending him to the clubhouse for an expected seven to ten days. It was Kansas City's tenth victory over Chicago in nineteen attempts; no one else had beaten the White Sox more than seven times. With Cleveland idle, Chicago's lead shrank by only half a game as they prepared for a coming series with Baltimore. Lopez announced that with Pierce out, his first two starting pitchers against Baltimore would be Early Wynn and Bob Shaw. Wynn, slated for game one, had won sixteen games and lost seven, while the twenty-six-year-old Shaw was twelve and three. Shaw had become a mainstay of Lopez's staff, even though his "glittering work" was unexpected. Barry Latman, at five and three, was set to pitch the final game against the Orioles. Lopez was also relieved at the diagnosis by Dr. Joseph Coyle of Billy Pierce's condition. Coyle, a bone and muscle specialist, after examining the veteran left-hander, said Pierce should miss only one turn in the rotation, two at the most. While Pierce, with thirteen losses in twenty-five decisions, was experiencing his worst record in eight years, he did have a creditable 3.57 ERA.[28]

Before a Tuesday night crowd of 34,547, the White Sox moved into a four-and-a-half-game lead in the American League, defeating Baltimore 6–4. The lead was the longest of any American League team that year. "Making it still more rosy," Chicago led Cleveland by six games in the loss column. The victory was also the White Sox' fifteenth in their last seventeen games at Comiskey Park. The win, coming in spite of Wynn's premature exit, was garnered largely on the arms of relievers Gerry Staley and Ken McBride. Staley, who followed McBride into the contest in the seventh, earned the victory, his fourth out of the bullpen since the All-Star break. The hitting and speed of Luis Aparicio also played an important role in the decision. The "little shortstop," accounting for three runs, participated in each of the four run-scoring innings. Behind 4–2 after four and a half innings, the White Sox scored in the fifth and seventh to tie the game and then won it in the eighth on a two-out double by Nellie Fox.[29]

Fox's late-game heroics were becoming passé by this point in the season. David Condon of the *Chicago Tribune* had already endorsed him for the Most Valuable Player award and believed that "only the most blinded loyalist would dispute Fox's candidacy." Since joining the White Sox ten years earlier, Fox had become "a Chicago legend." Hall of Famer Rogers Hornsby first made that statement and few disagreed with him. Ted Williams, renowned for his own exceptional batting eye, commented that no one in the American League had Fox's vision at the plate. Exhibiting the heart of a lion, Fox was the soul of Lopez's lineup. By 1959 Fox had played in eight All-Star games, in spite of being "less endowed with natural ability" than many of his big-league counterparts. Condon wrote that while Fox might not compare to baseball's more gifted athletes, he more than made up for it with his competitive fire. Bill Veeck agreed and honored him with a Nellie Fox night at Comiskey Park on August 21, 1959, at which the "little second baseman" was saluted by Mayor Richard Daley and showered with gifts including two cars, a twenty-six-foot powerboat, two round-trip airline tickets to Hawaii with a week's hotel accommodations, a motorized scooter, a fox stole for his wife, $100 bank accounts for his two daughters, and more. The event was called "the greatest tribute ever given a Chicago professional baseball player."[30]

The day before Nellie Fox night was to be held, another occasion was celebrated at Comiskey, albeit on a much smaller scale. August 20 was Lopez's fifty-first birthday, and to honor it a large cake was brought to the field and enjoyed by the team before the game. It was a good thing the cake arrived before the contest rather than after it, a 7–6 loss to Baltimore. The defeat was Chicago's fourth in five games amid a skid that was "reaching alarming proportions." Taken with the prior day's loss to Baltimore, a 3–1 affair, the White Sox were now only two and a half games in front of Cleveland. On "Nellie Fox night," the White Sox displayed a "powder puff attack," besting Washington 5–4 to maintain their reduced lead. Once again, Gerry Staley, making his fifty-second appearance of the year, was called upon by Lopez in relief and proved effective. With Lopez up to his elbows in antacid tablets and Raymond Chandler novels, his White Sox manufactured another win against Washington, this time 1–0. The victory, Chicago's twenty-ninth in the season's thirty-seven games decided by one run, helped the White Sox preserve their two-game lead with thirty-five games to play.[31]

This last victory against Washington presented a good example of the inside brand of baseball that Lopez preferred. The White Sox put only four men on base during the entire outing, yet they prevailed. This was due in large part to sound defense and the shutout pitching of Barry Latman, who struck out eight batters and was unusually tough on Washington's three power men, Jim Lemon, Bob Allison, and Harmon Killebrew. The lone run came when Sherm Lollar walked to start the second inning, unexpectedly stole second albeit aided by Clint Courtney's drop of Billy Goodman's third strike, and then scored on Bubba Phillips's seeing-eye single that just made it past the outstretched glove of Harmon Killebrew at first. Lollar, a catcher, had stolen only four bases on the year and thirteen in his thirteen seasons.[32]

Chicago's two-and-a-half-game lead was trimmed by a game after they split a doubleheader with the Yankees on August 23. They rebounded the next day, 4–2, assisting in the "abdication of the champions" and boosting their lead back to two games. The contest was the last appearance of the season by the Yankees at Comiskey and was reported as illustrating "their retreat from greatness." The White Sox, with thirty-two games remaining, then prepared to close their home stand with a three-game series versus Boston before traveling to Cleveland for a "vital" four-game weekend match.

The anticipation leading up to the Chicago–Cleveland series placed a visible and understandable strain on both clubs. Aside from the league standings, one had only to examine the shared makeup of the two squads over the previous three or four years to grasp the familiar tone of the rivalry. In the front office, Veeck had come to Chicago after having been in Cleveland, while Frank Lane had chosen the reverse. Lopez had moved to Chicago from Cleveland, as had Early Wynn, Al Smith, and Harry Simpson. Minnie Minoso had gone from Cleveland to Chicago and back to Cleveland. The entire scenario might have proved difficult to keep track of and brought certain loyalties into question, but it did not. On Friday, August 28, 70,398 highly partisan Indians fans jammed Cleveland Stadium for the start of the four-game series that might very well decide the American League pennant winner.

In game one, "silent" Sherm Lollar stroked a three-run homer in the seventh inning to tie things at three apiece before his teammates padded the score, winning 7–3. Bob Shaw, battling both the Indians and the "oppressive humidity," went all the way, despite Cleveland's having twice tied the score. Lollar's homer, his twentieth of the year and only the seventy-seventh homer hit by the White Sox, was nearly brought back into the park by Minnie Minoso. On the play, the mercurial Minoso raced back into left-center toward the wire screen that circled the outfield and leaped for the ball. For an instant, Minoso had the ball in his glove, but suddenly he turned and frantically tried to scramble up the barrier. The ball had dropped out of his hands over the fence. Lollar was merely doing what was becoming common for the thirty-five-year-old receiver, having either scored or knocked in the winning run in five of Chicago's last seven games. The seven runs were also the highest total for Chicago's "runless wonders" in their last sixteen games. The win positioned the White Sox another half game in front of Cleveland.[33]

In the second game of the series, Chicago's Dick Donovan, pitching because Ken McBride came down with a case of tonsillitis, hurled a five-hit shutout in leading the White Sox to another win over Cleveland, 2–0. Edward Prell of the *Chicago Tribune* described the scenario as "what may have been the most fortunate and correctly timed case of tonsillitis in baseball history." Donovan, scoring his eighth victory in fourteen decisions, restricted the Indians attack to five singles and, except for a walk, shut down the "fearsome" Rocky Colavito, fanning the slugger twice. Only one Indian reached second base after the second inning, the only inning in which Cleveland threatened. It had been a scoreless pitching duel featuring Donovan and Jim Perry, "a rookie from the North Carolina hills," until Jim Landis beat out a high bounder to shortstop to start the seventh. Sherm Lollar and Billy Goodman each flied out, but Earl Torgeson then slammed a single over shortstop into left-center. Minnie Minoso, who had made the valiant attempt on Lollar's homer the day before, streaked into the area, hoping to throw Landis out at third. But Minoso, in haste, bobbled the ball and Landis scored, just ahead of George Strickland's relay to the plate. This was the only run that Donovan needed, but Chicago's "Go-Go" style generated another that at least relieved the pressure on the shutout. Jim Rivera, playing in place of Jim McAnany in right field, lined a single to right to lead off the top of the eighth. Donovan then sacrificed him to second, followed by Aparicio's beating out a high bouncer in the damp infield that moved Rivera to third. When Nellie Fox flied to Tito Francona on the next pitch, Rivera came home with the insurance run.[34]

After the game, Earl Torgeson, "between pulls on a can of beer," said "It's about time someone gave that guy on the third base coaching line some credit." He was referring, of course, to Tony Cuccinello. "Tony's the best third base coach I've ever seen," said Torgeson. "He's stolen at least three runs for us in recent games." Cuccinello's theft of Saturday's game had come when he waived Jim Landis home on Minoso's fumble of Torgeson's single. Torgeson also reminded that the prior Saturday in Comiskey, Cuccinello had given Landis the go sign when he scored from first on John

Romano's single to help establish an early 2–0 lead against the Red Sox. While Lopez himself was jubilant after the contest, "exploding" from the pent-up tension and excitement of the pennant race, he refused to predict that Chicago had the championship wrapped up. "They're not mathematically out of it, are they?" he asked. "We're still going to keep going like hell. Nothing has been easy for us this year. We've won the hard way and we'll have to keep doing it that way to win."[35]

On Sunday, with Lopez's charges continuing to go "like hell," the White Sox completed their sweep of Cleveland, winning a doubleheader 6–3 and 9–4. Sunday's convincing victories, coming after the hard-earned wins of Friday and Saturday, surpassed Chicago's "wildest dreams," moving them into a five-and-a-half-game lead and rendering irreparable harm to Cleveland's pennant hopes in the process. Upon their return to the Windy City, the team was greeted with a hero's welcome from thousands of "pennant mad fans," still overcome by the White Sox sweep. Lopez and his players, having been advised to expect a massive crowd, had prepared for the hectic greeting. To avoid the jam, the players were instructed to leave their bags after departing the aircraft, rather than retrieve them inside the airport. With the crowd swarming the runway and surrounding the plane almost before it came to a halt, "the jam was on." As the players were leaving the plane, a group of fans made a rush for Jim Rivera and carried him aloft outside the airline waiting room. They then carried him all the way to his car. One of the more prominent signs displayed proclaimed, "Welcome Home, Champs." Another, reading "Saludos, Amigos, White Sox," was assumed to have come from the Latin-American contingent that "worships at the winged feet of Luis Aparicio." While the players danced in the aisles during the flight home, Lopez had been his usual quiet self. He was in the forward compartment "refueling" with some reporters, when one wag asked a blonde stewardess if she would like a beer. "It wouldn't help my ulcers," she replied. "Which club do you manage?" asked Lopez.[36]

Lopez's apprehension over an early celebration proved somewhat prophetic after Chicago followed their victories at Cleveland with two losses to the Indians in Chicago. However, the White Sox continued to play well and Cleveland, lacking any more head-to-head encounters, was put in the position of relying on someone else to close the gap. On September 7, Cleveland won two against Kansas City but remained a distant four and a half games behind the White Sox.[37]

With the countdown begun toward Chicago's first American League pennant since 1919, the city sizzled with White Sox fever. On September 13 Chicago bested the Red Sox 3–1, while Cleveland dropped two to the Yankees, moving Lopez's club five and a half games in front and within six games of the pennant. The White Sox front office subsequently announced that they would be accepting orders for World Series tickets that were postmarked before midnight of the coming Wednesday. Bill Veeck declared that an impartial committee composed of eleven civic leaders and an "average fan" would draw letters by chance to fill the ticket orders for World Series games played at Comiskey Park. The ticket applications themselves were to be sorted into bins according to zones of origin before the drawing took place. The plan, however, had its faults, as was divulged on the first day of the drawing when to Veeck's horror, the first application drawn belonged to a Cubs fan. A "red-faced" Veeck was at a loss for an explanation, quipping, "Now, how did that get in there?"[38]

By September 18, the White Sox were in position to "shoot" for at least a share of the title. With Detroit coming into Comiskey Park and the magic number at three, Lopez admitted that perhaps he was the only "jittery" member of "the White Sox ensemble." It was his hope that his club would clinch soon, thereby allowing him the chance to rest some of his regulars, such as Fox and Aparicio. Fox, who had started 662 consecutive games, an American League record for a second baseman, was removed after he had recorded one at-bat, thereby preserving his streak. At the same time, Lopez was eager to get Jim Landis back in the lineup. Landis, who was in Mercy Hospital being treated for an infected and broken blood vessel in his right thigh that had resulted in an eruption of boils on his leg, was equally excited about returning. That day, Chicago maintained their five-and-a-half-game lead, beating Detroit 1–0 on another Sherm Lollar homer, while Cleveland topped Kansas City 11–2. A few hours after the Cleveland game, manager Joe Gordon, culminating a feud with general manager Frank Lane that had become bitter and public in recent days, announced that he would not return to the Indians the following year. In a statement, Gordon said that it had become obvious that he and Lane could not work together and that he was resigning because the Cleveland fans deserved "better cooperation" in their club's management.[39]

The next day Chicago fell to Detroit 5–4 when Norm Cash, the rookie first baseman sent by the White Sox to the Tigers earlier in the season, spanked a two-run homer in the ninth inning to win it for the Tigers. The loss rendered Chicago's pennant plans stationary, making it still necessary for the White Sox to win two, Cleveland to lose two, or a Chicago victory and a Cleveland defeat. The defeat itself angered Lopez to the point that he became visibly upset after the game when two photographers attempted to take his picture. "You only take pictures when we get beat," shouted Lopez. "Why don't you come in here when we win? Where were you last night?" "We'll be here every day from now on," one of the cameramen said, but Lopez was having none of it. After a brief argument ensued, the two cameramen left, but Lopez was still unhappy. "They shouldn't take pictures when a club gets beat," he declared. "Just when a club wins and you feel good. Why don't they go over and take pictures in the Detroit clubhouse? They're feeling pretty good." Lopez then turned his attention to a base-running mixup that he felt had cost his club the game. In the third inning, Al Smith had been trapped between second and third base on Jim Rivera's smash to right, when Sherm Lollar held at third. "How can you run without watching the runners in front of you?" Lopez asked. "You can't keep running if the other guy stops." Smith's running gaff may have had something to do with the fact that Lopez taught his players never to hold at first when a runner was trying to score. An extension of this, albeit a riskier one, would be for Smith to try to draw the outfielder's throw to third, away from the plate where he *assumed* Lollar would be heading. The problem, of course, is that you never assume on the basepaths, and because Smith did so, Lopez correctly chastised him for it.[40]

By this point in the season, Lopez had seen a lot that he liked about his Chicago baseball team. He felt they were similar to St. Louis's famed Gas House Gang of the 1930s and in a detailed column explained his reasoning to Edward Prell:

> The Cardinals of those years had speed and dash. They didn't steal as much as we do, but they had fellows who could take that extra base. Both clubs had great spirit. We can't match their power, perhaps, because the Gas Housers had Ducky Medwick, Johnny Mize, Jim Bottomly, and Frankie Frisch among the others. But I think we're equally interesting, if not more so. The fans expected the Gas Housers to score. They are not too sure about us in that respect. Our defense is as good as any I've seen in all my years. How are you going to top Lu Aparicio and Nellie Fox and that kid in center [Jim Landis]? Jim's as good as any I've seen in a long time. Our pitching, starters and relievers, are tops.[41]

One of the season's surprises had been the performance of Lopez's pitching staff, especially his bullpen. Its two most important contributors were "castoff hurlers" Gerry Staley and Omar "Turk" Lown. Two years before, these aging veterans, Staley thirty-nine and Lown thirty-five, had been among the most unlikely World Series competitors one could find. Under Lopez and his fellow "pitching scientist, Coach Ray Berres," however, Staley and Lown became the best bullpen duo in the American League. Their mop-up performances were arguably as important to the club as the starting assignments hurled by Early Wynn and Bob Shaw. But on the eve of the 1959 season, neither had shown recently that they were ready to step up in such a fashion. "Lown has a great arm and at times his fast ball matches that of any other pitcher in the league," Lopez said. "First time he pitched to Mickey Mantle, Lown threw three fast balls past him. Think he was thrilled?... When the White Sox bought Staley, he was depending mostly on his knuckle ball. Here he throws mostly the sinker, a real good one with great control. He just shows the knuckler once in a while." Lopez credited Ray Berres with "getting the best from the pitching skills of those two fellows." But it might have been another case of where, as Berres noted earlier, Lopez simply saw something that no one else perceived.[42]

Certainly one of the strengths of Lopez's teams in Chicago was the closeness and continuity of his coaching staff. The core group of Cuccinello, Gutteridge, Berres, and Johnny Cooney remained with Lopez throughout most of his tenure there. While Cuccinello and Cooney had come over to Chicago with Lopez, Berres and Gutteridge had been there when he arrived, gladly remaining. Ray Berres, who had been with the White Sox since 1949, remembers that he was not sure what to expect until Lopez called and told him not to go anywhere. All five men had either played with or against each other for years before getting into coaching and so their relationship came naturally. Berres described the staff in Chicago as "the envy of the league.... We all had similar styles and honored the opinions of each other," he said.[43] Don Gutteridge echoed Berres's sentiments, remarking,

> Our coaching staff in Chicago was the best crew in Baseball....
> Lopez gave us all the free hand we needed to do our jobs and
> we did them. Some managers won't do that because they are
> afraid that you might be after their job. But Lopez was never
> threatened by it. We were all good friends and besides, he knew
> that none of us wanted to be a manager. Everybody worked

hard because we liked what we were doing and each other. That's the way that Al wanted it.[44]

Still needing a win and a Cleveland loss for the pennant, Chicago went to the field again facing Detroit and came away losers once more. The loss was largely the result of Detroit's Johnny Groth, a reserve outfielder playing in place of Charley Maxwell, who made an incredible diving catch of a Jim McAnany drive that cost the White Sox two runs. Many observers believed it impossible for Groth to make the catch. The White Sox stranded eleven runners in the game and made some costly errors to boot. "We had a lot of chances … a lot of chances," said Lopez. "And that guy [Groth] made the catch that saved the game for Detroit." Even though Jimmy Dykes, the Tigers' skipper, was willing to discuss the pennant race and Chicago's chances of winning it, Lopez would not. After a writer asked an involved question about whether winning the flag early or having the fight go right down to the wire gave a team the advantage in the World Series, Lopez refused to be drawn out. "I haven't talked about any series," said Lopez. "I haven't talked about winning the pennant. There's been a lot of talk about clinching the pennant, but I haven't done any of it. I'm trying to win this thing. I'm not concerned with the world series." His chance to finally win "this thing" came the following night when his club traveled to Cleveland in a series promising everything to its victor.[45]

Near midnight on December 4, 1957, in Colorado Springs, Lopez had told *Tribune* sports columnist Edward Prell why he supported a trade of Minnie Minoso, a Comiskey Park favorite, to Cleveland for Early Wynn and Al Smith. "If there was one game I had to win," said Lopez, "my pitcher would be Early Wynn." On September 22, 1959, Lopez, faced with that one victory he "had to win," named Wynn as his pitcher to confront the Indians. The most crucial game of the season matched the aging hurler against Cleveland's Jim Perry. If the White Sox won, the pennant was theirs. Going into the affair, Wynn knew that five of his twenty wins that year had come at the expense of his former club. Chicago had beaten Cleveland fourteen out of twenty-one times that season. But, since sweeping the Indians in that critical series during the final days of August, the White Sox had slumped into reverse, winning only eleven of twenty-one games. With another crucial series about to begin, the bottom line was that Chicago had four games left, the Indians five. The Pale Hose needed only two favorable results in the nine final outings to clinch the elusive championship.[46]

Chicago's decades-long chase ended when the "magic number" turned to zero upon their besting Cleveland 4–2. Lopez, "the first White Sox pennant winning manager since Kid Gleason" led the 1919 "Black Sox," had said it would not be easy and it was not. Al Smith and Jim Rivera hit consecutive home runs off Mudcat Grant in the sixth inning for the deciding runs of the "nerve wracking battle." Except for the unexpected show of power, it was a typical Chicago team victory. Lopez and Joe Gordon, the "abdicating" Cleveland manager, maneuvered as though they were in the World Series. The Indians used four pitchers, four pinch hitters, and two pinch runners. In addition to three pitchers and three catchers, Lopez used Bubba Phillips to sub for Landis in center and also at third base. When the end came, Billy Pierce and Turk Lown were up and throwing in the bullpen.

Bubba Phillips began the two-run rally that broke open the scoreless battle in the third, knocking a single off Jim Perry, who was beaten for the third time of the season by the White Sox. He was followed by Aparicio and Billy Goodman, who both stroked run-scoring doubles to put Chicago ahead 2–0. Woodie Held opened the fifth for Cleveland by drawing a walk, but Wynn, after pitching at least five minutes to pinch hitter Chuck Tanner, who fouled off five pitches, got the strikeout on a three and two count. It was a good thing he did, because Gordon Coleman, a rookie just called up from the Southern Association, where he hit thirty homers for Mobile, beat out a grounder fielded by Aparicio behind second. Jimmy Piersall followed with a single to deep left-center field, scoring Held and advancing Coleman to third. But Vic Power then bounced an easy grounder to Aparicio, who moved it along to Fox for the "handy" double play. After the home runs were hit off Grant in the sixth, Phillips singled, but Wynn forced him at second and was in turn forced by Aparicio for the third out.

After pushing a run across in the bottom of the sixth, Gary Bell, Cleveland's third pitcher, sailed through the White Sox without interruption in the seventh. But Bob Shaw, on in relief of Wynn, struggled. After eliminating the Indians' third and fourth pinch batters, Jimmy Piersall "rifled" a single through Shaw's legs into center field. Power followed, beating out a high bounder to Fox, who charged it in front of second base but failed to handle the ball on the short hop. With the noise in Cleveland Stadium at a "deafening" pitch, Tito Francona grounded sharply to Fox, who after bobbling it, recovered in time to get him at first for the third out. It was Chicago's defense in the ninth inning that finally proved fatal to Cleveland. The Indians half of the inning began quietly enough when Fox drifted back on the grass to his left for Held's popup. But then, with two strikes on him, Jim Baxes lined a single off Shaw's glove that was run down by Fox behind second, but not in time for the out. Harshman then delivered a single to right that sent Ray Webster, running for Baxes, to third. Piersall followed with a single that hit in front of the busy Fox, "squirting off his glove," filling the bases. Lopez, having seen enough, then emerged slowly from the dugout, gave Shaw a friendly tap, and waited for the automobile carrying Gerry Staley to pass through the outfield grass to deliver his reliever. With the bases loaded and one out, Staley answering his sixty-fifth summons of the year, threw one pitch, "a sinker low and outside," to the always dangerous Vic Power. Power, refusing to go the other way, grounded up the middle to Aparicio, who after considering the toss to Fox at second, "flashed three or four steps, hit the base with his spikes, and rifled the ball to Ted Kluszewski at first base" for the six-three game-ending double play. With an elated Lopez "shouting for joy" and leading the charge, the White Sox stormed out of their dugout, pounding and hugging Staley in jubilation.

Early Wynn and Billy Goodman, who had been "relieved of their duties" earlier in the day, were listening to the final inning on the radio in the clubhouse with three dozen reporters and newsreel and television men. As Aparicio made the play that ended it, Wynn, dragging nervously on a cigarette, jumped to his feet shouting "One pitch!" Earl Torgeson, the first player to reach the room, was promptly mobbed by Goodman. Earl Battey, talking to no one in particular, shouted "Yes sir, Whooo-e-e-e. What a heart attack." Don Gutteridge was pounding Ray Berres on the back, and all over the room people were jostling each other, shouting, laughing, shaking hands, being interviewed, photographed, and hugged. Staley, commenting on the fateful sinker ball thrown to Power and watching Aparicio make the play, said, "It was the most wonderful feeling I ever had." An animated Lopez, coming into the clubhouse, spotted a Chicago reporter, pointed a finger, and announced, "Now we won the pennant. It wasn't a blankety bit easy. Can you print that?"[47]

Lopez also indicated, as was his norm, that he would be back the following season to manage the White Sox. "If we had lost," said Lopez, "I would have quit. Now I guess I'll have to sit down and talk to Bill Veeck within the next few days." Veeck, who called Lopez's 1959 managing performance the "best job I have ever seen," was no doubt glad to hear it. Before the World Series commenced, Veeck signed Lopez to "the biggest contract of any White Sox player or manager in history." Veeck, who declined to hint at the deal's financial figure, said the contract was for one year because Lopez wanted it that way. "I think maybe the reason he didn't want a longer contract is that he enjoys this flurry each fall," said Veeck. Estimates on Lopez's salary ranged from $50,000 to $60,000. It was believed to have been around $40,000 for the previous three seasons.[48]

The White Sox victory indirectly caused near panic among thousands of Chicago residents who believed an air raid was under way when allegedly unauthorized sirens blared at 10:30 p.m. announcing the win. One man told the *Chicago Tribune* that upon hearing the sirens he jumped into his car and headed for Wisconsin, while another claimed to have gone into a closet "with a bottle of beer." One logical individual reasoned that there would be no air raid because Nikita Khrushchev was then visiting Iowa. Undeterred by the threat — just as they had after the Cleveland series in August — an estimated 25,000 faithful turned out in force to greet their heroes' arrival at Midway airport in Chicago. Mayor Richard J. Daley, caught up in the euphoria of the victory, brushed aside questions about the sirens and a possible federal probe into the matter, saying the city council had authorized it. "This is a great night in the history of Chicago," Daley beamed. The crowd at the airport agreed, many hanging from rooftops, telephone poles, and the tops of buses, cars, and trucks. There was at least one sign recommending Al Lopez for president of the United States.[49]

Chicago's opponent in the 1959 World Series was the Los Angeles Dodgers. Having moved to California from Brooklyn two years earlier, the Dodgers boasted a strong lineup featuring Brooklyn holdovers Gil Hodges, Carl Furillo, and "Duke" Snider and young pitchers Johnny Podres, Don Drysdale, and Sandy Koufax. Walter Alston, the Dodger manager, however, opted to open the series with journeyman hurler Roger Craig. While Alston may have preferred to use Drysdale or Podres in the opener, his staff had been worn thin under the pressures of the National League pennant race. Through the stretch, Los Angeles had been shuttling back and forth across the country almost daily. They closed out their regular season at home, flew to Milwaukee that same night for a league playoff game against the Braves, winning 3–2, then back to Los Angeles a day later, winning again 6–5. With just one day to rest and prepare, they had to travel to Chicago for the start of the series. Because of this, the White Sox were listed as early six-to-five favorites.[50]

The late-season strain may have taken its toll on Los Angeles, for it was a "listless crew in Dodger blue" that took the field in Comiskey Park for game one. Craig was simply ineffective. The White Sox chased him in the third inning after building a 9–0 lead assisted by two Duke Snider "misplays," then put two more runs across in the fourth. Ted Kluszewski, the powerful veteran first baseman who had come to Chicago from Pittsburgh in late August, led the attack with a single and two home runs that drove in five runs. His second homer was a "terrific liner" off a Chuck Churn fastball, landing against the facade separating the upper and lower decks. Jim Landis, who hit safely in the first, third, and fourth innings, was on base each time "Big Klu" connected. The Dodgers' offense, meanwhile, offered no response. Lopez's seasoned tandem of Early Wynn and Gerry Staley shut them out on eight hits for a huge 11–0 decision. Wynn, loser of his only World Series start while in Cleveland, exhibited sharp control, striking out six and walking one. Three of the Dodgers' six singles off him were in the infield, with three runners reaching second and none third.[51]

Getting some much-needed rest after their opening loss, the Dodgers fought back the next day to win 4–3. Chicago again jumped out to an early lead, scoring two runs in the first off Johnny Podres, Brooklyn's 1955 World Series hero. The Dodgers, however, awoke when Charlie Neal homered off Bob Shaw in the fifth inning. In the sixth, with two out, Chuck Essegian, pinch hitting for Podres, belted a home run to tie the score at two apiece. Jim Gilliam then walked and Neal hit his second homer of the day, putting the Dodgers ahead. Larry Sherry, a twenty-four-year-old right-hander who had rescued Alston's club during the playoff series with the Braves and was a high school teammate of the White Sox' Barry Latman, was then called upon to close the door on Chicago. He had his back to the wall in the eighth inning, however, when Kluszewski and Sherm Lollar singled for the Sox. But when Al Smith doubled to deep left-center, scoring Torgeson, who was on for Kluszewski, Sherm Lollar, being waved in by Cuccinello, raced home only to be nailed at the plate on short-stop Maury Wills's relay to catcher Johnny Roseboro. Cuccinello's aggressiveness ran the White Sox out of the inning, the game, and possibly the series. Sherry, who may have been rattled with no outs and the tying and go-ahead runs on second and third, calmly closed out the inning and went the rest of the way for the Dodgers, emerging as the series' most dominant performer.[52]

In the locker room, Cuccinello "didn't wait for the question" about the game's defining moment. "I sent him all the way," he said. "He's running on the 3-2 pitch.... I figure the way the ball's hit he's got to score.

I was watching the ball, not Lollar, and didn't know he slowed up at second. So I kept waving him on. I was yelling, 'go! go!' I know if they throw to third he's got to score and if they throw to the plate, Smith will be at third with the winning run." A reporter then asked Cuccinello when he knew that the Dodgers had Lollar on the play. "When he went by me, then I could tell," Cuccinello responded. "If I'd figured the relay was going to be done that way, I wouldn't have sent him in." When Lollar was asked why he had hesitated at second, he responded, "I thought there was a chance it might be caught. I couldn't tell, so I stopped dead at second. Otherwise, if he does catch it, I have no chance to get back to first." Al Smith agreed with Cuccinello on the call. "I'm no coach or anything," said Smith, "but I thought Cuccinello figured since there wasn't anybody out he'd gamble and get him home, then I'm at third with the winning run." Don Gutteridge, who was coaching first, also agreed, remarking that "you couldn't blame Tony." "I don't believe that Tony saw Lollar hesitate, he was watching the ball at that point. We had very few runners over the course of the year who were thrown out at home and Tony, who was a very good third base coach, sent them, but on that play it hurt us."[53]

Lopez, sitting "ghostlike" for his postgame interview, acknowledged that Lollar, his catcher, had slowed up at second when left fielder Wally Moon decoyed as though he might make the play, but agreed with Cuccinello's decision to send him. "Tony was watching the ball and figured Lollar was going to score. With his eye on the ball, Tony couldn't see that Lollar had hesitated, so he kept waving Lollar on. He figured that Lollar would score behind Torgeson and that on the throw to the plate, Smith would move to third with the winning run. I can't criticize Tony. It was the right play." But it didn't work, and so an aggressive play, checked flawlessly by the opponent, was stopped. The irony of the play is that Cuccinello, by yelling for Lollar to "go! go!" hung his team on its own nickname, possibly costing them the series.[54]

After an open date for travel, the series resumed before a crowd larger than 90,000 at the Los Angeles Memorial Coliseum. The Coliseum, originally constructed for college football games and later used as a track-and-field venue for the 1932 Olympics, was a terrible baseball facility. Its fences, dismally one-sided, measured 251.6 feet in left field and 390 in right. The shallow left-field porch was protected by a screen that extended 140 feet into left-center field from the foul pole. The screen was forty-two feet high, and began sloping to the ground at a 30° angle from the 320 mark to 348, or for a distance of twenty-four feet. Baseball Commissioner Ford

Frick had attempted to order the Dodgers to construct a second screen in left, in the seats at 333 feet, to make home runs more difficult to come by. He argued that a ball clearing both screens would constitute a home run, while a ball passing over only the first would be a ground rule double. The California Earthquake Code, however, made construction of the second screen illegal. The concrete outfield wall at the screen's base was also misshapen. In left-center it jutted out twice where its height changed. In right, it sloped sharply away from home plate, creating a situation in which a long drive near the foul line would be an out, but a shorter fly right down the line would be a homer. The Coliseum's irregular foul territory consisted of a "tremendously" large area on the third-base side, but almost none along first.[55]

In this misshapen arena and facing a mounting Dodgers attack, Lopez's charges began to waver. Carl Furillo, "the Reading Rifle," emerged as the Dodger hero in game three, breaking open a scoreless tie in the seventh with a two-run, pinch-hit single. Larry Sherry, again on for Alston and getting stronger as the series progressed, recorded his second consecutive save in relief, this time for Don Drysdale, who earned the 3–1 victory. The next day, game one starters Roger Craig and Early Wynn faced off again, but with a different result. Los Angeles chased Wynn in the third inning when, with two outs, they were able to push four runs across. Craig, who was in frequent trouble, managed to fend off the White Sox until the seventh, when Sherm Lollar, with a run in, two on, and two out, launched a game-tying homer. Alston, not hesitating, looked again to Larry Sherry, who did not disappoint, holding Chicago in check from then on. Gil Hodges later blasted a Gerry Staley pitch just to the right of the screen in left-center, sealing the 4–3 victory for the Dodgers.[56]

In game five, the White Sox, down to their last breath and playing before a record crowd of 92,706, scratched out the victory in typical fashion, winning 1–0. The lone Chicago score came off Sandy Koufax in the fourth inning when Nelson Fox singled, moved to third on a base hit by Landis, and came home on Lollar's double-play grounder. The Dodgers were threatening in their half of the seventh, when with two out, two men on, and Charlie Neal up, Lopez sent Jim Rivera in to replace Al Smith in right field. "Jungle Jim" responded by making the play of the game, a running over-the-shoulder catch of Neal's long drive to right that ended the inning, thereby preserving the lead. Lopez, downplaying the move, remarked, "I just wanted to get Al Smith into left field because he was more used to playing the screen, and we figured that Neal would hit that way instead of to right." Alston, however, praised Lopez for the decision, judging that he "made the right move at the right time."[57]

The victory was again threatened in the eighth inning when Carl Furillo, whose pinch single had doomed Chicago in game three, stepped to the plate against "Deliberate" Dick Donovan, on in relief, with the sacks full and one out. Donovan was the third pitcher Lopez had sent out that day, following Bob Shaw, who had "shackled the Dodgers" over seven and a third, and Billy Pierce, who was lifted after intentionally walking Rip Repulski to load the bases. Donovan, recognizing that "it was all or nothing," threw a ball on his first pitch to Furillo. It was "the only pitch that wasn't exactly where he wanted it to be during the one and two thirds trying innings he worked." Furillo next took a strike. He followed by lifting a high foul ball that hit the screen just off the fingertips of Sherm Lollar. With Wally Moon lurking menacingly down the third-base line, Donovan fed Furillo the low fastball "he wanted to deliver," causing the Dodger to pop it up to Bubba Phillips at third for the important second out. With Don Zimmer coming to the plate, Sherm Lollar went to the mound to discuss strategy with his pitcher. Whatever he said must have worked, because "suddenly," Al Smith was making a catch on Zimmer's fly to deep center field and the White Sox were out of the inning. Donovan went out again to protect the slim one-run margin after White Sox batters were summarily set down in the ninth. Before leaving the dugout, Lopez admonished him to "Get it over, and keep it low." Donovan, purposeful by nature, was determined to concentrate "on the guy at the plate and what I was going to give him." Larry Sherry, stepping into a pinch hitter's role, led off the inning grounding to Phillips at third for the first out. Junior Gilliam then grounded out the other way to Fox at second, and Donovan retired Charlie Neal for out number three, thus preserving the win. After the game Lopez confidently exclaimed, "I said if we won this one, we'd win the series, and that's still the way I feel!" He had reason to be optimistic with the series moving back to Chicago and Early Wynn, his stopper, scheduled to start game six with Lown and Staley in relief if needed. Alston looked to counter with his ace, Johnny Podres, the winner of game two.[58]

Contrary to what Lopez might have expected, the change in venue offered little in the way of a White Sox advantage. In game six, the series finale, Larry Sherry once again proved to be the difference, pitching five and two-thirds scoreless innings in relief of Podres to assure the 9–3 win. Sherry ultimately finished all four of the Dodgers victories, winning two and saving the others. In all he pitched twelve and two-thirds innings, yielding only one run and eight hits, and was named the series' most valuable player.[59]

After the series, Lopez was again honored by Tampa with a celebration welcoming him and his family home. The city held a parade as it had done in 1954, and several presentations were made; Lopez was even sworn in as a deputy sheriff in the West Tampa Sheriff's Association. In Tampa, Lopez responded to reports that Bill Veeck was talking trade with anyone who would listen in an attempt to add punch to the Chicago lineup by insisting that the White Sox could win again and with the same lineup. "We've got some young ball players and if they can come through for us they'll help tremendously," said Lopez. When asked about the series, Lopez offered no excuses, nor did he judge Lollar's being thrown out at the plate in game two as the series turning point. "We just didn't hit with men on base," said Lopez. "We had bad playing conditions at the Coliseum, but mainly we just didn't hit at the right time." One of the reasons the White Sox did not hit was the effectiveness of the Dodgers pitching staff, particularly Larry Sherry, whom Lopez conceded was "the big difference." "He just stopped us every time we thought we could get going throughout the whole series," said Lopez.[60]

In retrospect, Lopez recalls the 1959 series as another when the unexpected player rose to the occasion, carrying his team to victory:

> That happens in the World Series. You watch the World Series and there are always one or two guys that you don't expect to do any trouble, you know, do the harm, and those are the guys that kill you. The stars never hurt you that much because, I guess, you concentrate more on those guys. We had never heard of that pitcher [Sherry]. We never heard of him and he came up there and by God he was striking everybody out. They had a guy by the name of Charlie Neal, second base, did a tremendous job. He hit everything. [Neal batted .370 in the series.] Roseboro, our report was that he had a strong arm but was a little erratic. We had a good running ball club. But every time somebody tried to run, he made a perfect throw — every time![61]

Upon being asked whether in hindsight there was anything he thought that he might have done differently, Lopez responded, "Nothing. I always tried to give the best I had. Tried to work percentages and I don't think there was anything different that I could have done."[62] Lopez might have

done more homework, given time, on some of the lesser-known princi-
pals he spoke of. While Sherry was thought by many to be a minor-league
"flop," he had rebounded nicely that season after learning to throw a slider
in Venezuela the prior winter. "I wanted a third pitch, one that would come
off the fast ball," Sherry recalled. Using the slider, Sherry had been very
effective for the Dodgers down the stretch. His seven and two-thirds of
"stalwart relief" against the Braves in the first game of the National League
playoff series proved indicative of what awaited Lopez and the White Sox.
Lopez, who attended at least part of the Dodgers–Braves series, must have
dismissed Sherry's performance as a rarity and left it at that. The Dodgers'
Charlie Neal, however, had hit .287 that season batting leadoff, belted
nineteen home runs, and collected a league-leading eleven triples. His
fourth-inning homer off the Braves' Lew Burdette in game two of the series
with Milwaukee proved decisive. With numbers such as these, it is difficult
to imagine how Lopez might have overlooked him. But, in the manager's
defense, there were of course other players, the "stars," to consider.[63]

In recounting the 1959 season, Lopez remembers most the gladness
he found when running his team. "That club took managing and I enjoyed
that. It took a lot of time to squeeze a run here and get a run there. We
didn't have much power you know. Every game in Chicago you had to
struggle to win. You had to play advantages and maneuver around to try
and win it. But that is how you play the game."[64] Both Gutteridge and
Berres agreed, remarking that it was a team that relied on good defense
and pitching and made few mistakes while exhibiting exceptional "harmony."[65]

There was at least one instance that year when Lopez was called upon
to give the kind of order that is not always detected by casual observers.
Lopez:

> There was this pitcher, he wore these real thick glasses and for
> whatever reason he didn't like our center fielder, Jim Landis.
> He used to knock poor Landis down every time he faced him.
> What the hell was that pitcher's name? Anyway, we were in
> spring training and Landis came to bat against him and damned
> if he doesn't knock him down again. I say, "Holy Jesus," here
> Landis is on the ground, and I go over to him and asked if he
> was all right, because it burned me up. It burns you up when
> they knock one of your players down during the regular sea-
> son, but in spring training, my God. What the hell was the
> name of that goofy guy? I told Yogi to tell him that the next

time he throws at Landis, I'm going to get somebody to throw
at him, because pitchers hit in those days. I guess Yogi told him
but then the season started and early on the Yankees came over
to Chicago to play us and Casey brings him, Ryne Duren, in
to pitch. Well the first time Landis comes up, Duren throws
at him again, with a 7–1 lead! By God I called down to the
bullpen and I said, "Get me someone down there, I want him
drilled in the ribs." There were no volunteers except for this
young Cuban boy name of Rodolfo Arias. He volunteered sure
enough. I spoke to him in Spanish, because he couldn't speak
English. He was a lefty and I had wanted a right-handed sinker
ball pitcher [Staley?] because a sinker in the ribs hurts more.
So I put him in and instructed him to make the first pitch outside so Duren wouldn't be suspicious. So Arias puts the first
pitch outside, but the next one comes inside real tight and I
guess it must have dawned on Duren because he looks over at
me in the dugout. I said, "Yeah, you Godamned right we're
gonna getcha." The next one hits Duren high on the hip bone
and he yelled to Arias, "You son of a bitch, wait until you come
up." But I said from the dugout, "You ain't gonna get him
because I'm taking him out."[66]

Lopez also recalls a special honor he received after the season in the
form of a personal note from one of baseball's immortals. "After the season was over Ty Cobb wrote me a real nice letter congratulating me on
managing the way I did, the old-fashioned way. He claimed that was how
they managed in the old days, scrap for a run, bunt, steal."[67]

"This club," said Lopez, immediately after the 1959 World Series,
"with only a little help, is good enough to win the pennant again." Unfor-
tunately for Lopez, the help never arrived. Over the next three seasons,
White Sox fortunes steadily declined as they dropped to third, fourth, and
fifth place respectively. They simply did not have the talent to keep pace
with the resurgent New York Yankees or emerging powers such as Detroit
and Baltimore. However, in 1963 and 1964, Lopez again surprised the
pundits by spurring his troops to second-place finishes, chasing the Yankees up to the wire before conceding the pennant (one game behind in
1964). During the 1963 season, Lopez introduced a new wrinkle into his
repertoire, involving the American League rule requiring that pitchers take
their place in the on-deck circle while awaiting their time at bat. During
a July 28 encounter at Baltimore, Lopez sent infielder Al Weis to the on-
deck circle in place of pitcher Gary Peters during the fifth inning. When

protests were lodged by Orioles manager Billy Hitchcock, they were turned
down by umpire Nestor Chylak who explained, "I can't tell Lopez or any
other manager how to manage his club. As far as I could tell, Lopez wanted
to use Weis as a pinch hitter. But a pinch hitter isn't officially in the game
until he steps to the plate." The maneuver gave Peters a few minutes' extra
rest in the shade while winning 4–1. It also clearly indicated that Lopez's
desire to win and to seek every advantage for his club had not waned.[68]

To Lopez, however, there was a noticeable difference in the players
during these years. No longer were they, in general, as concerned with the
welfare of the team and winning ballgames as he felt they should have
been. In the 1960s, issues involving race, politics, economics, and personal
freedom played a larger role in how players conducted themselves on and
off the field. While maintaining his pleasant demeanor, Lopez, some
argued, had lost touch, he could not communicate. Baseball's "generation
gap" it seemed, had caught up with him. Leonard Koppet writes that
Lopez "learned what all managers find out sooner or later, that there's a
limit to satisfying the craving to be 'understood.'" Older managers, according to Koppett, stop trying to explain themselves, especially where lineup
changes are concerned, because they believe that players are merely looking for excuses. Explanations that Lopez might intend as instructive could
turn up as raw material in a player's grievance. In this new and changing
environment, Lopez found that his patience was "best kept under control
by silence."[69]

No more suitable example of this could be given than the rift that
developed between Lopez and Al Smith when the latter was traded to Baltimore in mid-January 1963. Smith and Lopez had always gotten along
well, both in Cleveland and Chicago. The former's compliance in doing
whatever was necessary to help his team had endeared him to Lopez. But
when Smith was traded to Baltimore along with Luis Aparicio, he lashed
out at his longtime manager, accusing him of fostering dissension on the
club. The charges were, at the time, flatly denied by Lopez. In fact, Lopez
took the opportunity to lash back at all the "backbiting and crybaby tactics" that he argued had become the rule with traded players in recent
years. Lopez:

> I've been in this game a long time, thirty-nine years, in fact,
> but I've never before heard so much complaining by players
> after they've been dealt somewhere else. Trades have always
> been a part of baseball. We don't go around rapping the play-
> ers we've traded. We hope they do well and that the players we

Casey Stengel (left) and Al Lopez upon Lopez's retirement. (Courtesy *The Tampa Tribune*.)

get do a good job for us. The reason for a trade is that you are trying to strengthen certain positions and so is the other club. There's nothing personal about trades. It's an organizational matter. I was traded three times as a player. Casey Stengel dealt me away twice.... I never got mad at Casey. In fact, he's one of the best friends I have in baseball.... I understand Smitty squawked about being moved back and forth between the outfield and third base. You know, he never said boo to me about it when I talked it over with him. In fact, he was very nice to me about it. Smitty and I always got along fine. After all, I had him in Cleveland too.[70]

Gary Peters, who won twenty games at Chicago in 1964, surmised that Lopez simply grew tired of being accessible to everyone. Peters felt this was especially true because of the modern player's propensity to put himself and his own goals before the team. Peters:

> Over the years, [Lopez] remained accessible to players and sportswriters. He tried to make everyone happy, and I think it finally got to be too much. He was such a generous person all those years, and it finally got to him. It is sad to say, because I always idolized Lopez, but for the last couple of years we thought he was physically sick ... his stomach. ... [H]e became more temperamental. Until the 1960s, when things ran smoothly, he didn't have to lose his temper with us. I think this was because in those early days the players had more love for the game. The dollar hadn't taken over and players were more willing to put their bodies on the line. Beginning in the 1960s, the Sox players worried about themselves more as individuals. It moved away from strong unity, not drastically, but gradually. I think Lopez had a hard time with this change.[71]

After another second-place finish in 1965, Lopez, tiring of the headaches and seeking to spend more time with his family and on the golf course, retired to his home in Tampa. Lopez, fifty-seven at the time, remained with the White Sox as a vice president or "sort of a super-scout and a consultant for General Manager Ed Short." His successor was Eddie Stanky, who was similar to Lopez in his understanding of the game's nuances but differed dramatically in temperament. After two fourth-place finishes and a poor beginning to a third, Ed Short turned to Lopez for help and El Señor, "like MacArthur," returned in 1968. It was understood by all parties, however, that his stay would be temporary and viewed "more to soothe the atmosphere than to perform miracles." The lack of continuity showed as the White Sox finished a dismal ninth place, thirty-six games behind the eventual 1968 World Series champion, Detroit. During the season Lopez was also sidelined for a month after undergoing an emer-

Lopez upon learning of his selection for the Hall of Fame, 1977. (Courtesy *The Tampa Tribune*.)

gency appendectomy pre-scribed to rid him of pain he had endured as far back as July 1965.[72]

As scripted, this second stint with the White Sox was short-lived. After winning only eight of his first seventeen games in 1969, Lopez, adhering to the interim nature of the agreement, turned the team over to Don Gutteridge and called it quits for good. Having spent portions of seventeen sea-sons as a big-league pilot, Al Lopez wrapped up his much-admired career tied for ninth place on the all-time winning percentage list with a .584 average. In 1977 he was en-shrined in baseball's Hall of Fame as a manager.[73]

No-Nonsense
or Prejudiced?

Dignity and respect are terms long associated with Al Lopez, both in and out of baseball. However, accusations made by Larry Doby, the first black player in American League history and one who played with and for Lopez, have raised questions about the way Lopez treated black baseball players, particularly Doby, during his tenure in the game. Did Lopez treat black players differently from their white counterparts? As a manager, did Lopez show marked indifference toward the plight of black players who helped to desegregate baseball in the 1940s and 1950s? Or was Lopez merely a no-nonsense, aggressive leader who demanded the utmost in hustle, drive, and ability and who failed to tolerate perceived excuses? Other managers of Lopez's era — Casey Stengel comes to mind — were also alleged to have had negative attitudes toward, or difficulty relating to, black players. Did these attributes constitute racism?

In spite of having collected several world championships with the New York Yankees, Stengel is remembered by some for his racist comments about Elston Howard, the Yankees' first black player. "When I finally get a Nigger," Stengel told the press, "I get the only one that can't run." This statement, pointedly cruel and unworthy of someone in Stengel's position, is held as evidence by those who argue that Stengel was in fact a racist. But Howard, the subject of the remark and one whom Stengel also unkindly dubbed "eightball," insisted, perhaps naively, that his manager treated him and other blacks with respect. Neither Maury Allen nor Robert Creamer, Stengel's primary biographers, thought he was prejudiced. While both recognized that he may have exhibited racist shortcomings, they defended him as a man of his times. Creamer surmised that Stengel "was racist only in the casual, unthinking way that most of his generation of Americans were."[1] Allen described him as "a nineteenth century white mid-Westerner who had to be pulled kicking and screaming into the racial liberalism of the twentieth century."[2] Jackie Robinson, however, argued "until his death" that Stengel was a bigot who never gave black players an equal chance.

This "casual, unthinking" or latent brand of racism that Creamer concludes many of Stengel's generation possessed has been alternately labeled as "modern" racism or its subtype, "aversive" racism. Modern racism has been described as an outgrowth of the recognition that more traditional racism [i.e., the overt belief that blacks are innately inferior to whites] is no longer acceptable and so alternative means of expressing prejudice need be implemented. Aversive racism, however, refers to those who believe that they are not prejudiced or discriminatory toward minorities, yet exhibit, perhaps unconsciously, racist tendencies. Aversive racists typically endorse racial equality and do not discriminate against minorities in situations in which it would be obvious to others or themselves.[3]

Solly Hemus, the abrasive, driven manager of the St. Louis Cardinals from 1959 to 1961, was labeled a racist by two of his players, Bob Gibson and Curt Flood. In his own defense, Hemus, as an "aversive" racist might, denied the charges. In doing so, he alluded to the fact that he had grown up in an ethnically mixed poor section of San Diego, where like the Ybor City of Lopez's youth, children of diverse races mingled. But coming of age in baseball during the 1940s, Hemus became accustomed to the sharp ethnic epithets still being tossed about, such as "dago and guinea, Polack and kike." When opponents, like Lew Burdette and Warren Spahn, believing Hemus was Jewish, hurled antisemitic verbal high ones in his direction, he returned them up the middle. Later as a manager, Hemus thought little of lobbing the same form of "razzing" toward opposing players, because he had been conditioned to believe that was how it was done in baseball. The fact that such overt displays might upset those black players on his own team did not matter. Their concern, argued Hemus, should be winning ballgames, not the feelings of their opponents.[4]

The questionable styles of Stengel and Hemus also illustrate the difference between managerial ability in the sense of strategies and tactics and interpersonal relationships. While their behavior may have been accepted in an earlier era, the socially conscious game that baseball was evolving into by the 1950s and 1960s could not tolerate it. No longer were a field manager's tactical concerns and efforts to implement them enough. New methods of understanding and motivation, relationships and feelings emerged as part of the job description, and some managers, ill at ease with it all, walked away.

Lopez initially called it quits after the 1965 season and then retired for good seventeen games into 1969, tiring, as Leonard Koppett believes, of dealing with many of these new distractions. Was race or the altered complexion of baseball one of the new distractions that Lopez grew tired of? The reality of blacks in the major leagues is something that Lopez had dealt with as a player and manager virtually since its inception. In his last year as a player, 1947, Lopez teamed with Larry Doby in Cleveland, and as a manager he always had black players on his club. Doby, Luke Easter, and Harry Simpson all started for Lopez in Cleveland, and at Chicago, Doby, Minnie Minoso, Al Smith, Earl Battey, and others played for him. In fact, Lopez and the Indians' failure to capture the pennant in 1953 was "widely attributed" to the club's having been oversaturated with black players.[5]

Lopez never spent a great deal of time personally interacting with them — or any of his other players, for that matter. If he had something to say to a player, he usually said it through one of his assistant coaches. Did this impersonal style, in and of itself, constitute some latent reflection of the manager's bias against certain players or races? Was it "aversive" racism? Doby believed so, especially in light of other incidents occurring while he played for Lopez. Lopez's impassiveness, however, might also have reflected his wish that players come to the park ready to play and leave their problems in the clubhouse. "He tried to keep it all in the game," recalled Al Smith. "Do not let it interfere with your playing and you would be O.K.... He had a team to manage and tried to keep that stuff off the field, when he could."[6]

Earl Battey, another former black member of the White Sox, agreed, saying that "Lopez was Spanish and surely he understood what we were going through. But he did not let it interfere with the day to day running of the club. He tried to keep it off the field. No nonsense!"[7] According to Smith, Hank Greenberg "would sit around and tell us of the antisemitic treatment he received in the minors, but Lopez never did that."[8] The more personal a manager's relationship with his players became, the more likely it was that personal problems might enter into it, and Lopez could not accept that and expect to win games, which was his job.

As noted above, Lopez himself had emerged among the first wave of Latin ballplayers into the major leagues and was subject to overt verbal abuse from both fans and players. While progressing through the minors, he played in front of many hostile crowds who thought little of using expletives to bait and rile opposing players. But Lopez says that he never allowed the abuse to bother him. Nevertheless, the effect of such treatment and its lasting impression on him may offer some insight into the perspective he later maintained regarding the mistreatment of other players. Lopez, like Hemus, considered the abuse to be part of the game. "They do that all over in baseball," said Lopez. "They want to get under your skin. People would call me a Cuban Nigger or something like that, and I'm not even Cuban." Lopez also thinks that maybe he was just too young to have realized the extent to which prejudicial behavior was in fact being directed at him. "I treated everybody like I wanted to be treated and if a guy treated me badly then I just didn't bother with him," he said. "I never had this minority thing handicap me in any way. I'm Spanish and proud of it."[9]

It is easier for someone of Lopez's racial background to maintain such indifference to racism. There was a gulf of difference between the way most blacks and Latins, particularly white Latins, were treated during this period.

Lopez is less than tactful when expressing his perception of the treatment afforded those first black players in organized baseball. He insists that the news media made more out of it than there actually was and that all players suffer verbal abuse in some form or another, not simply blacks or minorities.[10] Aside from the fact that this comment is patently untrue, statements like this by Lopez perhaps suggest the nature of the problem — that Lopez may not have been a racist, but he probably did not have any idea about racist practices and how they might be taken by black players.

When questioned about the off-the-field discrimination that Larry Doby, Jackie Robinson, and other blacks endured, including death threats, and the separate, substandard living accommodations allotted to them, Lopez abruptly responded that he knew little of it. His concern was on the field and as such, he may have blinded himself to many of the indignities that black players suffered during the game's desegregation. But not knowing about or ignoring circumstance does not mean that it did not exist, and Lopez's alleged ignorance in the matter is negligent at best given his role as a manager. Furthermore, Lopez must have witnessed more than he cared to discuss, since as Doby's manager he had to regularly pick him up at segregated hotels before games. The fact that his manager did so little to alleviate the pressure he felt or to even acknowledge that such tension existed must have also grated on the deepening resentment Doby harbored against Lopez. Smith, a black teammate of Doby's, was stunned to hear that Lopez said the news media overstated things:

> I believe that someone must have put words into Lopez's mouth for him to blame the media. He saw the mistreatment on a daily basis, particularly in spring training when we had to stay in segregated hotels. More than that, because we stayed across town we had to leave often in the third inning so we could get back and change to catch our train. Lopez knew that this was going on. I think maybe it is his way of just putting it behind him ... but it happened.[11]

It is Lopez's opinion that the pressure of being the first black in the American League and feeling that he was fighting everybody effected Doby's career, rendering him somewhat less productive than he should have been.[12] This sentiment is indicative of Lopez's mind-set, which framed the racial question in terms of baseball and kept the issue between the chalked lines. But was Lopez laying down a smokescreen or giving an accurate portrayal of Doby? The day after Larry Doby was traded from Cleveland to Chicago in 1955, sportswriter Franklin Lewis of the *Cleveland Press* criticized Doby by stating that his "opportunities for immortality in baseball ended where his complexes began — at the neckline." Lewis also referred to Doby as "[h]ighly gifted" yet "frequently morose, sullen and, upon occasion, downright surly to his teammates and his public." Lewis concluded by blaming much of this on "the load" Doby carried since entering the majors. "He thought of himself ... as the symbol of the Negro in his league."[13] Gordon Cobbledick of the *Plain Dealer* admitted that Cleveland would miss his bat but disparaged Doby's temperament as problematic and agreed with the trade.[14] "Sheep" Jackson of the *Call and Post*, however, believed that the trade was imbalanced and referred to Doby as "the heart of the team."[15] While Doby rejects the charges of Lewis and Cobbledick, it is conceivable that Lopez, who supported the trade for reasons discussed above, agreed with them and felt that such "problematic" behavior hurt the team in the short run and Doby over his career.

Perhaps it was because Lopez more easily fit into the overtly "Caucasian" world of organized baseball that he failed to acknowledge the disparities in treatment afforded minorities of a different skin tone. Lopez does not possess the stereotypical dark-complected physical traits often associated with Latin people. Would Lopez's career have been less successful had he physically fit such a profile? It is not coincidental that Lopez outwardly seems so oblivious to the abuse rendered himself and other minority ballplayers. Perhaps racial slurs did not bother Lopez because he never really considered himself a minority. "I treated everybody like I wanted to be treated.... I never had this minority thing handicap me in any way. *I'm Spanish and proud of it* [emphasis added]. People would call me a Cuban Nigger or something like that, and I'm not even Cuban." This last statement may be indicative of what Lopez viewed as a distinct class difference. Cubans and blacks might properly be lumped as one and the same, for often Cubans were black, but not Spaniards and blacks nor even Spaniards and Cubans, for in the predominantly Spanish Ybor City of Lopez's youth, the differences between the groups were obvious and accepted. Perhaps Lopez never felt like a minority because his Asturian pride in racial purity could not conceive of it.

Taking this profile of Lopez and placing it into the context of his career as a big-league player and manager, we find an individual who, perhaps in spite of his own exposure to ethnic prejudice, did not relate as closely to the plight of Doby and other early black players as one might expect. As noted above, Lopez managed with a self-imposed rule that if his players respected him he would respect them.[16] But for Lopez, respecting a player and his ability did not necessarily transcend the playing field to society at large, at least to the extent to which Lopez might act as a buffer of sorts to relieve the pressures of outside society felt by one of his players. This might be particularly true if the player were viewed by Lopez as imposing much of the unwanted pressure on himself and worse, of bringing it to the ballpark with him.

Lopez and Doby's relationship began in 1947, during the former's rookie year with the Cleveland Indians. At the time Lopez was winding down his own playing career, performing primarily as a backup catcher for the team. Doby's biographer, Joseph Moore, indicated that the source of the strained relationship between the two might possibly date back to that season. Moore quotes Lopez as telling some players in the dugout, after Doby's first official at-bat, that he was glad that it was Bryan Stephens and not he whom Doby had pinch-hit for. In other words, according to Moore, Lopez was relieved not to have been the first player in American League history to have a black man replace him in the lineup. Moore gives other minor instances in which Lopez, in his capacity as manager, was purported to have treated Doby badly, including an incident that occurred in 1952 while Doby was playing for Lopez in Cleveland. The episode occurred during a game when Doby, after having reached first base, failed to advance to third on a single to right field by Luke Easter. When Lopez angrily confronted him over this failure to advance, Doby responded in kind and was summarily benched.[17]

While Moore and Doby list this as a case in point supporting their allegations, it can also be viewed as an authoritative manager acting against a perceived threat to his leadership and the team's chemistry. Moreover, little angered Lopez more than careless mental lapses during a game. Recall his reaction to Al Smith overrunning Sherm Lollar at third base while at Chicago in 1959. It would have been one thing if Smith, running aggressively, had simply been thrown out on a good play. But it was something else entirely for him to overlook the guy running in front of him. In a game in 1965, Lopez benched outfielder Floyd Robinson, also black, in the first inning for failing to run out a ground ball to first base and following it with a lazy attempt in the outfield. A few years earlier he had benched Jim Rivera for casually making high looping throws from the outfield. Lopez:

> I warned him that the next time he did it, he'd be jerked right out of the game. Well, it was only about two or three innings later when Jim let fly with another of those boomerang throws and, of course, as usual, the batter continued on to second base and he got nobody at the plate. When he came in, he nonchalantly flipped his glove on the bench and went for the water cooler. I yelled at him. "Pick up your glove and keep right on going to the clubhouse. You're through for the day." Well, Jim started to alibi about the ball getting away from him or something, but I just turned away from him. There are times when you've got to use your authority and lower the boom on some of these players. If you don't, the whole club will begin getting lackadaisical on you. A good scrappy, hustling player can inspire a team, but a lazy, careless player can do just as much damage the other way.[18]

Lopez could not afford to have team leaders like Doby making careless plays on the basepaths. When Doby compounded the error by arguing over it, Lopez had no choice but to bench him. If he had not, the whole club might have begun "getting lackadaisical" on him.

Jerome Holtzman, who covered the White Sox for the *Chicago Sun-Times*, agreed that Lopez was never the easiest manager to play for. "For the guy who is putting out every day, there is evidently no problem, but ballplayers don't put out every day, and that's when they run into trouble with Lopez."[19] Jim Frigley, a former player of Lopez's at Cleveland, supports this contention. He recalled that if

> you did something wrong with [Lopez], he made you pay: I remember being on first and Early Wynn was on second. There was a base hit and I slid into third, thinking Wynn had scored. But Wynn was standing there [on third]. Lopez didn't say a word; he didn't have to. I knew what to expect from him. He sat me down and I got splinters in my rear end because I was there so long.[20]

After his trade from Chicago to Baltimore in 1957, Doby told "Doc" Young of *Jet* that Lopez's racism had affected his play with the White Sox. This revelation came after Doby had already expressed dismay at finding out about the trade, one he had expected, from his daughter, who heard about it on television. In that statement Doby chastised Paul Richards of Baltimore and Chuck Comiskey of Chicago for not informing him of the deal, but acknowledged that he had not borne up to the pennant-winning expectations in Chicago and that someone had to pay the price. In *Jet*, however, Doby argued that it was Lopez's lack of respect for black players, as evidenced by the trade of himself and Minnie Minoso, the popular Afro-Cuban outfielder, that had resulted in his not meeting the aforementioned expectations. "I can't have any respect for a man who lacks regard for a man because he's in a minority [group] and acts as if we're always wrong and they're always right," said Doby. "I just didn't care to play for him."[21]

As noted earlier, Lopez had no misgivings about trading Doby. "We've just traded away 100 strikeouts," he said. But Lopez, while exerting some influence, was not the last word on trades in Chicago. In 1957, that responsibility fell to John Rigney and Chuck Comiskey, the White Sox's two vice presidents. Both believed that the thirty-three-year-old Doby and Jack Harshman were the biggest disappointments of the prior season and also looked forward to relieving themselves of Doby's $30,000 contract.[22]

While the Doby deal caused few surprises, the trade of the popular Minnie Minoso back to his original club in Cleveland merited some questioning. Minoso was coming off a year in which he batted .310, won a golden glove for his performance in the outfield, and played in the All-Star game. It was also the second time that Minoso had been traded away from a Lopez-managed club.[23] Minoso, who like Doby read about the deal in the newspaper, could not understand it and, searching for someone to blame, found Lopez:

> I had no idea such a trade was pending. I tried to clarify things in my mind, but nothing seemed to make sense. Then a thought crossed my mind, a fleeting thought this time. It had been the second time in my career that I had been traded.... Perhaps it was just a bit coincidental, but both times the manager of the club that traded me happened to be Al Lopez.[24]

For his part, Lopez "hated" to trade Minoso, but he felt that Early Wynn and Al Smith gave his club better balance. "I was for the Wynn deal because I thought we were getting thin on pitchers," said Lopez. Lopez also believed the multifaceted Smith was a more consistent outfielder, despite Minoso's golden glove. Although Lopez supported the trade, it was not Lopez who sent Minoso back to Cleveland. Chuck Comiskey handled it on the Chicago end and Frank Lane, Cleveland's new general manager, pursued it for the Indians. When Lane assumed the Cleveland post after Greenberg was fired, he was given a "free hand" to rebuild the club, and the player he wanted more than any other was Minoso, who referred to Lane as his "second father." Lane had also traded for Minoso when he was the G. M. in Chicago, and now he had an opportunity to make amends to Cleveland's fans, who had cursed that deal since 1951.[25]

It is remarkable that Minoso was traded or released from a Lopez-managed club three times, the last after the 1964 season — during which he made a mere thirty-one plate appearances — when he was granted his outright release. Like Doby after the 1957 season, and Bob Feller after the 1954 World Series, Minoso questioned why, "with a pennant on the line," Lopez had not used him more. In his autobiography, Minoso implies that Lopez did not care for him and was behind all three trades. While he does not say it openly, the indirect tone he uses to describe each of the transactions and the impersonal manner in which Lopez is alleged to have handled them leaves little to ponder. "There were no soothing words, no warmth, no show of appreciation. Just, 'Minoso, you've been traded'.... That was it," he notes. Minoso has declined on numerous occasions to elaborate, leaving one to assume that he is either too good-natured to do so or that it no longer means anything to him. Whatever the reason, Minoso refuses to discuss the matter further.[26]

Al Smith, labeled by some teammates as "Little Bobo" because they viewed him as "Lopez's favorite," claims that Lopez did have a hand in the trade sending Minoso to Cleveland, although to what extent he is not sure. He remembers that Lopez told him in advance to expect it. "In 1956 he told me that I was coming to join him in Chicago and the trade happened with me and Wynn going there for Minoso and Fred Hatfield."[27] Did that mean that Lopez was behind the deal or merely in favor of it? And what if he was behind it? As a player Lopez was traded twice by Casey Stengel, a future business partner and longtime friend. Did the two Lopez deals alone constitute antihispanic tendencies on the part of Stengel? Of course not. Trades are a part of the game. As Lopez was quoted earlier, "The reason for a trade is that you are trying to strengthen certain positions and so is the other club. There's nothing personal about trades. It's an organizational matter."[28] Ray Berres agreed, adding plainly that "trades aren't personal, you might just be filling a need."[29] Jerome Holtzman failed to note anything of a personal nature about it. It was a trade that while initially unpopular with many White Sox fans, proved to be a plus, as Smith and Wynn both excelled in leading the club to the 1959 pennant. Smith, upon being traded by the White Sox after the 1963 season, lashed out at Lopez and club management for doing so, but he harbors no longterm resentment over it. He certainly did not believe that racism had played a factor in the decision to send him to Baltimore. In fact, as witnessed above, he remains one of Lopez's biggest supporters.[30]

Fred Hatfield, a teammate of Doby's and Minoso's on Lopez's 1957 Chicago White Sox squad and part of the deal sending Minoso back to Cleveland, recalls Doby as being labeled, perhaps unfairly, a "Johnson & Johnson ballplayer," because he used about $25 worth of tape and rubdown every day. Hatfield explains that although Doby was honestly hurt, in those days a manager did not have much respect for an injured player. "A manager figured that you were a professional ballplayer and you weren't supposed to get hurt.... If Lopez ever did anything to Doby, it was probably over his always being hurt." Hatfield reasons that the combination of Doby's sensitive nature and Lopez's lack of respect for an injured player may have led to the bitter feelings between them.[31] If, as Hatfield presumes, managers had little respect for injured players, someone like Lopez, with a record of durability and playing hurt, might have exhibited even less. This variable, placed within the context of Lopez and Doby's off-the-field tensions, might have then spoiled the playing field as a forum of respect between the two men, further increasing resentment.

Hatfield offers additional insight on the two personalities that bares mention. He frankly recalls Doby as being thin-skinned about his race. "Doby realized that he was in a minority group and it showed," said Hatfield. "I got around it by kidding with him all the time. But you couldn't kid him about his race." Hatfield depicts Lopez, on the other hand, as a grudge holder and a man who was unable to let things go easily. "If you did something to get on Al's bad side," insisted Hatfield, "he could hold it against you." Hatfield, a white player from the deep South, recalls that as an opponent, he had given Lopez quite a bit of razzing, for which he believes Lopez never forgave him:

> I used to be a pretty good bench jockey and I remember get-
> ting on him real bad when he was managing Cleveland. The
> year they set the record, 1954, I was with Detroit and we were
> a game or so out of fourth place and the fourth-place clubs got
> money. Well, Cleveland had already clinched the pennant, but
> when we played them he pitched his big four anyway, Lemon,
> Garcia, Wynn, and I think Houtteman. During the series ...
> I got all over Lopez about pitching his big four against us when
> he could have thrown somebody else. I got on him about being
> Spanish, called him Señor or something like that. We were try-
> ing to get into fourth place.[32]

When Lopez came to the White Sox in 1957, Hatfield, feeling that his new manager was holding a grudge against him, saw his playing time diminish noticeably, and then he was traded. The volatile traits offered by Hatfield, on both Lopez's and Doby's parts, may have further increased tensions.

Earl Battey describes Lopez as being the nicest guy in the world and an excellent teacher but a manager who ruled with an iron hand. "He was no-nonsense on the field," Battey recalled. "He did much of his coaching through his assistants. If he had something to say to you personally, you were usually in trouble."[33] With this in mind, the question arises whether such an "iron hand" was best suited for the stroking that Doby's "thin skin" may have required. A contemporary of Lopez's during this period was Johnny Keane, manager of the St. Louis Cardinals. Like Lopez, Keane was viewed by his players, black and white alike, as somewhat rigid in his approach to the game, but unlike Lopez and Hemus, Keane's predecessor, he openly acknowledged the pressure that his own black players, particularly Bob Gibson and Curt Flood, faced. Keane felt his job "was to reduce, not increase, the pressure on them, to reduce extraneous distractions."[34] Assuming that Lopez did recognize the pressure Doby was under, self-imposed or otherwise, why did he not act to help reduce it rather than allowing his own indifference to the issue and intolerance for injuries to increase it?

Al Smith provides a plausible response to this question by pointing to the distance Lopez maintained from the majority of his players. "Lopez was the person who was hardest to get to know," Smith said. "He didn't talk too much, but he'd watch you, and if you did well, then he gained confidence in you. Sometimes he could be a difficult man to get along with."[35] Jim Landis, however, recalls a Lopez that "always had the door open ... he knew how to handle players as individuals, always."[36] Which was it? Was Lopez distant and difficult all the time or merely, as Landis and Smith suggest, when he lacked confidence in a player? In the Landis-Smith scenario, it can be inferred that Lopez had lost confidence in Doby. Such a lack of confidence might also bring with it the distance and difficulty of which Smith spoke, as well as an understanding of why Doby, like Minoso, was traded or released from Lopez-managed clubs on three separate occasions.

In personal notes recorded by Joseph Moore in 1980, Doby is said to have alleged that Lopez purposely farmed Luke Easter out to the minor leagues after the 1953 season because the black first baseman was dating a white woman. Doby is further quoted as commenting that other black players were treated likewise by Lopez for the same behavior.[37] But little is presented in the way of evidence to support this claim, and Lopez's response to direct questioning on the subject from Doby's biographer, that Easter simply did not have it anymore, is credible. Luke Easter had a history of not starting many games for Cleveland, but he consistently hit the long ball and drove in runs. He started in only sixty-eight games in 1953 and hit a respectable .303 that season, but his power stats were way down. Since also he was probably older than he would admit, Cleveland was justified in releasing him early the next season. Earl Battey, however, may be a counter example. He insists that Lopez had ample opportunity to trade him away "on several occasions" but opted to keep him as long as he could. "He went out of his way to teach me things," said Battey. "Much of what I was able to take from Lopez came either directly from him or indirectly through his coaches. If he was prejudiced, I don't believe he would have taken the time."[38]

If Lopez treated Doby and others in a racist fashion, then why do

Battey and others reject the notion as wrong? Bob Shaw, the surprising winner of eighteen games for Lopez's 1959 "Go-Go" White Sox, refuses to believe that Lopez ever acted in a prejudiced manner to anyone. Shaw, who is white, claims that as far as he is concerned, Lopez should not have to defend himself. "As a manager," intoned Shaw, "Lopez did absolutely nothing that I can possibly construe as being prejudiced; he is not that way…. He is the best manager I ever played for; not even close."[39] Walt Dropo, another of Doby's former white teammates under Lopez, called him a "fair manager" and recalled at no time witnessing any discrimination by Lopez against a certain group of players. Dropo noted that Lopez was a great manager who would discipline whites as well as minorities *and in the same manner* (emphasis added).[40] Al Smith agreed with Dropo, claiming that all players, "white, black, and Hispanic," received the same treatment from Lopez. "It didn't matter," said Smith. "You had better hustle or you wouldn't be in there — white or black."[41] This is an important observation, for if Lopez had treated white players differently from blacks when doling out punishment, the iron hand theory would be suspect.

Others, both in and around baseball, give adequate assurance that Lopez is deeply respected and loved within the game. Could a racist in the mold described by Doby garner such adulation? John Kuenster, the editor of *Baseball Digest*, once referred to Lopez as the "finest gentleman I have ever met on the major league beat."[42] Monte Irvin, the black Hall of Famer and longtime friend of Larry Doby, who never played for Lopez but played against him, remembers Lopez as a "a great manager who was a decent and kind human being."[43] Roland Hemond, the former general manager of the Baltimore Orioles, describes Lopez as "unquestionably one of the finest men ever to have been associated with Baseball."[44] Longtime baseball executive Gabe Paul, who has known Lopez since 1937, touts him as a "great tribute to Baseball, both on and off the field."[45] Mickey Vernon, a longtime major leaguer who served in the Pacific with Larry Doby during World War II, refers to Lopez as "a great manager and a great guy; I wish I could have played for him!"[46] Gene Woodling, another of Lopez's former players, remembers him as "a great person, a ballplayer's manager."[47] While testimonials often come cheap, Lopez's sterling reputation does strengthen the opinions of Battey, Smith, Shaw, and Dropo that he was a good man with no predetermined axe to grind. Smith describes him simply as "a good manager." "He wasn't 'rah rah' or anything like that. He just kept to himself," said Smith. "Maybe that is why some people felt that he wasn't on their side. Me, I never had any problems with him."[48]

How then does one reconcile Doby's accusations with the above claims? Doby accepts that Lopez has mellowed lately and that as an aging institution within the game he is simply being afforded the accolades that would naturally come his way. He does not, however, forgive Lopez for what he views to have been the prejudice of his youth. He insists that as an adult, Lopez was responsible for his own actions, and those actions were harmful and prejudicial to Doby and his race.[49]

On the other hand, those individuals who reject Doby's charges counter that Lopez was a no-nonsense manager who only sought the best from his players and refused to accept excuses. Jerome Holtzman recently commented that in his years of covering Lopez-led ball clubs he never witnessed any evidence of prejudice on the manager's part. Lopez, according to Holtzman, was always fair, regardless of the player's color.[50] Al Smith agreed: "Definitely a no-nonsense type of manager.... Although he was not vocal one way or the other, he would lay down the law in spring training and you followed it."[51]

While the reasons for Doby's defensiveness may have been understandable given the circumstances, Lopez, true to his "iron hand," showed little empathy. This might seem particularly odd for a man with Lopez's background. However, the only category that Lopez should be placed in is that of baseball player and manager with the emphasis always on *performance*. To Lopez, being a minority in a white man's game was no reason not to live up to your potential. Larry Doby's crime, in the eyes of Al Lopez, was just that; a failure to live up to his potential, thereby warranting the loss of confidence that Lopez displayed. Furthermore, Lopez was quite aware of his own actions and the reasons for any loss of confidence in Doby. If there was some hidden, less than obvious, brand of racism wafting through the clubhouses in Cleveland and Chicago, it did not emanate from the manager. Lopez, in typical no-nonsense fashion, simply tired of waiting for what he believed was Doby's "Hall of Famer" potential to mature. The fact that the outfielder was traded away from various teams on multiple occasions and with the press generally approving indicates that Lopez was not alone in his assessment.[52]

Conclusion

Al Lopez is today a tremendously popular and physically fit retiree living in Tampa. Upon meeting him for the first time, one cannot help but be impressed at how well he appears for his age. While his hands bear the scars of nineteen big-league campaigns behind the plate, his waist is trim, his eyes clear, and his biceps tight. Widowed now,[1] but still residing in his modest bayfront home, Lopez spends the bulk of his days golfing in the hot Florida sun and evenings visiting with his son's family or perhaps watching a baseball game, preferably the St. Louis Cardinals, on television. As one might expect, Lopez appreciates the Cardinals' aggressive "go-go" inside game and their manager Tony LaRussa.[2]

He is quick to display his pride in the growing reputation of the Tampa Bay area as a proving ground for baseball player development. Lopez also beams at the mention of LaRussa and Lou Piniella, the two "Tampa kids" who faced each other in the 1990 World Series as managers of the opposing clubs. He boasts, "We had two kids — well, not kids anymore — who are managers in the big leagues and managed in the World Series against each other. That's amazing. I doubt if that has ever happened. Two guys managing in the World Series from the same area, one from Ybor City and the other from West Tampa."[3]

For some time, Lopez was dismayed with the destruction of ballparks in and around Tampa with no new ones built. He explained, "I've said this before. Instead of tearing down ballparks, they should be building them. They tore down Al Lopez Field [a baseball stadium named for Lopez that housed the Class A Tampa Tarpons and was razed in 1989 to make

227

Top: Al Lopez at home in Tampa, Florida, 1992. (Photo by author.) *Bottom:* Spring training for the Cincinnati Reds (Pete Rose on third) at Al Lopez Field, ca. 1970. This field was razed in 1989. (Courtesy Florida State Archives.)

Statue commemorating Lopez's career. Al Lopez Park, Tampa, Florida. (Photo by author.)

room for a sports facility], which was a great disappointment to me, not because it was named after me, but because we lost the Tarpons.... They also tore down the old baseball diamond at Cuscaden Park [in Ybor City] and made a soccer field."[4] Since Lopez made these remarks, however, the New York Yankees have relocated their spring training program to Tampa, where they are housed at the new Legends Field, a marvelous ten-thousand-seat replica of Yankee Stadium. Lopez welcomed the move because he felt that the demise of professional baseball in the city, as well as the removal of local parks, had an adverse effect on Tampa's youth. As a child, Lopez learned much about the game by attending major-league and minor-league contests played in the city. Accordingly, it is important to Lopez that today's local children have a place to play and enjoy baseball, just as he did, so that they can continue to build upon and enrich the game's legacy in the community.

Toward this aim, the City of Tampa, Hillsborough County, and the State of Florida decreed October 3, 1992, to be "Al Lopez Day." As part of their official proclamations, they ordained that a popular preexisting community park would henceforth bear his name. The proclamation read in full:

Proclamation

State of Florida
Executive Department
Tallahassee

WHEREAS, on Saturday, October 3, 1992, the residents of Tampa will celebrate Tampa's first national sports celebrity, Al Lopez, by dedicating the Al Lopez Park, located adjacent to their stadium as part of that city's sports complex, and by unveiling a statue honoring him as an outstanding major league catcher, manager and Hall of Famer; and

WHEREAS, Floridians have followed with pride the career of Tampa's native son, Al Lopez, rejoicing in his achievements and recognitions as an elected member of the Baseball Hall of Fame as well as election into the Sports Hall of Fame of the State of Florida and the City of Tampa, and as one of Florida's Professional Athletes of the Year, and as Dr. Al Lopez when in 1989 he received an Honorary Doctorate Degree from the University of South Florida; and

WHEREAS, Floridians have proudly followed his baseball career from the days of the Tampa Smokers and his 36 years in the major leagues playing for the Brooklyn Dodgers, the Boston Braves, the Pittsburgh Pirates, the Cleveland Indians, as well as watching him play in two All Star Games and then as Manager for six years of the Cleveland Indians and then as Manager for 11 years of the Chicago White Sox and managing the American League in numerous All Star Games and as the 1991 Captain of the American League All Star Game at Chicago's Wrigley Field.

NOW, THEREFORE, I, Lawton Chiles, by virtue of the authority vested in me as Governor of the State of Florida, do hereby proclaim October 3, 1992, as

AL LOPEZ DAY

throughout this state and call upon all residents and visitors to join in recognizing this sports hero, who is a man of strong character, loyalty and humility, by celebrating and dedicating Al Lopez Park and unveiling the Al Lopez statue honoring Al Lopez, an outstanding lifelong native and resident of our great state.

IN WITNESS WHEREOF, I have hereunto set my hand and caused the Great Seal of the State of Florida to be affixed at Tallahassee, the Capital, this 1st day of October in the year of our Lord nineteen hundred and ninety-two.

Governor

An impressive bronze statue of Lopez, resplendent in Brooklyn Dodgers regalia and "the tools of ignorance," was commissioned by Tony Saladino and the "Friends of Al Lopez" committee and erected by Steve Dickey, a local sculptor, as an enduring tribute and placed at the southern end of the park, where it waits patiently under an imagined pop foul.[5] Few honors could have so markedly portrayed the essence of Lopez than a field to play on. The former Horizon Park had long served Tampa as a recreational area, providing weekend fun for all who came to romp on its spacious lawns or enjoy its two lakes. As Al Lopez Park it continues to provide a venue for Tampa's citizens, particularly its youth, to par-

Al Lopez Park, Tampa, Florida. (Photo by author.)

ticipate in outdoor activities while reminding them of the sporting heritage passed on to them by the park's namesake.

As serene and graceful in retirement as he was during his career, Dr. Lopez (he received an honorary doctorate from the University of South Florida in 1989) takes the accolades of his twilight in stride. While grateful for the many honors directed toward him, he would rather that people understand that he was merely enjoying his life in baseball. For Lopez, the chase was always the game; he left the applause to others. Avoid the distractions, keep to the basics, come to work, and compete. These were the traits that Lopez personified as a player and manager and continues by example to embody today. In this resolute fashion he remains yesterday's understated diamond gentleman, El Señor.

Notes

Introduction

1. *Tampa Tribune*, 16 Oct. 1925.
2. *Tampa Tribune*, 30 Oct. 1925.
3. *Ibid.*
4. With Lopez behind the plate, the Cuban Stars lost 12–5 to the Primo Lord "Undertakers" a few days day before the professional exhibition. The *Tribune* reported it as the first loss for the Cuban Stars all summer and fall (27 Oct. 1925).
5. Donald Honig, *The Man in the Dugout: Fifteen Big League Managers Speak Their Minds*, p. 180.
6. Lopez interview with Gary Mormino, 4 Apr. 1980.
7. Scheer played parts of two seasons for the Philadelphia Athletics, 1922 and 1923, batting .212 lifetime.
8. *Tampa Tribune* 31 Oct. 1925.
9. Honig, *Man in the Dugout*, p. 181.
10. Al Hirshberg, *Baseball's Greatest Catchers*.
11. Steven Lawson, "Ybor City and Baseball: An Interview with Al Lopez," *Tampa Bay History* (Fall/Winter 1985): 59.

Chapter 1

1. Gary Mormino and George Pozzetta, *The Immigrant World of Ybor City*, pp. 70–71.
2. Lopez interview with Gary Mormino, 4 Apr. 1980.
3. *Ibid.*
4. Michael Gannon, *Florida: A Short History*, p. 95; Mormino and Pozzetta, *Immigrant World*, p. 75.

5. Passenger lists of vessels arriving at Key West, Florida, vol. 10, Jan. 1– May 26, 1906; Charlton Tebeau, *A History of Florida*, pp. 312, 321; Mormino and Pozzetta, *Immigrant World*, p. 75. The *Olivette* had earlier gained a semblance of fame by transporting the survivors of the battleship *Maine* back to Key West after their ship was blown apart in Havana harbor on Feb. 15, 1898, precipitating U.S. involvement in the Spanish-American War.

6. Passenger lists of vessels arriving at Key West, Florida, vol. 10, Jan. 1– May 26, 1906.

7. Lawson, "Ybor City and Baseball," p. 60.

8. *1910 Census*, vol. 19, Hillsborough 1–225, #119; Al Lopez and wife Connie, the last of the family to occupy the 12th Avenue residence, moved to 3501 Beach in 1960. *Tampa City Directory* (Richmond, Va.: R.L. Polk & Co., 1959–60).

9. Mormino and Pozzetta, *Immigrant World*, p. 77.

10. Tony Pizzo, "Reminiscences of Ybor City," *Sunland Tribune* 17 (1991): p. 50.

11. *Ibid.*

12. *Tampa Tribune*, 12 Sept. 1977.

13. Lopez interview with Mormino. Buffalo Avenue has since been renamed Martin Luther King Avenue.

14. Lopez interview with Mormino.

15. *Ibid.*

16. *Ibid.*

17. This was particularly true in matters of labor relations. The Spanish-born cigar manufacturers often joined Tampa's "Anglo" business leaders in supporting "citizens' committees" and other vigilantism to suppress cigar-worker strikes or demonstrations. Such tactics not only led to resentment on both sides of the societal spectrum but to mob violence and death. See Robert P. Ingalls, *Urban Vigilantes in the New South: Tampa, 1882–1936*.

18. Mormino and Pozzetta, *Immigrant World*, p. 245.

19. Lopez interview with the author, 10 June 1992; See Steven A. Riess, *Sport in Industrial America: 1850–1920*.

20. *Ibid.*

21. *Ibid.*

22. Mormino and Pozzetta, *Immigrant World*, p. 248.

23. Eric A. Wagner, "Baseball in Cuba," *Journal of Popular Culture* 18 (Summer 1984):115.

24. Mormino and Pozzetta, *Immigrant World*, p. 247.

25. Lawson, "Ybor City," p. 61.

26. *Ibid.*

27. Mormino and Pozzetta, *Immigrant World*, pp. 248–50.

28. Lopez interview with Mormino.

29. Ferlita's was best known for its fresh Cuban bread, which was made daily and delivered throughout Ybor City. According to Lopez though, this Cuban bread was not actually Cuban but Tampa bread. He explains: "I've been to Cuba many times and what they serve there mostly is French bread. There is quite a bit of difference in the taste. In Tampa, first they would mix the dough from flour, lard and other ingredients, rolling it by hand, and then place a split palmetto leaf on each of the two sides, top and bottom. Then it was baked, leaf intact, and this

big palmetto leaf gave it a unique taste. It also made the bread open up so that you had a split in the top of the loaf." Although the original wooden structure of the bakery burned years ago, the subsequent brick building stands today as an Ybor City, State of Florida, museum. Lawson, "Ybor City and Baseball," p. 64.

30. *Tampa Tribune*, 15 Sept. 1925.
31. *Tampa City Directory*, 1925.
32. *Tampa Tribune*, 15 Sept. 1925.
33. *Ibid.*
34. Lawson, "Ybor City," p. 64.
35. *Tampa Tribune*, 15 Sept. 1925.
36. Lawson, "Ybor City," p. 64; *Tampa City Directory*, p. 434; See Charles J. Foreman, "Major League Debutantes," 1928 (Al Lopez file, National Baseball Library and Archives).
37. Lopez interview with the author, 10 June 1992.
38. John Bowman and Joel Zoss, *Diamonds in the Rough: The Untold History of Baseball,* pp. 130–33.
39. *Ibid.*, p. 131.
40. *Tampa Tribune*, 28 Oct. 1925.
41. Lawson, "Ybor City," p. 69.
42. *Ibid.*, p. 70.
43. *Ibid.*, p. 71.
44. *Ibid.*
45. *Ibid.*
46. *Ibid.*, p. 73.
47. *Ibid.*, p. 75.
48. Lopez interview with Mormino.
49. *Tampa Tribune*, 15 Sept. 1925.
50. Lawson, "Ybor City," p. 65.
51. *Ibid.*, p. 68.
52. *Tampa Tribune*, 15 Sept. 1925; See career statistics sheet maintained in the Al Lopez file, National Baseball Library and Archives.
53. *Tampa Tribune*, 26–27 Aug. 1925.
54. Estrada made it to the major leagues in 1929 with the St. Louis Browns. His stint, however, was short-lived. He pitched one inning of one game, giving up a hit and a walk.
55. *Tampa Tribune*, 29–30 Aug. 1925.
56. *Tampa Tribune*, 1–2 Sept. 1925.
57. *Tampa Tribune*, 3 and 5 Sept. 1925.
58. *Tampa Tribune*, 8–9 Sept. 1925.
59. *Tampa Tribune*, 11–13 Sept. 1925.
60. *Tampa Tribune*, 15 Sept. 1925.
61. Mormino and Pozzetta, *Immigrant World*, p. 251.
62. Marcelo Maseda interview with the author, 12 June 1992.
63. *Tampa Tribune*, 30 May 1926.
64. *Tampa Tribune*, 4, 5, and 9 June 1926.
65. *Tampa Tribune*, 15–17 June 1926.
66. *Tampa Tribune*, 18 June 1926.
67. *Tampa Tribune*, 18–19 June 1926.

68. *Tampa Tribune,* 25 June 1926.
69. *Tampa Tribune,* 26 June 1926.
70. *Tampa Tribune,* 27 June 1926.
71. *Tampa Tribune,* 29 June and 6 July 1926.
72. *Ibid.*
73. After the sanctions were imposed, Sanford clinched the first half on 1 July, with a 10–7 win over Fort Myers. Tampa finished in seventh place at 24–33. *Tampa Tribune,* 2 and 4 July 1926.
74. *Tampa Tribune,* 30 June 1926.
75. *Tampa Tribune,* 10 and 23 July 1926.
76. *Tampa Tribune,* 14–25 Aug. 1926.
77. *Tampa Tribune,* 25 Aug. 1926.
78. *Tampa Tribune,* 27 Aug. 1926.
79. *Tampa Tribune,* 7–9 Sept. 1926.
80. *Tampa Tribune,* 9 Sept. 1926.
81. *Tampa Tribune,* 11 Sept. 1926.
82. *Ibid.*
83. *Tampa Tribune,* 12–13 Sept. 1926.
84. *Tampa Tribune,* 14 Sept. 1926.
85. *Ibid.*
86. *Tampa Tribune,* 15 Sept. 1926.
87. *Tampa Tribune,* 16 Sept. 1926.
88. *Ibid.*
89. Charles J. Foreman, "Major League Debutantes," 1928 (Al Lopez file, National Baseball Library and Archives).
90. Lawson, "Ybor City," p. 65.

Chapter 2

1. Clifford Bloodgood, *Who's Who in Baseball; Florida Times-Union,* 2 Oct. 1927; Foreman, "Major League Debutantes," 1928 (Al Lopez file, National Baseball Library and Archives.)
2. *Florida Times-Union,* 8 Mar. 1927.
3. *Florida Times-Union,* 8 Apr. 1927.
4. Lopez played the 1928 season with the Macon Peaches while under contract to the Brooklyn Dodgers.
5. *Florida Times-Union,* 9 Apr. 1927.
6. *Florida Times-Union,* 2 May 1927. Townsend was re-signed when Lopez's backup broke a finger and later re-released; *Florida Times-Union,* 23 May 1927.
7. *Florida Times-Union,* 25 Apr. and 3 May 1927.
8. *Florida Times-Union,* 1–9 May 1927.
9. *Florida Times-Union,* 14–15 May 1927.
10. *Florida Times-Union,* 27 May 1927.
11. *Florida Times-Union,* 31 May 1927.
12. *Florida Times-Union,* 5 June 1927.
13. *Florida Times-Union,* 12 June –23 July 1927.
14. *Florida Times-Union,* 2 Aug. 1927. On August 4, in his last Jacksonville

performance of the year, Cantwell defeated Albany again for his twenty-fifth win of the season (*Florida Times-Union*, 5 Aug. 1927).

15. *Florida Times-Union*, 2 Aug. 1927. Cantwell went on to enjoy a marginally successful major-league career, winning 20 games in 1933 with the Boston Braves and posting 76–108 career numbers. Bear-Cat Ben was also reunited with Al Lopez for the 1936 season in Boston, after the catcher had been traded from Brooklyn.

16. *Florida Times-Union*, 12 Sept. 1927.

17. *Florida Times-Union*, 7–10 Aug. 1927.

18. Sacco and Vanzetti were two Italian-born anarchists who were arrested on May 5, 1920, for a robbery and murder in South Braintree, Massachusetts. They were brought to trial before a judge who allowed the prosecutor to exploit the Red Scare then sweeping America and thus to divert the jury's mind away from the issue at hand. The question of Sacco and Vanzetti's guilt remains in doubt, though the bias of the court does not, and the belief persists that they were sentenced for their beliefs and their ethnic origins rather than for any crime they committed. Despite pleas for mercy and public demonstrations on behalf of the two men, they died in the electric chair on 23 Aug. 1927.

19. *Florida Times-Union*, 11 Aug. 1927. See also Mormino and Pozzetta, *Immigrant World*, pp. 160–62, 298.

20. *Florida Times-Union*, 2–31 Aug. 1927.

21. Lopez interview with Mormino.

22. *Ibid.*

23. *Florida Times-Union*, 27 Aug. 1927.

24. *Florida Times-Union*, 11 Sept. 1927.

25. *Florida Times-Union*, 13–21 Sept. 1927.

26. *Florida Times-Union*, 21 Sept. 1927.

27. *Florida Times-Union*, 23 Sept. 1927.

28. *Florida Times-Union*, 1 Oct. 1927.

29. *Florida Times-Union*, 24 Sept.–1 Oct. 1927.

30. *Florida Times-Union*, 1 Oct. 1927.

31. *Ibid.*

32. *Atlanta Constitution*, 6 Apr. 1928. Though Macon began the season winning seven of their first eight, they eventually cooled, losing the Sally League pennant to Asheville, NC, who posted a .664 winning percentage. This represented the first time in Lopez's professional career when his club did not have at least a mathematical chance at the title on the final day of the season.

33. Bloodgood, *Who's Who in Baseball*.

34. Lopez interview with the author, 10 June 1992. Lopez had actually turned 20 on August 20.

35. *Ibid.*

36. John Thorn and Pete Palmer, eds., *Total Baseball*. The following list contains the names of the first fifteen "Floridians" to make it to the major leagues, in the order of their major-league debut. Note that the designation (P) beside a player's name designates that player as a pitcher:

Ralph McLaurin, Kissimmee, deb. 1908.
Stuffy Stewart, Jasper, deb. 9-13-16.

Bob "Slim" Gandy, Jacksonville, deb. 10-5-16.
Red Causey (P), Georgetown, deb. 4-26-18.
Horace "Pug" Allen, Deland, deb. 6-15-19.
James "Zach" Taylor, Yulee, deb. 6-15-20.
Lance Richbourg, Defuniak Springs, deb. 7-4-21.
Paul "Von" Schreiber (P), Jacksonville, deb. 9-2-22.
Herb Thomas, Sampson City, deb. 8-28-24.
Hank Johnson (P), Bradenton, deb. 4-17-25.
Ned Porter (P), Apalachicola, deb. 8-7-26.
Johnny Burnett, Bartow, deb. 5-7-27.
Al Lopez, Tampa, deb. 9-27-28.
Russ Scarritt, Pensacola, deb. 4-18-29.
Elliot "Babe" Bigelow, Tarpon Springs, deb. 4-18-29.

37. Bloodgood, *Who's Who in Baseball.*
38. Lopez interview with the author, 10 June 1992.
39. *Atlanta Constitution*, 18–30 Mar. 1929; *Tampa Tribune*, 26 Mar. 1929. Lopez went two for four in his return to Tampa against the Senators, a 7–6 loss. The photograph that accompanied the March 26 story was taken during Lopez's days as a batting-practice catcher for Washington and showed a prominent "W" on his left sleeve.
40. *Atlanta Constitution*, 29–30 Mar. 1929.
41. *Atlanta Constitution*, 30 Mar. 1929.
42. *Atlanta Constitution*, 31 Mar. 1929.
43. *Atlanta Constitution*, 6 Apr. 1929.
44. *Atlanta Constitution*, 9 Apr. 1929.
45. *Atlanta Constitution*, 5–10 Apr. 1929. The Birmingham Barons, defending champions of the Southern League, returned only six of the eighteen Barons who had won the pennant in 1928.
46. *Atlanta Constitution*, 11–12 Apr. 1929.
47. *Atlanta Constitution*, 14 Apr. 1929.
48. Elberfield, while an assistant coach with Montgomery in the Southern League in 1912, taught a young Casey Stengel much regarding the niceties of inside baseball and behaving in big-league fashion. See Robert W. Creamer, *Stengel: His Life and Times*, pp. 53–55.
49. *Atlanta Constitution*, 17–18 Apr. 1929.
50. *Atlanta Constitution*, 14, 17–18 Apr. 1929.
51. *Atlanta Constitution*, 19 Apr. 1929.
52. *Atlanta Constitution*, 21 Apr. 1929.
53. *Atlanta Constitution*,
54. *Atlanta Constitution*, 1 July 1929.
55. *Atlanta Constitution*, 4, 6, 7 July 1929.
56. *Atlanta Constitution*, 4 July 1929. Later in the season, Spiller opposed a proposed sale of the Chattanooga Lookouts to Griffith for the very reasons cited by the Washington owner when he backed away from purchasing the Crackers. *Atlanta Constitution*, 15 Sept. 1929.
57. *Atlanta Constitution*, 21 July 1929.
58. *Atlanta Constitution*, 24 July –1 Sept. 1929.

59. *Atlanta Constitution*, 10 Sept. 1929.
60. *Atlanta Constitution*, 15, 16, 18 Sept. 1929.
61. Lopez interview with the author, 10 June 1992.

Chapter 3

1. Stanley Cohen, *Dodgers! The First 100 Years*, p. 22.
2. Lopez interview with the author, 10 June 1992.
3. George F. Will, *Men at Work: The Craft of Baseball*, p. 7.
4. Lopez interview with the author, 10 June 1992.
5. Cohen, *Dodgers!*, p. 20.
6. *Ibid.*, pp. 20–21.
7. *Ibid.*
8. Charles C. Alexander, *John McGraw*, pp. 170–71.
9. Cohen, *Dodgers!*, p. 36.
10. *Ibid.*, pp. 36–37.
11. Lopez interview with the author, 10 June 1992.
12. Unidentified article contained in the Al Lopez file, National Baseball Library and Archives, "Lopez Shows His Class as Catcher."
13. *New York Times,* 22 and 25 Apr. 1930.
14. *New York Times*, 28 Apr. 1930.
15. *New York Times*, 29–30 Apr. 1930.
16. *New York Times*, 11 and 13 July 1930.
17. *Atlanta Constitution*, 1930 (Ralph McGill, "Al Lopez, Ybor City Kid, Already Great Catcher" — Al Lopez file, National Baseball Library and Archives). Ralph McGill, as a later long-time editor of the *Constitution*, emerged as a leading regional journalist supporting individual liberties and liberal programs such as the New Deal while opposing backward, "malignant aspects of southern life" like "political demagoguery," the Ku Klux Klan, and "sentimental" traditionalism. Dewey W. Grantham, *The South in Modern America*, p. 149.
18. *New York Times*, 2–3, 21 and 24 Sept. 1930.
19. *New York Times*, 29 Sept. 1930.
20. Cohen, *Dodgers!*, p. 41.
21. Bill James, *The Bill James Historical Baseball Abstract*.
22. Lopez interview with the author, 10 June 1992.
23. Honig, *Man in the Dugout*, p. 187.
24. Lawrence Ritter, *The Glory of Their Times: The Story of the Early Days of Baseball Told by the Men Who Played It*, p. 167.
25. Lopez interview with the author, 10 June 1992.
26. *Ibid.*
27. *Tampa Tribune*, 17 Oct. 1931; Lopez scored another hole-in-one thirty-three years later, on 23 Nov. 1964, at the Temple Terrace Golf Club, near Tampa. Lopez dropped a six-iron shot 165 yards into the fifteenth cup to help finish a six-over-par 78. Playing with Lopez was Tony Cuccinello, long-time teammate and assistant coach. *Tampa Tribune*, 5 Dec. 1964.
28. Onis interview with the author, 20 July 1993.

29. Lopez interview with Mormino.

30. Mormino and Pozzetta, *Immigrant World*, pp. 131, 289.

31. Creamer, *Stengel*; p. 63; Maury Allen, *You Could Look It Up: The Life of Casey Stengel*, p. 59.

32. *New York Times*, 28 Mar. 1934.

33. Allen, *You Could Look It Up*, p. 109. Since Randy Moore was sent to Brooklyn in the trade that sent Lopez to Boston, Lopez must have been visiting Brooklyn when the dinner occurred.

34. *New York Times*, 21 Mar. 1934.

35. *New York Times*, 22–24, 27 Mar. 1934.

36. *New York Times*, 27 Mar. 1934. Career pitching records for Stengel's 1934 staff are Mungo, 120–115; Leonard, 191–181; Benge, 101–130; Beck, 38–69; Carroll, 64–90; Munns, 4–13; Herring, 34–38; Lucas, 1–1; Perkins, 0–3; and Page, 3–3.

37. *New York Times*, 31 Mar. 1934. Wilson, who hit a National League record 56 home runs in 1930, played in only 67 games for Brooklyn in 1934, batting .262 with 6 homers.

38. *New York Times*, 1 Apr. 1934. Allen, *You Could Look It Up*, pp. 115–16; Creamer, *Stengel*, p. 182. Max Carey, who was still Brooklyn's manager at the time of Terry's initial remark and who refused to respond to it, was fired shortly thereafter when it became obvious that he and Bob Quinn disagreed over a proper reply. See Creamer, *Stengel: His Life and Times*, p. 182.

39. *New York Times*, 2–3 Apr. 1934.

40. *New York Times*, 4–5, and 10 Apr. 1934.

41. *New York Times*, 15 April 1934.

42. *Ibid.*

43. *New York Times*, 18 Apr. 1934.

44. *New York Times*, 19–23 April 1934.

45. *New York Times*, 25–30 April 1934.

46. *New York Times*, 1 July 1934.

47. *New York Times*, 2 July 1934.

48. *New York Times*, 4 July 1934.

49. All five of these catchers made it into baseball's Hall of Fame; Cochrane, Dickey, Ferrell, and Hartnett as players and Lopez as a manager.

50. Thorn and Palmer, *Total Baseball*, p. 260.

51. *New York Times*, 4 and 10–11 July 1934.

52. *New York Times*, 4 July 1934.

53. *New York Times*, 1–4, 21, 23, 26, and 27 Sept. 1934.

54. *New York Times*, 30 Sept. 1934.

55. *New York Times*, 1 Oct. 1934.

56. *Ibid.* The day was also noteworthy in that Babe Ruth made his "last bow as a regular" while playing for the New York Yankees at Washington. The St. Mary's school band was on hand, participating in the festivities. Lou Gehrig also recorded his 49th homer of the season.

57. *New York Times*, 2 Oct. 1934.

58. Lopez telephone interview with the author, 19 Sept. 1995.

59. Allen, *You Could Look It Up*, p. 124.

60. Marshall Smith, "A Plot to Whip the Yanks," *Life*, 5 May 1958, p. 83.

61. *Ibid.*
62. *Ibid.*
63. Onis interview with the author, 20 July 1993.
64. *Ibid.* Upon being cut, Onis never returned to the majors. The reasons stem from an altercation with an umpire over a disputed failure to call a third strike. Onis:

> We [Dayton, Mid-Atlantic League] were playing in Wilkes-Barre, Pennsylvania, and had lost four games in a row. Everybody was upset and so was I.... Late in the game the first baseman for Wilkes-Barre came up to bat and we had him two strikes and two balls. Then my pitcher threw a pitch that was right down the middle. I swear today that it was right down there and the ump called it a ball! Oh boy, that started it right then; I was steamed up about it. The next pitch, the guy hits a home run. Well, you know how I felt and so I raised hell with the umpire. "I'm going to charge this ballgame to you," I kept arguing. He said, "Get down there and catch or I'm going to throw you out." I said, "If you throw me out I'm going to hit you in the head!" So he threw me out and I hit him in the head. I hit him with my catcher's mask and it cracked open his head and he was bleeding there at home plate. I started pounding him with my fists, but they separated us and I was out of the ballgame.... The umpire was all right, but I got suspended without pay for thirty days and fined twenty-five dollars. You can imagine, I was only making a hundred fifty dollars a month to begin with and now on top of the fine I was suspended. The team sent me back to Brooklyn because the umpires wouldn't even let me stay on the field. Then after that, Brooklyn released me; I think they feared trouble with the umpires. My temper cost me a lot.

65. Honig, *Man in the Dugout*, p. 192.

Chapter 4

1. Harold Kaese, *The Boston Braves*, p. 236.
2. Lopez interview with the author, 10 June 1992; Lopez telephone interview with the author, 28 Feb. 1996.
3. *Ibid.*
4. Kaese, *Boston Braves*, p. 237; Lopez interview with the author, 10 June 1992.
5. *Chicago Tribune*, 18 Apr. 1937.
6. *Boston Herald*, 18 Apr. 1937.
7. *Boston Herald*, 20 Apr. 1937.
8. *Boston Herald*, 21 Apr. 1937.
9. *Chicago Tribune*, 24–26 Apr. 1937.
10. *Chicago Tribune*, 26–29 April 1937.
11. *Chicago Tribune* and *Boston Herald*, 30 Apr. 1937.

12. *Chicago Tribune*, 1 May 1937; *Boston Herald*, 19 Apr. 1937.
13. *Chicago Tribune*, 2–4 May 1937.
14. *Chicago Tribune*, 5–6 May 1937.
15. *Chicago Tribune*, 8–10 May 1937.
16. *Chicago Tribune*, 14 Aug. 1937.
17. *Chicago Tribune*, 17 Aug. 1937.
18. *Boston Herald*, 18–19 Aug.; 28 Sept. 1937.
19. Creamer, *Stengel;* p. 191.
20. Lopez interview with the author, 10 June 1992.
21. Hirshberg, *Baseball's Greatest Catchers*, p. 103.
22. Honig, *Man in the Dugout*, pp. 192–93.
23. Al Lopez, Jr. interview with the author, 20 July 1993.
24. *Ibid.*
25. *Ibid.*
26. *Ibid.*
27. Lopez interview with the author, 19 Sept. 1995.
28. *Boston Herald*, 15 June 1940.
29. *Ibid.*
30. Berres telephone interview with the author, 3 July 1996.
31. Richard Goldstein, *Spartan Seasons: How Baseball Survived the Second World War.*
32. *Ibid.*
33. *Ibid.*; Ira Berkow, ed., *Hank Greenberg: The Story of My Life.*
34. Lopez telephone interview with the author, 18 Oct. 1995; Peter Calvo-coressi, Guy Wint, and John Pritchard, *Total War: The Causes and Courses of the Second World War,* rev. ed., pp. 549–51.
35. *St. Louis Post-Dispatch*, 16 Apr. 1944.
36. Bob Smizik, *The Pittsburgh Pirates: An Illustrated History*, pp. 64–66.
37. *St. Louis Post-Dispatch*, 19–20 Apr.; 2 July 1944.
38. *St. Louis Post-Dispatch*, 2 Aug. 1944.
39. Smizik, *Pittsburgh Pirates*, p. 63.
40. *St. Louis Post-Dispatch*, 2–6 Aug. 1944.
41. *St. Louis Post-Dispatch*, 13–14 Aug. 1944.
42. *St. Louis Post-Dispatch*, 3 Sept. 1944.
43. *St. Louis Post-Dispatch*, 19 and 21 Sept. 1944.
44. Lee Lowenfish, *The Imperfect Diamond: A History of Baseball's Labor Wars*, p. 141.
45. Lowenfish, *Imperfect Diamond*, p. 144.
46. *Pittsburgh Post Gazette*, 5 June 1946.
47. Lowenfish, *Imperfect Diamond*, p. 144.
48. Lopez telephone interview with the author, 18 Oct. 1995.
49. *Pittsburgh Post Gazette*, 6 June 1946.
50. *Pittsburgh Post Gazette*, 7 June 1946.
51. *Ibid.*
52. *Ibid.*
53. *Pittsburgh Post Gazette*, 7–8 June 1946.
54. *Pittsburgh Post Gazette*, 8 June 1946; Lopez telephone interview with the author, 18 Oct. 1995; Lowenfish, *Imperfect Diamond*, pp. 144–146; Smizik, *Pitts-*

burgh Pirates, p. 67. See also Mormino and Pozzetta, *Immigrant World*, pp. 119–134, and Ingalls, *Urban Vigilantes in the New South*, pp. 87–115, regarding the 1910 Ybor City cigar makers strike.

55. *Pittsburgh Post Gazette*, 8 June 1946.
56. *Pittsburgh Post Gazette*, 10 June 1946; Lowenfish, *Imperfect Diamond*, pp. 147–150.
57. *Pittsburgh Post Gazette*, 21 Aug. 1946; Lowenfish, *Imperfect Diamond*, pp. 147–50.
58. United Press International, 6 Sept. 1946.
59. Lopez interview with the author, 10 June 1992.
60. *Ibid.*
61. Honig, *Man in the Dugout*, p. 194; Veeck and Boudreau ironed out enough of their problems the next season to win the 1948 World Series.

Chapter 5

1. Leonard Koppett, *The Man in the Dugout: Baseball's Top Managers and How They Got That Way*, p. 178.
2. Gene Karst and Martin Jones, *Who's Who in Professional Baseball*, pp. 574–76. See also Bill Veeck, *Veeck — As in Wreck: The Autobiography of Bill Veeck*.
3. Gilbert Rogin, "The Valiant Yankee Chaser," *Sports Illustrated*, 22 Mar. 1965.
4. Tom Saffell telephone interview with the author, 26 June 1996.
5. Jack Cassini telephone interview with the author, 26 June 1996.
6. Ted Beard telephone interview with the author, 26 June 1996.
7. Rogin, Valiant Yankee Chaser," p. 28.
8. Jack Torry, *Endless Summers: The Fall and Rise of the Cleveland Indians*, p. 9.
9. Koppett, *Man in the Dugout*, p. 179.
10. Al Lopez, Jr. interview with the author, 20 July 1993.
11. Ernest Havemann, "Low Pressure Lopez," *Sports Illustrated*, 6 Sept. 1954; Torry, *Endless Summers*, p. 9.
12. Robert J. Moskin, "Big League Manager Agony," *Look*, 10 May 1960, p. 115.
13. Rogin, "Valiant Yankee Chaser," p. 28.
14. Leonard Koppett incorrectly wrote that Indianapolis was the top farm club of the Cleveland Indians (*Man in the Dugout*, p. 181).
15. *Indianapolis Star*, 24 Mar. 1948.
16. Frank "Red" Barrett interview with the author, 16 July 1994.
17. *Indianapolis Star*, 24 and 27 Mar. 1948.
18. Lopez interview with the author, 10 June 1992.
19. Cassini telephone interview with the author, 26 June 1996.
20. "Bitsy" Mott interview with the author, 30 July 1994.
21. Ted Beard telephone interview with the author, 26 June 1996.
22. *Indianapolis Star*, 29 Mar. 1948.
23. *Indianapolis Star*, 30 Mar. and 5 Apr. 1948.

24. *Indianapolis Star*, 13 Apr. 1948.

25. *Indianapolis Star*, 15 Apr. 1948.

26. *Indianapolis Star*, 16 Apr. 1948.

27. *Indianapolis Star*, 16 Apr.–30 June 1948.

28. *Indianapolis Star*, Sept.–Oct. 1948.

29. Jack Cassini telephone interview with the author, 26 June 1996.

30. *Indianapolis Star*, 3 Apr. 1949.

31. *Ibid.*

32. *Indianapolis Star*, 12 Apr. 1949.

33. *Indianapolis Star*, 17 and 19 Apr. 1949.

34. *Indianapolis Star*, 20–21 Apr. 1949.

35. *Indianapolis Star*, 22–23 Apr. 1949.

36. *Indianapolis Star*, 24 Apr. 1949.

37. *Indianapolis Star*, 25–30 Apr. 1949.

38. *Indianapolis Star*, 8 May 1949.

39. *Indianapolis Star*, 2 June 1949; Nanny Fernández telephone interview with the author, 26 June 1996.

40. *Indianapolis Star*, 3 June 1949.

41. *Indianapolis Star*, 4 June 1949.

42. *Indianapolis Star*, 10 June 1949; Tom Saffell telephone interview with the author, 26 June 1996. Restelli, the "24-year-old sensation," played parts of two seasons in Pittsburgh, compiling a .241 average.

43. Robert Peterson, *Only the Ball Was White: A History of Legendary Black Players and All-Black Professional Teams*, pp. 235–36.

44. John B. Holway, *Black Diamonds: Life in the Negro Leagues from the Men Who Lived It*, p. 131.

45. *Indianapolis Star*, 10 June 1949.

46. *Indianapolis Star*, 11–12 June 1949.

47. *Indianapolis Star*, 15 June 1949.

48. *Indianapolis Star*, 16 June 1949.

49. *Indianapolis Star*, 16–30 June 1949.

50. *Indianapolis Star*, 2 Aug. 1949.

51. *Indianapolis Star*, 3 Aug. 1949.

52. *Indianapolis Star*, 4 Aug. 1949; Gutteridge telephone interview with the author, 3 July 1996.

53. *Indianapolis Star*, 5 Aug. 1949.

54. *Indianapolis Star*, 6 Aug. 1949.

55. *Indianapolis Star*, 7–11 Aug. 1949.

56. *Indianapolis Star*, 13–15 Aug. 1949.

57. *Indianapolis Star*, 10 Sept. 1949.

58. *Indianapolis Star*, 11 Sept. 1949.

59. *Indianapolis Star*, 12–13 Sept. 1949.

60. *Ibid.*

61. *Indianapolis Star*, 13–15 Sept. 1949.

62. *Indianapolis Star*, 16 Sept. 1949.

63. Holway, *Black Diamonds*, pp. 134 and 144.

64. *Indianapolis Star*, 16 Sept. 1949.

65. *Indianapolis Star*, 17–18 Sept. 1949.

66. *Indianapolis Star*, 19 Sept. 1949.
67. *Indianapolis Star*, 20 Sept. 1949; Holway, *Black Diamonds*, p. 144.
68. *Indianapolis Star*, 21 Sept. 1949.
69. *Indianapolis Star*, 21–24 Sept. 1949.
70. *Indianapolis Star*, 24–30 Sept. 1949.
71. *Indianapolis Star*, 26 Sept. 1949.
72. *Indianapolis Star*, 1–3 Oct. 1949.
73. *Indianapolis Star*, 4–5 Oct. 1949.
74. *Indianapolis Star*, 7 Oct. 1949.
75. *Indianapolis Star*, 8 Oct. 1949.
76. Fernández telephone interview with the author, 26 June 1996.
77. Cassini telephone interview with the author, 26 June 1996.
78. *Indianapolis Star*, 9 Oct. 1949.
79. *Ibid.*
80. *Indianapolis Star*, 12 Oct. 1949.
81. *Indianapolis Star*, 3 Apr. 1950.
82. Gutteridge telephone interview with the author, 3 July 1996.
83. *Indianapolis Star*, 4 Apr. 1950.
84. *Indianapolis Star*, 9 and 13 Apr. 1950.
85. *Indianapolis Star*, 4 July 1950.
86. *Indianapolis Star*, 30 Sept. 1950.

Chapter 6

1. Berkow, *Hank Greenberg*, p. 206.
2. *Ibid.*, 206–7.
3. Moskin, "Big League Manager Agony," *Look*, 10 May 1960, p. 112.
4. Honig, *Man in the Dugout*, p. 195.
5. Torry, *Endless Summers*, p. 8.
6. Bob Feller, with Bill Gilbert, *Now Pitching Bob Feller*, pp. 180–81.
7. Lopez interview with the author, 10 June 1992.
8. William Furlong, "That Positive Thinker, Al Lopez," *New York Times Magazine*, 27 Sept. 1959, p. 68.
9. Lopez interview with the author, 10 June 1992.
10. *Ibid.*
11. Torry, *Endless Summers*, p. 10.
12. Smith, "Plot to Whip the Yanks," p. 76.
13. Torry, *Endless Summers*, p. 11.
14. *Cleveland Plain Dealer*, 10 Apr. 1954.
15. Al Lopez, Jr. interview with the author, 20 July 1993.
16. Lopez interview with the author, 10 June 1992.
17. *Cleveland Plain Dealer*, 13 Apr. 1954.
18. Allen, *You Could Look It Up*, p. 169; *Cleveland Plain Dealer*, 12 Apr. 1954.
19. *Cleveland Plain Dealer*, 11 Apr. 1954; Torry, *Endless Summers*, p. 11.
20. *Cleveland Plain Dealer*, 9 Apr. 1954.

21. *Cleveland Plain Dealer*, 14 Apr. 1954.
22. *Cleveland Plain Dealer*, 15 Apr. 1954.
23. *Cleveland Plain Dealer*, 16 Apr. 1954.
24. *Cleveland Plain Dealer*, 18 Apr. 1954.
25. *Cleveland Plain Dealer*, 18 and 20 Apr. 1954.
26. *Cleveland Plain Dealer*, 19 Apr. 1954.
27. *Cleveland Plain Dealer*, 20 Apr. 1954.
28. *Cleveland Plain Dealer*, 16 May 1954.
29. *Ibid.*
30. *Cleveland Plain Dealer*, 23 and 25 May 1954.
31. *Cleveland Plain Dealer*, 24 May 1954.
32. *Cleveland Plain Dealer*, 26–27 May 1954.
33. *Cleveland Plain Dealer*, 28 May 1954.
34. *Cleveland Plain Dealer*, 29–31 May 1954.
35. *Cleveland Plain Dealer*, 1 June 1954.
36. *Cleveland Plain Dealer*, 31 May 1954.
37. *Cleveland Plain Dealer*, 2–3 June 1954. Bob Chakales won three games and lost seven in 1954. He won a total of fifteen games against twenty-five losses before his big-league career ended after the 1957 season. Vic Wertz, on the other hand, turned it around in 1954 as Lopez expected. He batted .275 with fourteen homers and enjoyed an outstanding World Series, batting .500 with eight hits in the four-game sweep of Cleveland by the Giants. His career continued until 1963 when, after seventeen seasons, he retired with a lifetime .277 average and 266 home runs, 106 of which came in Cleveland.
38. *Cleveland Plain Dealer*, 2–3 June 1954.
39. *Cleveland Plain Dealer*, 6 and 10–11 June 1954.
40. *Cleveland Plain Dealer*, 1 July 1954.
41. *Cleveland Plain Dealer*, 4 July 1954.
42. *Cleveland Plain Dealer*, 13 Sept. 1954; Allen, *You Could Look It Up*, p. 169.
43. Allen, *You Could Look It Up*, p. 170.
44. Torry, *Endless Summers*, p. 12.
45. *Ibid.*, p. 13; *Cleveland Plain Dealer*, 30 Sept. 1954.
46. Lopez interview with the author, 10 June 1992.
47. Geoffrey C. Ward and Ken Burns, *Baseball: An Illustrated History*, pp. 337–38.
48. Leonard Gettelson, *Official World Series Records*, p. 189.
49. Torry, *Endless Summers*, p. 14.
50. Roger Kahn, "One, Two, Three, Four & Bingo," *Sports Illustrated*, 11 Oct. 1954, pp. 16–17.
51. Lopez interview with the author, 10 June 1992.
52. Feller and Gilbert, *Now Pitching*, p. 200.
53. *Ibid.*
54. Lopez interview with the author, 10 June 1992.
55. Gettelson, *World Series Records*, p. 190; *Tampa Tribune*, 6 Oct. 1954.
56. Lopez interview with the author, 10 June 1992.
57. *Tampa Tribune*, 3, 4 and 6–7 Oct. 1954.
58. *Tampa Tribune*, 6 Oct. 1954.
59. Torry, *Endless Summers*, p. 15.

60. *Cleveland Call and Post,* 24 Sept. 1955.
61. *Ibid.*
62. *Ibid.*
63. *Cleveland Call and Post,* 1 Oct. 1955.
64. *Cleveland Plain Dealer,* 27 Oct. 1955.
65. *Cleveland Plain Dealer,* 26 Oct. 1955.
66. *Ibid.*
67. *Cleveland Plain Dealer,* 28 Oct. 1955.
68. Rogin, "Valiant Yankee Chaser."
69. Furlong, "Positive Thinker," p. 69.

Chapter 7

1. Furlong, "Positive Thinker."
2. Rogin, "Valiant Yankee Chaser," p. 42.
3. Furlong, "Positive Thinker."
4. *Associated Press,* 25 Oct. 1957.
5. *Chicago Defender,* 5 Dec. 1957; *Chicago Tribune,* 4–5 Dec. 1957; *New York Times,* 11 Sept. 1968. Ray Moore wasn't the success that Lopez foresaw, winning only eleven games in 1957 and thirteen more over the next three seasons before being sent to Washington.
6. *Chicago Tribune,* 4 and 16 Dec. 1957.
7. Charles Moritz, ed., *Current Biography Yearbook 1960,* p. 242.
8. Furlong, "Positive Thinker."
9. *Ibid.,* p. 17.
10. Lopez interview with the author, 10 June 1992.
11. *Chicago Tribune,* 8–14 Apr. 1959.
12. *Chicago Tribune,* 30 Apr.–1 May 1959.
13. *Chicago Tribune,* 14 Apr. 1959.
14. *Chicago Tribune,* 15–17 Apr. 1959.
15. *Chicago Tribune,* 18–19 Apr. 1959.
16. *Chicago Tribune,* 27–28 Apr. 1959.
17. *Chicago Tribune,* 28 Apr. 1959.
18. *Chicago Tribune,* 29 Apr.–1 May, 1959.
19. *Chicago Tribune,* 2 May 1959.
20. *Chicago Tribune,* 2 and 5–6 May 1959.
21. *Chicago Tribune,* 8 and 10 June 1959.
22. *Chicago Tribune,* 11–12 June 1959.
23. *Chicago Tribune,* 21 June 1959.
24. *Chicago Tribune,* 15 Aug. 1959.
25. *Chicago Tribune,* 16 Aug. 1959.
26. George F. Will, *Men at Work: The Craft of Baseball,* p. 39.
27. *Ibid.,* pp. 40, 68.
28. *Chicago Tribune,* 17–18 Aug. 1959.
29. *Chicago Tribune,* 19 Aug. 1959.
30. *Chicago Tribune,* 21 Aug. 1959.
31. *Chicago Tribune,* 20–23 Aug. 1959.

32. *Ibid.*

33. *Chicago Tribune*, 29 Aug. 1959.

34. Tito Francona was traded to Detroit during the 1958 season and was subsequently moved along to Cleveland.

35. *Chicago Tribune*, 30 Aug. 1959.

36. *Chicago Tribune*, 31 Aug. 1959.

37. *Chicago Tribune*, 8 Sept. 1959.

38. *Chicago Tribune*, 25 Aug. –14 and 18 Sept. 1959.

39. *Chicago Tribune*, 18–19 Aug. 1959.

40. *Chicago Tribune*, 20 Sept. 1959.

41. *Chicago Tribune*, 21 Sept. 1959.

42. *Chicago Tribune*, 22 Sept. 1959.

43. Ray Berres telephone interview with the author, 3 July 1996.

44. Don Gutteridge telephone interview with the author, 3 July 1996.

45. *Chicago Tribune*, 21 Sept. 1959.

46. *Chicago Tribune*, 22 Sept. 1959.

47. *Chicago Tribune*, 23 Sept. 1959.

48. *Chicago Tribune*, 30 Sept. 1959.

49. *Chicago Tribune*, 23 Sept. 1959.

50. *Chicago Tribune*, 29 Sept. – 1 Oct. 1959.

51. *Chicago Tribune*, 2 Oct. 1959; Cohen, *Dodgers!*, p. 132.

52. *Chicago Tribune*, 3 Oct. 1959; Cohen, *Dodgers!*, p. 132; Gettelson, *World Series Records*, p. 215.

53. *Chicago Tribune*, 3 Oct. 1959; Lopez telephone interview with the author, 28 Feb. 1996; Gutteridge telephone interview with the author, 3 July 1996.

54. *Chicago Tribune*, 3 Oct. 1959; Lopez telephone interview with the author, 28 Feb. 1996.

55. Philip J. Lowry, *Green Cathedrals*, pp. 168–169.

56. *Chicago Tribune*, 5–6 Oct. 1959; Gettelson, *World Series Records*, p. 215.

57. *Chicago Tribune*, 7 Oct. 1959.

58. *Ibid.*

59. *Chicago Tribune*, 9 Oct. 1959; Cohen, *Dodgers!*, p. 133.

60. *Tampa Tribune*, 9–11 Oct. 1959.

61. Lopez interview with the author, 10 June 1992.

62. *Ibid.*

63. *Chicago Tribune*, 29–30 Sept. 1959.

64. Lopez interview with Mormino, 4 Apr. 1980.

65. Berres and Gutteridge telephone interviews with the author, 3 July 1996.

66. Lopez interview with the author, 10 June 1992.

67. *Ibid.*

68. "New Lopez Wrinkle: 'On-Deck' Stand-In," 10 Aug. 1963. National Baseball Library and Archives, Al Lopez file.

69. Koppett, *Man in the Dugout*, p. 183.

70. "Seething Senor Aims Broadside at Smith's Gripe," 16 Mar. 1963. National Baseball Library and Archives, Al Lopez file.

71. Danny Peary, ed., *We Played the Game: 65 Players Remember Baseball's Greatest Era, 1947–1964*, p. 620.

72. Koppett, *The Man in the Dugout*, p. 183; Miscellaneous articles, National

Baseball Library and Archives, Al Lopez file. Lopez had been hospitalized in July 1965 with appendicitis.

    73. Koppett, *Man in the Dugout*, p. 183; Miscellaneous articles, National Baseball Library and Archives, Al Lopez File.

Chapter 8

    1. Creamer, *Stengel*, p. 282.

    2. Allen, *You Could Look It Up*, pp. 172–73.

    3. Bret L. Billet and Lance J. Formwalt, *America's National Pastime: A Study of Race and Merit in Professional Baseball*, p. 11.

    4. David Halberstam, *October 1964*, p. 110.

    5. Bowman and Zoss, *Diamonds in the Rough*, p. 185.

    6. Smith telephone interview with the author, 24 July 1995.

    7. Battey telephone interview with the author, 25 July 1995.

    8. Smith telephone interview with the author, 24 July 1995.

    9. Lopez interview with Mormino, 4 Apr. 1980.

    10. *Ibid.*

    11. Smith telephone interview with the author, 24 July 1995.

    12. Lopez interview with the author, 10 June 1992.

    13. Joseph Thomas Moore, *Pride against Prejudice: The Biography of Larry Doby*, pp. 110–11.

    14. *Cleveland Plain Dealer*, 27 Oct. 1955.

    15. *Cleveland Call and Post*, 5 Nov. 1955.

    16. Lopez interview with the author, 10 June 1992.

    17. Joseph Thomas Moore, personal notes of comments by Larry Doby about Al Lopez, 18 Dec. 1980.

    18. "Soft-Hearted Senor Can Crack the Whip, Floyd Quickly Finds," unidentified newspaper article, 17 July 1965. National Baseball Library and Archives, Al Lopez file.

    19. Rogin, "Valiant Yankee Chaser."

    20. Peary, ed., *We Played the Game*, p. 200.

    21. Doc Young, "Why Minoso and Doby Got Traded: Larry Doby says Al Lopez Affected Play with White Sox," *Jet*, 19 Dec. 1957; *Chicago Tribune*, 6 Dec. 1957.

    22. *Chicago Tribune*, 4 Dec. 1957.

    23. The first, a terrible three-team deal involving Cleveland, Chicago, and Washington, predominantly orchestrated by Hank Greenberg of Cleveland and Chicago's Frank Lane, sent Minoso to Chicago and brought 6'4" pitcher Lew Brissie to Cleveland (*Chicago Tribune*, 1 May 1951). John Fuster of the *Call and Post* defended the deal, saying that the Indians pitching staff, laden with right-handers, needed a lefty to beat the Yankees. After the season (Minoso won rookie of the year honors with a .330 batting average), Fuster defended his endorsement, arguing that Cleveland lost because Brissie had failed to be the answer, not because the deal was unsound (*Cleveland Call and Post*, 5 May and 6 Oct. 1951).

    24. Minnie Minoso with Herb Fagen, *Just Call Me Minnie: My Six Decades in Baseball*, p. 113; *Chicago Tribune*, 1 May 1951.

25. *Chicago Tribune*, 21 Sept. 1959; *Chicago Defender*, 15, 17, 23 Oct., 13 Nov. and 5 Dec. 1957.

26. Minoso, *Just Call Me Minnie*, pp. 48, 159. Minoso and Doby have both failed to respond to my repeated attempts to discuss these matters with them. On one occasion, Doby telephoned and asked that I send him the questions I had in written form and he would answer. A short while later, Joe Moore told me not to expect anything, that the phone call was Doby's way of being polite and I probably wouldn't hear from him again. I didn't.

27. Al Smith telephone interview with the author, 24 July 1995.

28. "Seething Senor," 16 Mar. 1963. National Baseball Library and Archives, Al Lopez file.

29. Ray Berres telephone interview with the author, 3 July 1996.

30. Jerome Holtzman telephone interview with the author, 15 June 1994.

31. Hatfield interview with the author, 11 Mar. 1994.

32. *Ibid.*

33. Battey telephone interview with the author, 25 July 1995; Rogin, "Valiant Yankee Chaser."

34. Halberstam *October 1964*, p. 117.

35. Smith telephone interview with the author, 24 July 1995.

36. Peary, *We Played the Game*, p. 379.

37. Moore, personal notes of comments by Doby, 18 Dec. 1980.

38. Battey telephone interview with the author, 25 July 1995.

39. Bob Shaw interview with the author, 19 July 1993.

40. Walt Dropo, letter to the author, 7 Nov. 1993.

41. Smith telephone interview with the author, 24 July 1995.

42. John Kuenster, letter to Tony Saladino, 25 Sept. 1992. Kuenster's letter was part of the campaign soliciting contributions for the Al Lopez monument erected in Tampa.

43. Monte Irvin, letter to Tony Saladino, 22 Sept. 1992.

44. Roland Hemond, letter to Tony Saladino, 24 July 1991.

45. Gabe Paul, letter to Tony Saladino, 5 Sept. 1992.

46. Mickey Vernon, letter to Tony Saladino, 26 Sept. 1992.

47. Peary, *We Played the Game*, p. 340.

48. Smith telephone interview with the author, 24 July 1995.

49. Moore, personal notes of comments by Doby, 18 Dec. 1980.

50. Holtzman telephone interview with the author, 15 June 1994.

51. Smith telephone interview with the author, 24 July 1995.

52. Doby was elected to Baseball's Hall of Fame in 1998.

Conclusion

1. Connie Lopez died from emphysema on 1 Oct. 1983.

2. Lopez interview with the author, 10 June 1992; Lopez telephone interview with the author, 28 Feb. 1996.

3. *Ibid.*

4. *Ibid.*

5. *Tampa Tribune*, 4 Oct. 1992; *La Gaceta*, 9 Oct. 1992.

Bibliography

Unpublished Sources

Barrett, Frank "Red." Interview with the author, 16 July 1994.
Battey, Earl. Telephone interview with the author, 25 July 1995.
Beard, Ted. Telephone interview with the author, 26 June 1996.
Berres, Ray. Telephone Interview with the author, 3 July 1996.
Bloodworth, Jimmy. Interview with the author, 9 July 1993.
Cassini, Jack. Telephone interview with the author, 26 June 1996.
Cuellar, Charlie. Interview with the author, 30 Mar. 1994.
Dropo, Walt. Letter to the author, 7 Nov. 1993.
Fernández, "Nanny." Telephone interview with the author, 26 June 1996.
Gutteridge, Don. Telephone interview with the author, 3 July 1996.
Hatfield, Fred. Interview with the author, 12 Mar. 1994.
Hemond, Roland. Letter to Tony Saladino, 24 July 1991.
Holtzman, Jerome. Telephone interview with the author, 15 June 1994.
Irvin, Monte. Letter to Tony Saladino, 22 Sept. 1992.
Kuenster, John. Letter to Tony Saladino, 25 Sept. 1992.
Lopez, Al. Interview with Gary Mormino, 4 Apr. 1980. Oral History Project, University of Florida, Gainesville.
Lopez, Al. Interview with Joseph T. Moore, 2 Aug. 1980.
____. Interview with the author, 10 June 1992.
____. Interview with the author, 20 July 1993.
____. Telephone interview with the author, 19 Sept. 1995.
____. Telephone interview with the author, 18 Oct. 1995.
____. Telephone interview with the author, 28 Feb. 1996.
Lopez, Al, Jr. interview with the author, 20 July 1993.
Maseda, Marcelo. Interview with the author, 12 June 1992.
Moore, Joseph T. Personal notes on Al Lopez and Larry Doby.
Mott, "Bitsy." Interview with the author, 30 July 1994.

National Baseball Library and Archives, Cooperstown, N.Y. Al Lopez file.
Onis, Manuel. Interview with the author, 20 July 1993.
Paul, Gabe. Letter to Tony Saladino, 5 Sept. 1992.
Saffell, Tom. Telephone interview with the author, 26 June 1996.
Shaw, Bob. Interview with the author, 19 July 1993.
Smith, Al. Telephone interview with the author, 24 July 1995.
Vernon, Mickey. Letter to Tony Saladino, 26 Sept. 1992.

Published Sources

Aaron, Henry, with Lonnie Wheeler. *I Had A Hammer: The Hank Aaron Story.* New York: HarperCollins, 1991.
Alexander, Charles C. *John McGraw.* New York: Viking, 1988.
_____. *Our Game: An American Baseball History.* New York: Henry Holt, 1991.
Allen, Maury. *You Could Look It Up: The Life of Casey Stengel.* New York: Times Books, 1979.
Alvarez, Mark, ed. *The Perfect Game.* Dallas, Tex.: Taylor Publishing, 1993.
Ashe, Arthur. *A Hard Road to Glory: A History of the African-American Athlete, 1919–1945.* New York: Warner, 1988.
_____. *A Hard Road to Glory: A History of the African-American Athlete, since 1946.* New York: Warner, 1988.
Berkow, Ira, ed. *Hank Greenberg: The Story of My Life.* New York: Times Books, 1989.
Billet, Bret L., and Formwalt, Lance J. *America's National Pastime: A Study of Race and Merit in Professional Baseball.* Westport, Conn.: Praeger Publishers, 1995.
Bloodgood, Clifford. *Who's Who in Baseball.* New York: Baseball Magazine, 1943.
Boudreau, Lou, with Ed Fitzgerald. *Player-Manager.* Boston: Little, Brown, 1952.
Bowman, John, and Zoss, Joel. *Diamonds in the Rough: The Untold History of Baseball.* New York: Macmillan, 1989.
Calvocoressi, Peter, Guy Wint, and John Pritchard. *Total War: The Causes and Courses of the Second World War,* rev. ed. New York: Pantheon Books, 1989.
Cohen, Stanley. *Dodgers! The First 100 Years.* New York: Carol Publishing Group, 1990.
Cooper, Patricia Ann. *Once a Cigar Maker: Men, Women and Work Culture in American Cigar Factories, 1900–1919.* Urbana: University of Illinois Press, 1987.
Creamer, Robert. *Baseball in '41.* New York: Viking, 1990.
_____. *Stengel: His Life and Times.* New York: Simon and Schuster, 1984.
Crepeau, Richard C. *Baseball's Diamond Mind.* Orlando: University Presses of Florida, 1980.
Daley, A. "Two Managers." *New York Times Magazine,* 26 Sept. 1954.
Dean, Susie Kelly. *The Tampa of My Childhood, 1897–1907.* Tampa: Dean, 1966.
Dunn, Hampton. *Yesterday's Tampa.* Miami: E.A. Seemann Publishing, 1972.
Durocher, Leo, with Ed Linn. *Nice Guys Finish Last.* New York: Viking, 1976.
Feller, Bob, with Bill Gilbert. *Now Pitching Bob Feller.* New York: Carol Publishing Group, 1990.

Firmite, Ron. "In Cuba, It's Viva El Grand Old Game." *Sports Illustrated*, 6 June 1977.

Flood, Curt, with Richard Carter. *The Way It Is.* New York: Trident Press, 1970.

Forker, Dom. *The Men of Autumn: An Oral History of the 1949–53 World Champion New York Yankees.* Dallas: Taylor Publishing, 1989.

Franklin, John Hope, and Alfred A. Moss. *From Slavery to Freedom: A History of Negro Americans,* 6th ed. New York: Alfred Knopf, 1988.

Furlong, William. "That Positive Thinker, Al Lopez." *New York Times Magazine,* 27 Sept. 1959.

Gannon, Michael. *Florida: A Short History.* Gainesville: University Press of Florida, 1993.

Gettleson, Leonard. *Official World Series Records.* New York: Sporting News, 1971.

Goldfield, David. *Promised Land: The South since 1945.* Wheeling, Ill.: Harlan Davidson, 1987.

Goldstein, Richard. *Spartan Seasons: How Baseball Survived the Second World War.* New York: Macmillan, 1980.

_____. *Superstars and Screwballs: 100 Years of Brooklyn Baseball.* New York: Dutton, 1991.

Grantham, Dewey. *The South in Modern America: A Region at Odds.* New York: HarperCollins, 1994.

Guttmann, Allen. *Whole New Ball Game.* Chapel Hill, N.C.: University of North Carolina Press, 1988.

Halberstam, David. *October 1964.* New York: Villard Books, 1994.

_____. *Summer of '49.* New York: William Morrow, 1989.

Havemann, Ernest. "Low Pressure Lopez." *Sports Illustrated,* 6 Sept. 1954.

Hirshberg, Al. *Baseball's Greatest Catchers.* New York: Putnam, 1966.

Holway, John B. *Black Diamonds: Life in the Negro Leagues from the Men Who Lived It.* New York: Stadium Books, 1991.

Honig, Donald. *Baseball When the Grass Was Real.* New York: Coward, McCann & Geoghegan, 1975.

_____. *The Man in the Dugout: Fifteen Big League Managers Speak Their Mind.* Chicago: Follett Publishing, 1977.

Ingalls, Robert P. *Urban Vigilantes in the New South: Tampa, 1882–1936.* Knoxville, Tenn.: University of Tennessee Press, 1988.

James, Bill. *The Bill James Historical Baseball Abstract.* New York: Villard Books, 1988.

Johnson, Harold "Speed." *Who's Who in Major League Base Ball.* Chicago: Buxton Publishing, 1933.

Kaese, Harold. *The Boston Braves.* New York: Putnam, 1948.

Kahn, Roger. "1...2...3...4...& Bingo." *Sports Illustrated,* 11 Oct. 1954.

Karst, Gene, and Martin J. Jones. *Who's Who in Professional Baseball.* New Rochelle, N.Y.: Arlington House, 1973.

Koppett, Leonard. *The Man in the Dugout: Baseball's Top Managers and How They Got That Way.* New York: Crown, 1993.

Lawson, Steven. "Ybor City and Baseball: An Interview with Al Lopez." *Tampa Bay History* 7, No. 1, (1985): pp. 59–76.

Litwack, Leon. *The American Labor Movement.* New York: Simon & Schuster, 1962.

Lowenfish, Lee. *The Imperfect Diamond: A History of Baseball's Labor Wars.* New York: DaCapo Press, 1991.

Lowry, Philip J. *Green Cathedrals.* Reading, Mass.: Addison-Wesley, 1992.

Meany, T. "Lopez and the Indian Signs." *Colliers,* 12 July 1952.

Mercurio, John. *Record Profiles of Baseball's Hall of Famers.* New York: Perennial Library, 1990.

Minoso, Minnie, with Herb Fagen. *Just Call Me Minnie: My Six Decades in Baseball.* Champaign, Ill.: Sagamore Publishing, 1994.

Moore, Joseph Thomas. *Pride against Prejudice: The Biography of Larry Doby.* New York: Greenwood Press, 1988.

Moritz, Charles, ed. *Current Biography Yearbook 1960.* New York: Wilson, 1960.

Mormino, Gary, and George Pozzetta. *The Immigrant World of Ybor City: Italians and Their Latin Neighbors in Tampa, 1885–1985.* Urbana: University of Illinois Press, 1987.

Moskin, J. Robert. "Big League Manager Agony." *Look,* 10 May 1960, pp. 112–15.

Obojski, Robert. *Bush League: A History of Minor League Baseball.* New York: Macmillan, 1975.

Pacheco, Ferdie. *Ybor City Chronicles: A Memoir.* Gainesville: University Presses of Florida, 1994.

Peary, Danny, ed. *Cult Baseball Players.* New York: Simon & Schuster, 1990.

_____, ed. *We Played the Game: 65 Players Remember Baseball's Greatest Era, 1947–1964.* New York: Hyperion, 1994.

Perez, Louis A. "Ybor City Remembered." *Tampa Bay History* 7, No. 1 (1985): pp. 170–171.

Peterson, Robert. *Only the Ball Was White: A History of Legendary Black Players and All-Black Professional Teams.* Englewood Cliffs, N.J.: Prentice-Hall, 1970.

Piniella, Lou, with Maury Allen. *Sweet Lou.* New York: G.P. Putnam's Sons, 1986.

Pizzo, Anthony. "Reminiscences of Ybor City." *Sunland Tribune,* vol. 17 (1991): p. 50.

_____. *Tampa Town 1824–1886: The Cracker Village with a Latin Accent.* Miami: Hurricane House, 1968.

Pope, Edwin. *Baseball's Greatest Managers.* Atlanta: Tupper and Love, 1960.

Porter, David L. *Biographical Dictionary of American Sports: Baseball.* New York: Greenwood Press, 1987.

Rader, Benjamin G. *Baseball: A History of America's Game.* Urbana: University of Illinois Press, 1992.

_____. *American Sports: From the Age of Folk Games to the Age of Television.* Englewood Cliffs, NJ: Prentice-Hall, 1990.

Riess, Steven A. *Touching Base: Professional Baseball and American Culture in the Progressive Era.* Westport, Conn.: Meckler, 1980.

_____. *City Games: The Evolution of American Urban Society and the Rise of Sports.* Urbana: University of Illinois Press, 1989.

Ritter, Lawrence. *The Glory of Their Times: The Story of the Early Days of Baseball Told by the Men Who Played It.* New York: Macmillan, 1966.

Rogin, Gilbert. "The Valiant Yankee Chaser." *Sports Illustrated,* 22 Mar. 1965.

Rosenthal, Harold. *Baseball's Best Managers.* New York: T. Nelson, 1961.

Schlossberg, Dan. *The Baseball Book of Why.* Middle Village, N.Y.: Jonathon David Publishers, 1984.

Seymor, Harold. *Baseball: The Golden Years.* New York: Oxford University Press, 1989.

Shatzkin, Mike. *The Ballplayers: Baseball's Ultimate Biographical Reference.* New York: Arbor House, 1990.

Singletary, Wes. "Señor: The Managerial Career of Al Lopez." *Sunland Tribune* 19 (1993):00–00.

_____. "The Early Baseball Career of Al Lopez." *Tampa Bay History.* 16, No. 1 (1994):00–00.

_____. "Opportunity Knocks Once: A Conversation with Manuel 'Curly' Onis." *Sunland Tribune* 20 (1994):00–00.

Smith, Marshall. "A Plot to Whip the Yanks." *Life,* 5 May 1958.

Smizik, Bob. *The Pittsburgh Pirates: An Illustrated History.* New York: Walker, 1990.

Tampa City Directory. Richmond, Va.: R. L. Polk, 1925–26.

Tebeau, Charlton. *A History of Florida.* Coral Gables: University of Miami Press, 1971.

Thorn, John, and Pete Palmer, eds. *Total Baseball,* 2d. ed. New York: Warner, 1991.

Torry, Jack. *Endless Summers: The Fall and Rise of the Cleveland Indians.* South Bend, Ind.: Diamond Communications, 1995.

Turner, Frederick. *When the Boys Came Back: Baseball and 1946.* New York: Henry Holt, 1996.

Tygiel, Jules. *Baseball's Great Experiment: Jackie Robinson and His Legacy.* New York: Oxford University Press, 1983.

Veeck, Bill. *Veeck—As in Wreck: The Autobiography of Bill Veeck.* New York: Putnam, 1962.

Voight, David. *America through Baseball.* Chicago: Nelson-Hall, 1976.

Wagner, Eric A. "Baseball in Cuba." *Journal of Popular Culture* 18 (Summer 1984): p. 115.

Ward, Geoffrey C., and Ken Burns. *Baseball: An Illustrated History.* New York: Alfred Knopf, 1994.

Will, George F. *Men at Work: The Craft of Baseball.* New York: Macmillan, 1990.

Woodward, C. Vann. *The Strange Career of Jim Crow.* New York: Oxford University Press, 1974.

Young, Doc. "Why Minoso and Doby Got Traded: Larry Doby Says Al Lopez Affected Play with White Sox." *Jet,* 19 Dec. 1957.

Newspaper Citations

Atlanta Constitution, **1928**: 6 Apr. **1929**: 18, 19, 20, 21, 22, 23, 24, 25, 26, 27, 28, 29, 30, 31 Mar.; 5, 6, 7, 8, 9, 10, 11, 12, 14, 17, 18, 19, 21 Apr.; 1 4, 6, 7, 21, 24, 25, 26, 27, 28, 29, 30, 31 July; 1, 2, 3, 4, 5, 6, 7, 8, 9, 10, 11, 12, 13, 14, 15, 16, 17, 18, 19, 20, 21, 22, 23, 24, 25, 26, 27, 28, 29, 30, 31 Aug.; 1, 10, 15, 16, 18 Sept.

Boston Herald, **1937**: 18, 19, 20, 21, 30 Apr.; 2, 3, 4, 5, 6, 8, 9, 10 May; 14, 17, 18, 19 Aug.; 28 Sept. **1940:** 15 June

Chicago Defender, **1957**: 15, 17, 23 Oct.; 13 Nov.; 5 Dec.
Chicago Tribune, **1937**: 18, 24, 25, 26, 27, 28, 29, 30 Apr.; 1 May **1951**: 1 May
    1957: 4, 5, 6, 16 Dec. **1959**: 14, 15, 16, 17, 18, 19, 27, 28, 29, 30 Apr.; 1, 2,
    5, 6 May; 8, 10, 11, 12, 21 June; 15, 16, 18, 19, 20, 21, 22, 23, 25, 29, 30, 31
    Aug.; 8, 14, 18, 20, 21, 22, 23, 29, 30 Sept.; 1, 2, 3, 5, 6, 7, 9 Oct.
Cleveland Call & Post, **1951**: 5 May; 6 Oct. **1955**: 24 Sept.; 1 Oct.
Cleveland Plain Dealer, **1954**: 10, 11, 12, 13, 14, 15, 16, 18, 19, 20 Apr.; 16, 23, 24,
    25, 26, 27, 28, 29, 30, 31 May; 1, 2, 3, 6, 10, 11 June; 1, 4 July; 13, 30 Sept.
    1955: 26, 27, 28, Oct.
Florida Times-Union, **1927**: 8 Mar.; 8, 9, 25 Apr.; 1, 2, 3, 4, 5, 6, 7, 8, 9, 14, 15,
    23, 27, 31 May; 5, 12, 13, 14, 15, 16, 17, 18, 19, 20, 21, 22, 23, 24, 25, 26,
    27, 28, 29, 30 June; 1, 2, 3, 4, 5, 6, 7, 8, 9, 10, 11, 12, 13, 14, 15, 16, 17, 18,
    19, 20, 21, 22, 23 July; 2, 3, 4, 5, 6, 7, 8, 9, 10, 11, 12, 13, 14, 15, 16, 17, 18,
    19, 20, 21, 22, 23, 24, 25, 26, 27, 28, 29, 30, 31 Aug.; 11, 12, 13, 14, 15, 16,
    17, 18, 19, 20, 21, 23, 24, 25, 26, 27, 28, 29, 30 Sept.; 1 Oct.
Indianapolis Star, **1948**: 24, 27, 29, 30 Mar.; 5, 13, 15, 16, 17, 18, 19, 20, 21, 22,
    23, 24, 25, 26, 27, 28, 29 30 Apr.; 1, 2, 3, 4, 5, 6, 7, 8, 9, 10, 11, 12, 13, 14,
    15, 16, 17, 18, 19, 20, 21, 22, 23, 24, 25, 26, 27, 28, 29, 30, 31 May; 1, 2, 3,
    4, 5, 6, 7, 8, 9, 10, 11, 12, 13, 14, 15, 16, 17, 18, 19, 20, 21, 22, 23, 24, 25, 26,
    27, 28, 29, 30 June; 1, 2, 3, 4, 5, 6, 7, 8, 9, 10, 11, 12, 13, 14, 15, 16, 17, 18,
    19, 20, 21, 22, 23, 24, 25, 26, 27, 28, 29, 30 Sept.; 1, 2, 3, 4, 5, 6, 7, 8, 9,
    10, 11, 12, 13, 14, 15, 16, 17, 18, 19, 20, 21, 22, 23, 24, 25, 26, 27, 28, 29, 30,
    31 Oct. **1949**: 3, 12, 17, 19, 20, 21, 22, 23, 24, 25, 26, 27, 28, 29, 30 Apr.;
    8 May; 2, 4, 10, 11, 12, 15, 16, 17, 18, 19, 20, 21, 22, 23, 24, 25, 26, 27, 28,
    29, 30 June; 2, 3, 4, 6, 7, 8, 9, 10, 11, 13, 14, 15 Aug.; 10, 11, 12, 13, 14, 15,
    16, 17, 18, 19, 20, 21, 22, 23, 24, 25, 26, 27, 28, 29, 30 Sept.; 1, 2, 3, 4, 5,
    7, 8, 9, 12 Oct. **1950**: 4, 9, 13 Apr.; 4 July; 30 Sept.
La Gaceta (Ybor City, Tampa), 9 Oct. 1992
New York Times, **1930**: 22, 25, 28, 29, 30 Apr.; 11, 13, July; 2, 3, 21, 24, 29 Sept.;
    1934: 21, 22, 23, 24, 27, 28, 31 Mar.; 1, 2, 3, 4, 5, 15, 18, 19, 20, 21, 22, 23,
    25, 26, 27, 29, 30 Apr.; 1, 2, 4, 10, 11 July; 1, 2, 3, 4, 21, 23, 26, 27, 30 Sept.;
    1, 2 Oct. **1968**: 11 Sept.
Pittsburgh Post Gazette, **1946**: 5, 6, 7, 8, 10 June; 21 Aug.
St. Louis Post-Dispatch, **1944**: 16, 19, 20 Apr.; 2 July; 2, 3, 4, 5, 6, 13, 14, Aug.;
    3, 19, 21 Sept.
Tampa Tribune, **1925**: 26, 27, 29, 30 Aug.; 1, 2, 3, 5, 8, 9, 11, 12, 13, 15 Sept.; 16,
    27, 28, 30, 31 Oct. **1926**: 30 May; 4, 5, 9, 15, 16, 17, 18, 19, 25, 26, 27 29,
    30 June; 2, 4, 6, 10, 23 July; 14, 15, 16, 17, 18, 19, 20, 21, 22, 23, 24, 25, 27
    Aug.; 7, 8, 9, 11, 12, 13, 14, 15, 16 Sept.; **1929**: 26 Mar. **1931**: 17 Oct. **1954**:
    3, 4, 6, 7 Oct. **1959**: 9, 10, 11 Oct. **1964**: 5 Dec. **1977**: 12 Sept. **1992**: 4 Oct.

Index

Page numbers in boldface indicate photographs